Sexual and Gender Minority History

A Counter-Narrative

JAMES I. MARTIN

OXFORD
UNIVERSITY PRESS

Oxford University Press is a department of the University of Oxford.
It furthers the University's objective of excellence in research, scholarship,
and education by publishing worldwide. Oxford is a registered trade mark of
Oxford University Press in the UK and in certain other countries.

Published in the United States of America by Oxford University Press
198 Madison Avenue, New York, NY 10016, United States of America.

© Oxford University Press 2025

All rights reserved. No part of this publication may be reproduced, stored in a retrieval system, transmitted, used for text and data mining, or used for training artificial intelligence, in any form or by any means, without the prior permission in writing of Oxford University Press, or as expressly permitted by law, by license or under terms agreed with the appropriate reprographics rights organization. Inquiries concerning reproduction outside the scope of the above should be sent to the Rights Department, Oxford University Press, at the address above.

You must not circulate this work in any other form
and you must impose this same condition on any acquirer.

CIP data is on file at the Library of Congress

ISBN 9780197765470
DOI: 10.1093/9780197765500.001.0001

Printed by Integrated Books International, United States of America

Contents

Preface	vii
Acknowledgments	xi
1. Introduction	1
2. Germany in the Late 19th and Early 20th Centuries	9
3. The Weimar Republic and National Socialism	21
4. Foundations in the United States	31
5. The Jazz Age	45
6. The 1930s and the Great Depression	57
7. The World at War	69
8. The 1950s and the Homophile Movement	83
9. A Rising Tide of Resistance	99
10. Stonewall and Its Aftermath	113
11. Turbulence and Visibility in the 1970s	129
12. The Deluge and Beyond	147
13. Summary and Conclusions	163
References	171
Index	191

Preface

This book is the culmination of many years of teaching and learning. I taught a graduate social work course on sexual and gender minority issues for 18 years at New York University, and within a couple of years of starting it, I began adding material about constructions of sexual and gender minority identities. George Chauncey's book *Gay New York* had influenced me strongly toward the belief not only that these identities were constructed but also that those constructions changed over time. Another early influence was Philip Cushman's book *Constructing the Self, Constructing America*, which examined changing constructions of American identities in relation to the social and political context. My interest in this area eventually brought me in contact with the developmental psychology literature on the impact of historical time on developmental pathways, and I began lecturing and writing about this topic with respect to sexual and gender minorities.

Meanwhile, I began traveling to Germany on a regular basis, and as I became immersed in the German history of sexual and gender minority people, I started to add some material about it to my course. Eventually I became friends with a German professor of social work at RheinMain University of Applied Sciences, and when she invited me to lecture to her students, the topic I chose was the construction of sexual and gender minority identities in Germany and the United States. Putting this lecture together strengthened my immersion in sexual and gender minority history. I was surprised to find that students and faculty at that university were as unfamiliar with the history of sexual and gender minority people in Germany as my own students were of the American history. Building on that presentation, I began lecturing at conferences and other universities about the changing constructions of sexual and gender minority identities, and I steadily expanded the historical material in my course until it was one-fourth of the entire semester. I learned about the construction of narratives, and the importance of stories, from my German colleagues, especially through our design and teaching of two "summer school" international courses that enrolled students from both

viii PREFACE

of our universities. It was in the last few years of teaching my course on sexual and gender minority issues that I began to frame the historical material as a counter-narrative.

The theoretical perspective of this book is partially based on standpoint theory, which asserts that all knowledge is constructed from specific social standpoints. Thus, it is important for readers to know about my own standpoint and life experiences, since they could have shaped my understanding of the history that this book examines and influenced my writing. I was born to a striving middle-class Jewish family six years after the end of the Second World War. Among my parents' generation, many Jews were progressing from a marginalized position in American society to the mainstream, and I was part of the generation that was fully mainstreamed or, in other terms, had attained whiteness. However, my gender expression was decidedly "nonconforming," which was more perilous in the 1950s and 1960s than it is today, and I rarely felt safe in the world because of it. A sense of belonging was, for me, elusive. By the time I graduated high school, exactly three weeks before the Stonewall Riots, I knew that I was gay. I found that prospect both exciting and terrifying, but I had no idea how to be gay. There were no guideposts and no internet then. And although I was aware of pre-Stonewall gay culture, I didn't participate in it. It would take several years of experimentation and retreat before I claimed a gay identity for myself and found a community. I experienced the freedom of young adult gay life in the late 1970s and early 1980s, and soon afterward I saw my community devastated by the AIDS epidemic in which I lost many friends.

Over the course of my career as a social work practitioner and then academic, I maintained a focus on sexual and gender minority issues, which I considered to be a matter of integrity and personal responsibility. My clinical work focused on lesbian and gay individuals and couples. As an academic I was active in developing structures to support sexual and gender minority faculty and students, and in creating and disseminating new knowledge primarily about sexual minorities. Being gay was integral to my career even from the beginning; one of the two social work students mentioned in chapter 11 who co-led one of the first gay youth groups in the United States was me. But irrespective of my gender expression and sexual orientation, I was still socialized to be a man. Being gay did not inoculate me from sexist assumptions and male privilege. Becoming aware of and challenging these ways of thinking and behaving would accompany my professional and personal development over many years.

This book is also shaped by my social work background in its examination of sexual and gender minorities within a larger national context, rather than in isolation. A defining characteristic of the social work profession is the belief that people's problems exist within their social and economic context, and to help people with those problems, one must understand, and sometimes intervene in, the contextual level. As a social worker, examining sexual and gender minority people within the context of social, economic, and political changes made sense to me. Social work also taught me that in addition to understanding whatever problems people might have, it is equally important to know about their strengths and the resources they might draw on to surmount those problems. Accordingly, this book concerns itself not only with the constructions of sexual and gender minority identities but also with the construction of sexual and gender minority communities as primary sources of strength and support.

Acknowledgments

I am indebted to Heidrun Schulze and Davina Höblich, colleagues at Rhein-Main University of Applied Sciences, for teaching me about narratives and the importance of stories. Their invitation to visit their university and lecture to their students was the launchpad for the work that eventually resulted in this book. And since the book grew from many years of teaching a course on sexual and gender minorities, I am also thankful for the students at New York University's Silver School of Social Work who engaged with me on this material, shared my enthusiasm for it, challenged my blind spots, and went on to do important work of their own. Over the years, a number of colleagues and friends encouraged me to write a book on this topic, but I considered it to be too great a challenge. For this reason, I am particularly appreciative of the push that Steven David gave me to just do it. Upon hearing of my interest in writing this book, my colleague Jeane Anastas encouraged me to pursue the idea with Dana Bliss, senior acquisitions editor at Oxford University Press. Thank you, Jeane, for this recommendation, since working with Dana and OUP has been an extraordinarily positive experience. And thank you, Dana, for your guidance and support from our initial discussions about the idea for the book, through the development of the proposal, to the final product. I also appreciate the care with which the reviewers examined and assessed my proposal and the thoughtfulness of their comments and suggestions. I am beyond thankful to good friends Christoph Marshall, Jo Pryce, and Peter Graves for taking the time to read several chapters as I completed them, for offering helpful comments, and for encouraging me to keep going. Finally, writing a single-authored book is an inherently solitary task, and in the case of this particular book, writing it gave rise to several periods of reflection about my own life experiences, some joyful and some painful. Consequently, I am truly grateful for the continuing support of friends and family whose patience, interest, companionship, and encouragement sustained me through this creative process, including Jim Ehlers, Marshall Feldman, Peter Graves, Peter Kamps, Randy Lavinghouse, George Marin, John and Connie Martin, Margaret Powers, Jo Pryce, Maureen Rotblatt, Peter Sichel, Joel Verdon, Roger Wedell, and the late Elliot Pollack.

Chapter 1
Introduction

By the time this book was being written, the legislatures of California, Colorado, Illinois, Nevada, New Jersey, and Oregon had mandated the inclusion of the contributions of sexual and gender minority people in the history that is taught in public schools. In the case of New Jersey, Adely (2020) noted that "middle and high school students [would] learn about the social, political, and economic contributions of LGBTQ individuals" beginning in academic year 2020–2021. Laws such as these are not supported by everyone. The Family Policy Alliance of New Jersey's director of advocacy voiced opposition to the state law because it would "normalize or promote certain desires and attractions" (Hyland as quoted by Adely 2020). The intent of positions like this one is to control the narrative about *who* New Jerseyans are and, more generally, who Americans are as a people. That is, the dominant US narrative has always erased the existence or importance of sexual and gender minorities, and some people want to keep it that way.

The last few years have provided numerous other examples of the effort to erase sexual and gender minorities from narratives where they had gained some inclusion or to prevent their visibility. For example, sexual and gender minority content or authorship characterized a significant proportion of the more than 4,000 books targeted for removal from school and public libraries in 2023; 7 of the 10 books most often targeted had such content (American Library Association 2024). At least 500 bills aimed at restricting sexual and gender minority rights were introduced in state legislatures in 2023, many seeking to prevent visibility of gender minorities through restrictions on drag performances (American Civil Liberties Union 2024). In perhaps the clearest example of efforts to erase the visibility of sexual and gender minorities, Florida prohibited teaching about sexual orientation and gender identity through eighth grade and prevented school employees and students, regardless of grade, from expressing a gender that did not correspond with their biological sex.

In states where instruction about the contributions of sexual and gender minorities is mandated, it's fair to ask *which* contributions are to be

Sexual and Gender Minority History. James I. Martin, Oxford University Press. © Oxford University Press (2025). DOI: 10.1093/9780197765500.003.0001

taught. From what history would these contributions be drawn? These questions point to the nature of history itself. It is the position of this book that history is a narrative, a constructed story about people and nations. More specifically, a narrative is "a structure of explanation used to account for the occurrence of events and human actions" (Munslow 2006, p. 201). To know about the past, we cannot actually experience past events or speak with people who are dead; the only way we can know about the past is through interpretations of it, which we call *history*. Jenkins (2003) provided the following illustration of the constructed nature of history: "Although millions of women have lived in the past . . . few of them appear in history, that is, in history texts. Women thus have been 'hidden from history,' that is, systematically excluded from most historians' accounts" (p. 26).

The historical narrative that most of us know is what we learned in school—*public history*, which Tosh (2018) defined as "the version of the past promoted for public consumption by the public authorities" (p. 30). Public history is frequently elaborated and disseminated through popular culture. In narrative terms, public history tends to be the *dominant narrative*, or the story that's constructed from the perspective of those who have the most power in society. The dominant narrative about the United States is constructed from the perspective of white, Christian, heterosexual, cisgender men. In this narrative, people who are nonwhite, non-Christian, nonheterosexual, noncisgender, and not men are nonnormative, and their perspectives are invisible or, at best, ancillary. Thus, a critical examination of the national narrative reveals patterns of power, domination, and marginalization in society. In the case of sexual and gender minorities, the tacit or explicit exclusion of them from history, "and the lack of discussion of sex, gender and sexuality more generally, has been a key part of the ways that institutions and discourses of public history reinforce power structures" (Gowing 2018, p. 295).

This book presents sexual and gender minority history as a *counter-narrative*. Counter-narratives are stories told from the perspectives of people who are marginalized in society, and thus they serve to resist the domination and marginalization perpetuated by the dominant narrative. Telling the history of sexual and gender minority people is an act of resistance against oppression that is perpetuated by the dominant narrative. In addition, the lessons provided by pulling back the curtain on invisible patterns of dominance and marginalization in society can benefit everyone.

In his essay "The White Man's Guilt," James Baldwin (1965, p. 47) argued that history is much more important than most people recognize.

> History, as nearly no one seems to know, is not merely something to be read. And it does not refer merely, or even principally, to the past. On the contrary, the great force of history comes from the fact that we carry it within us, are unconsciously controlled by it in many ways, and history is literally present in all that we do. It could scarcely be otherwise, since it is to history that we owe our frames of reference, our identities, and our aspirations.

Baldwin was referring primarily to the history of enslavement of Africans and their descendants and how that legacy continues to influence contemporary American life through racist social, cultural, political, and economic patterns that remain invisible to many people. Similar observations could be made about other aspects of American history and, for that matter, the history of other countries. How does the past exert an invisible but powerful influence on the present and future? In the novel *1984* (Orwell 1949), the Party proclaimed that those who control the past control the future, and whoever controls the present can control the past. In other words, control of the historical narrative is central to the maintenance of power in society.

Why Learn About Sexual and Gender Minorities?

For 18 years I taught a graduate social work course on sexual and gender minorities, and often, at the very beginning of the course, I asked this question: *Why should we bother to learn about sexual and gender minority people?* The answer given by most students was about the importance of learning to be culturally competent when working with sexual and gender minority people. Although this was a correct answer, another possible answer to this question may be more important. That is, sexual and gender minority people have unique experiences and perspectives that can help all people to better understand themselves and the world in which they live. This idea comes from standpoint theory.

Standpoint theory helps to conceptualize why learning about people who are different, especially marginalized and disempowered minority people, is so valuable for our understanding of the world. The theory originated in the writing of Nancy Hartsock (1983). According to standpoint theory, all knowledge is socially situated; our position in society is our standpoint, and it is from this standpoint that we experience and understand the world. Hartsock drew directly from Karl Marx's theory about social class in capitalist society and applied it to gender, specifically the relationships between women and men, which is why the theory is often called feminist standpoint theory. Feminist standpoint theory is concerned with the relationship between knowledge and power. Social groups with the most power in society have considerable investment in maintaining both the knowledge and lack of knowledge that perpetuate that power. For example, men are less likely than women to recognize the existence or effects of sexism. Therefore, women's experiences are especially valuable for advancing social justice in society (Harding 1997). In a sense, those who are on the margins of society have a more complete understanding of social reality.

However, feminist standpoint theory was critiqued by some African American writers as overgeneralizing about women. They argued persuasively that women don't all have the same position in society, or the same standpoint (Collins 1997). Among American women, those who are white or of European descent are the mainstream, and African American and other women of color are on the margins. Thus, the standpoints of racial and ethnic minority women are especially valuable for advancing social justice. Audre Lorde (1984) was an important contributor to the development of black feminist standpoint theory with her watershed speech "The Master's Tools Will Never Dismantle the Master's House," which she gave at the Second Sex Conference in 1979. It is from black feminist standpoint theory that the concept of intersectionality originated, especially through the writing of Kimberlé Crenshaw. Intersectionality refers to the fact that people's identities are multifaceted, and any of these facets can be targets of harm from society. Crenshaw (1989) described traffic going in all four directions as a metaphor for intersectionality. Let's say a black lesbian with a disability is injured in an accident involving more than one car while she is crossing an intersection. To understand the cause of the accident, we need to consider the contributions of cars going in all four directions. And to understand the harms she experiences in life from discrimination, we must consider, at minimum, discrimination on the basis of her race, her sexual orientation, and her ability status.

By applying the major concepts of standpoint theory to examination of the historical narrative, we can see why counter-narratives are so important. Since they represent the experiences of people who are marginalized in society, they allow for a much more complete and accurate understanding of society. Sexual and gender minority history provides a particularly important counter-narrative precisely because it is so invisible. Examination of this history allows us to view the dominant narrative, or public history, more critically. Who and what have been left out of that narrative, and why? Who wrote the history that we learned? From what social position was that narrative constructed? What is the impact on sexual and gender minorities of being rendered invisible in the national narrative? And what is the impact on society in general? How does it suffer from the way in which the dominant narrative has been constructed? I hope you'll think about these questions as you read this book.

As you will see, there is also a dominant narrative among sexual and gender minorities that has been constructed by those who are less marginalized, that is, white, male, cisgender, and middle class or affluent. Thus, sexual and gender minority history can easily replicate many aspects of the dominant narrative unless an effort is made to uncover experiences of those who are doubly or triply marginalized due to their race, sex, gender identity or expression, or social class. Applying an intersectional lens to this history, then, will also identify patterns of racism, sexism, cisgenderism, and classism.

Who Are Sexual and Gender Minorities?

But who are sexual and gender minority people? The answer to this question is not as simple as it might seem. There is evidence of same-sex sexual behavior, same-sex relationships, and varied patterns of gender expression throughout history and across cultures. For example, Sappho (seventh to sixth century BCE), considered to be one of the greatest poets of the ancient world, wrote poetry that is renowned for its focus on love and passion, especially love for women. The term *lesbian* derives from Lesbos, the Greek island where she was born (Aldrich 2012). The Sacred Band of Thebes was the elite force of the Theban Army composed of 150 pairs of male lovers who were virtually unbeaten on the battlefield for more than 40 years until they were martyred at the Battle of Chaeronea by the army of King Philip of Macedon and his son Alexander in 338 BCE (Romm 2021). Emperor Ai, who ruled Han dynasty China from 6 BCE until 1 CE, is said to have cut off his own sleeve when he awoke so as not to disturb his sleeping male lover, Dong Xian. This ancient story is the origin of the phrase "cut sleeve" (*duan xiu*) as a Chinese synonym for homosexuality (Chou 2000). In 1886, in Buganda (now Uganda), King Mwanga II ordered the execution of 45 of his male subjects who converted to Christianity, which had been brought to Buganda by European colonizers. According to those who condemn the king and consider the subjects martyrs, he did so because they refused to have sex with him. However, Blevins (2011) criticized this narrative as being colonialist. According to Blevins, there is no evidence that Bugandans at that time disapproved of sex between King Mwanga and his male subjects, and the executions were ordered because the subjects had converted to the religion of the colonizers.

These examples from world history show that same-sex sexual behavior is neither new nor limited to one part of the world. However, the meaning of same-sex sexual behavior, and the patterns in which it occurs, varies greatly across historical time and culture; patterns of gender expression also vary according to culture, and they too change over time. None of the people mentioned above were thought of, or could have thought of themselves, as lesbian, gay, bisexual, transgender, or queer since these identities did not exist during their lifetimes. As you will see in this book, these identities originated in the second half of the 19th century in Germany before developing further in the United States during the 20th century. By focusing primarily on 20th-century US history, this book tells only one part of a global story about sexual and gender minorities. Today, people who identify as lesbian, gay, bisexual, transgender, or queer live in countries throughout the world, and the particular histories of which they are a part may have some commonalities with the one examined in this book, but also many points of divergence.

Some Basic Concepts

The following concepts are centrally important for this examination of sexual and gender minority history. But since they have been defined and used by previous authors and in popular culture in a variety of ways, the definitions used in this book are provided below.

Gender and sex: While *sex* is a biological status (e.g., female, male) that is usually assigned at birth, *gender* is a social status. Prior to the 1950s gender was a linguistic term that categorized words as female, male, or neuter, and in many languages other than English nouns continue to have gender.

In the mid-1950s the sexologist John Money (1955) adapted this term to show how biological and social influences interact in the development of women's and men's identities. There are two common and very powerful assumptions about gender. First, there are only two genders, which can be called the assumption of binary gender. Second, gender and sex are congruent, which can be called the assumption of gender-sex congruence. In other words, the only genders are *woman* and *man*; women are *biologically female*, and men are *biologically male*. Both of these assumptions are incorrect. In fact, there may be an unlimited number of gender constructions (woman and man being arbitrary), and there is no necessary connection between sex and gender (Hyde et al. 2019). Likewise, there are two common assumptions about sex (Fausto-Sterling 2000). First, there are only two sexes, which can be called the assumption of binary sex. Second, biological sex is a real thing, that is, not a social construction. These assumptions are also incorrect. More than 65 years ago, Money (1955) commented that "there is no absolute dichotomy of male and female" (p. 73). The existence of intersex people provides evidence that the two categories of sex, female and male, are constructions as arbitrary as those for gender (Fausto-Sterling 2000).

Sexual orientation: A social construction referring to sexual and/or romantic attraction to members of the same and/or another sex. John Money reportedly coined this term as a replacement for *sexual preference* because the older term suggested a process of choice that did not actually occur (Ehrhardt 2007). Research indicates that genetic and intrauterine environmental factors combine to determine sexual orientation (Cook 2021).

Same-sex sexual behavior: Sexual behavior directed toward a member of the same sex.

Sexual minority identities: Identities that are constructed around a sexual orientation that is not exclusively other-sex oriented (e.g., lesbian, gay, bisexual). Among the attempts to formulate an umbrella term to represent all these identities, most notable is the acronym LGB (representing lesbian, gay, and bisexual identities). However, this acronym fails to represent identities that are fluid or that fall outside the three defined categories in other ways. The umbrella term *sexual minority identities* is used in this book to avoid these limitations.

Gender identity: The innate sense of one's own gender (e.g., woman, man). Research on gender identity development indicates that it becomes stable in most children by age 6 (Perry et al. 2019). Money (1985) noted that it was necessary to invent this term because the expression of one's gender through behavior and appearance was not necessarily congruent with the private experience of one's gender.

Gender expression: The way that one's gender identity is expressed outwardly through behavior and appearance. Money (1985) originally called it *gender role*.

Gender minority identities: Identities constructed around experiences of gender that are nonbinary and/or noncongruent with the biological sex or gender assigned at birth. *Cisgender* identity is constructed around experiences of gender that are binary and congruent with the biological sex and gender assigned at birth (Schilt and Westbrook 2009). Identifying an umbrella term for all noncisgender identities is particularly difficult. Transgender, or trans, is the most common umbrella term used today, but many people with noncisgender identities reject it. Use of the umbrella term *gender minority identities* is an attempt at greater inclusivity.

Sexual and gender minority identities: Sexual minority identities and gender minority identities are not mutually exclusive. For example, the self-identifiers *queer* and *two spirit* may incorporate elements of both sexual orientation and gender identity. The umbrella term *sexual and gender minority identities* will be used in this book except when addressing issues that are specific to experiences of sexual orientation versus experiences of gender, or when focusing on specific identities such as lesbian or transgender.

Chapter 2
Germany in the Late 19th and Early 20th Centuries

The Offense of Sodomy

Some authors suggest that Christianity was tolerant of same-sex relationships until the 13th century. In particular, Boswell (1994) found evidence throughout Europe of official Christian liturgy for the blessing of same-sex unions dating from as early as the 4th century to as late as the 16th century. However intolerance and denunciation of same-sex sexual behavior (primarily among men) became increasingly common in Europe during the time of the Crusades (12th to 13th century), when hatred of non-Christians and heretics proliferated. In the second half of the 13th century, Thomas Aquinas codified doctrine on virtually every issue of concern to the Catholic Church, including sexuality, in the *Summa Theologiae*. Aquinas imported into the *Summa* popular xenophobic attitudes about same-sex sexual behavior among both men and women and constructed a theological explanation for them. Subsequently, the *Summa* strongly influenced European laws. By the beginning of the 14th century, laws throughout much of Europe prescribed the death penalty for same-sex sexual behavior (Boswell 1980). The first criminal code of the Holy Roman Empire, issued in 1523, proclaimed in Article 116 that anyone who committed "impure intercourse with beast, man with man or woman with woman shall be burnt" (Schwules Museum Berlin and Sternweiler 2008, p. 15).

Laws that criminalize same-sex sexual behavior are called sodomy laws in reference to the biblical city Sodom, which, according to the popular interpretation of Genesis 19, God destroyed because its men engaged in same-sex sexual relations. However, quite a few authors (e.g., Carden 2014; Downey 2017; Gnuse 2015) have advanced interpretations of this text that don't involve same-sex sexuality at all. Nevertheless, for centuries men who had sex with other men were referred to as *sodomites*. Sodomy laws have varied greatly with respect to the behaviors they address, which include not

Sexual and Gender Minority History. James I. Martin, Oxford University Press. © Oxford University Press (2025).
DOI: 10.1093/9780197765500.003.0002

only sexual acts between men and penetrative sexual acts between women but also masturbation, anal sex between men and women, and sex with nonhumans (Hofman 2020).

Capital punishment for the offense of sodomy in Europe was not just theoretical; hundreds of people lost their lives (Crompton 1981). For example, in 1578, five Catholic monks were burned to death in the Flemish city of Ghent for the offense of sodomy, and their remains were put on public display (Roelens 2015). Between 1730 and 1732 more than 300 men were put on trial for sodomy in the Netherlands, and those found guilty were executed (Boon 1989). In the year 1806 alone, 50 men were hanged to death in England for sodomy (Harvey 1978). John Smith and John Pratt were the last two men executed for sodomy in England; they were hanged in front of London's Newgate Prison in 1830. It has generally been accepted that sodomy laws rarely applied to women. Although this might be true of more recent laws, Crompton (1981) claimed that between the 13th and 17th centuries they applied to both men and women throughout Europe. There are comparatively few records of executions of women for sodomy, but Puff (2000) identified several examples in the Low Countries and the German-speaking lands between the 14th and 18th centuries.

By the late 1700s the philosophers of the Enlightenment began to have an influence on laws in Europe. With its emphasis on reason and science, as opposed to religious authority or tradition, the Enlightenment led to a reduction in the harshness of sodomy law penalties (Sibalis 2006). In 1787, Austria became the first European country to abolish the death penalty for sodomy (Schwules Museum Berlin and Sternweiler 2008). A few years later, an even more radical reform was undertaken by revolutionary France.

The French Revolution, which began in 1789, swept away the *ancien régime* based on the authority of the monarchy and Catholic Church. The revolutionary penal code enacted in 1791 did not mention sodomy at all, thereby removing from criminality consensual sex acts between men and between women (Sibalis 2006). The intent of the penal code was to decrease the interference of government into people's personal lives, especially with respect to victimless offenses (Johnson 2020). With the Penal Code of 1810 the postrevolutionary French Empire confirmed that private sexual acts would not be regulated by the state. Under Napoleon I, France conquered much of Europe, and the French legal system either was imposed in these lands or significantly influenced legal reforms. Sodomy was removed from the penal codes of Holland and many of the Italian and German states. For example, the Bavarian Criminal Code of 1813 did not mention sodomy at all (Sibalis 2006).

Sodomy in Prussia and the German Empire

The country of Germany that we know today is a modern invention. In the mid-19th century, there were more than 30 independent German states and kingdoms, the largest and most powerful being the Kingdom of Prussia. Prussia's system of laws was strongly influenced by French Enlightenment ideas. For example, capital punishment for sodomy was discontinued in 1794. That influence had its limits, though, as sodomy was not decriminalized (Schwules Museum Berlin and Sternweiler 2008). Later, sexual behavior between women was omitted from the Prussian Criminal Code when it was revised in 1851 (Leck 2016). In the decades following Prussia's 1815 defeat of the French Empire, it became increasingly interested in uniting the other German states and kingdoms under its leadership. In 1868 this goal was partially accomplished with the formation of the North German Confederation and then fully realized with the establishment of the German Empire in 1871. Prussian law regarding sodomy was incorporated into the German Empire's criminal code as Paragraph 175, which outlawed "unnatural sexual acts committed between persons of the male sex, or by humans with animals." The punishment was imprisonment for up to five years (US Holocaust Memorial Museum 2021). Notably, in many parts of the new empire where sodomy had been decriminalized for a couple of decades, a sodomy law was now imposed. It is within this context that the first constructions of sexual and gender minority identities emerged and the first movement for the rights of people with same-sex desires occurred. Interestingly, the German government's proposal for a revised criminal code in 1909 included a change to Paragraph 175 that would have recriminalized same-sex behavior between women. However, the revision was never completed or implemented (Matysik 2004).

Karl Heinrich Ulrichs, 1825–1895

The first European person known to have declared publicly that he had same-sex desires was Karl Heinrich Ulrichs, born in the Kingdom of Hannover in 1825. Ulrichs had studied law and worked in a district court for

12 SEXUAL AND GENDER MINORITY HISTORY

several years until he resigned in 1854, apparently due to rumors about his same-sex desires. In Hannover, same-sex sexual behavior was not illegal unless it caused *public offense*, that is, until it was annexed by Prussia in 1866. Because Ulrichs was a public official, his desires—and rumors of his acting on them—were considered to cause public offense (Beachy 2014). In 1862, if not earlier, he openly discussed his desire for other men in letters to members of his family, who generally were not supportive (Pretsell 2020). Over the course of the next few years he published under a pseudonym several monographs on same-sex sexuality in which he explicated an original theory about it and argued for its decriminalization. He also advocated for decriminalization directly with government officials. For example, in an 1864 letter to the Hannover government he wrote, "We want equal rights just as other citizens do, and protection of our social existence. . . . The state does not have the right to take punitive action against the simple sexual acts of [those with same-sex desires] or to invade their privacy by the vice squad" (Pretsell 2020, p. 155). In 1867 he appeared before the Sixth Congress of German Jurists, more than 500 judges, lawyers, and administrators, to argue against the Prussian sodomy law. Unfortunately, he was shouted down and had to leave the podium before finishing his speech (Beachy 2014).

His groundbreaking public advocacy notwithstanding, Ulrichs is perhaps most important for articulating the first modern theory about those who desired same-sex others as being *a people*. He proposed that attraction to members of one's own sex was inborn, not learned, and not due to any moral failing. In other words, having same-sex desires constituted *who one was* rather than *what one did*, and thus it represented the first construction of a sexual or gender minority identity. According to Ulrichs's theory, men who desired other men (like himself) had a female soul in a male body, which influenced not only his sexual desire but also what today we would call his gender expression. He called such men, including himself, Uranians (in German, *Urning*). In his formulation, women who desired other women had a male soul in a female body, and he called them Uraniads (in German, *Urningin*). Ulrichs's word for other-sex-desiring people was *Dioning*. Over the course of several years, Ulrichs further elaborated this theory to account for variation in gender sensibility and behavior among same-sex-desiring people as well as for people whose desires were for both the same and other sex.

In an 1865 letter, Ulrichs proposed bylaws for a Federation of Uranians, which would have among its purposes:

a. To wrest Urnings out of their previous isolation and to unite them into a compact body united in solidarity.
b. To defend the innate human rights of Urnings in the face of public opinion and State institutions, in particular to ensure Urnings equal status with Dionings before the law and in all of human society. (Pretsell 2020, p. 173)

The proposed federation would also "assist individual urnings who face discrimination because of their Uranism, in every need and danger, to help them, if need be, to obtain an appropriate position in life" (Pretsell 2020, p. 173).

Karl Heinrich Ulrichs influenced virtually every other German activist for the cause of same-sex-oriented men and women during the late 19th and early 20th centuries, and his ideas were also adopted by the Victorian-era British writers John Addington Symonds and Edward Carpenter, who were among the earliest English-language advocates for the rights of sexual minority people.

Károly Mária Kertbeny, 1824–1882

Among the authors influenced by Ulrichs was Károly Mária Kertbeny, an Austrian journalist of Hungarian parentage who introduced the term *homosexuality* in two monographs he published anonymously in 1869 that argued for the "legal emancipation of homosexuals" (Takacs 2004, p. 29) on the basis of the state having no right to interfere in private behavior between consenting adults. Kertbeny was the first author to reference Ulrichs's early work, which had been published pseudonymously, and the two men subsequently exchanged letters and ideas between 1865 and 1868. They both had significant concerns about the number of same-sex-oriented men who were driven to suicide due to the effects of sodomy laws, and they also shared distress about the increasing power of militaristic Prussia. However, Kertbeny never adopted Ulrichs's terms for same-sex-desiring people, and he disagreed with Ulrichs's belief that the inborn nature of same-sex desire was a sound argument for decriminalization. In his final letter to Ulrichs, written in 1868, he argued, "While it challenges prejudice against urnings, it also multiplies it ever more by making them special, peculiar, abnormal unfortunates" (Pretsell 2020, p. 204). In the same letter, Kertbeny used the invented terms *monosexual, heterosexual, homosexual,* and *heterogenit* to describe the sections of a volume on sexuality that he was writing (but never completed); these terms referred to sexual acts directed toward the self, the other sex, the same sex, and nonhumans (Leck 2016).

Richard von Krafft-Ebing, 1840–1902

Another important person from this era was Richard von Krafft-Ebing, a German psychiatrist whose book *Psychopathia Sexualis* became the authoritative source of medical and legal knowledge about sexuality in the late 19th and early 20th centuries. First published in 1886, the book was revised and expanded through 12 editions, each lavishly illustrated with case studies drawn from forensic records, court proceedings, and Krafft-Ebing's clinical practice. An English-language version was published in 1892. Although Krafft-Ebing's primary achievement was the medicalization and pathologization of nonprocreative sexual behavior, his work also contributed to the development of sexual and gender minority identities by providing case examples and, in some cases, names for behaviors and feelings that were previously hidden. Through his work, people who shared these feelings or engaged in these behaviors learned that they were not alone and, in some cases, now had a name for what they did or who they were (Oosterhuis 2012). As an illustration, the main character of Radclyffe Hall's groundbreaking lesbian novel of 1928, *The Well of Loneliness,* "discovered her true nature when she finds a copy of . . . *Psychopathia Sexualis*" (Rupp 2006, p. 239). Krafft-Ebing disagreed with the criminalization of homosexuality, and he supported efforts to repeal Paragraph 175. However, he believed that homosexuality was pathological and that homosexuals should be treated as patients. Thus, the idea of same-sex desire being a mental health problem began its establishment in the new profession of psychiatry.

Magnus Hirschfeld, 1868–1935

Magnus Hirschfeld was a German Jewish physician who was one of the founders, in 1897, of the *Scientific Humanitarian Committee,* the world's first organization to fight for the decriminalization of same-sex sexual behavior. In 1898, 1922, and 1925 the committee submitted petitions to the Reichstag (German Parliament) to repeal Paragraph 175. The petitions were signed by thousands of people, including famous authors and scientists like Thomas Mann, Emile Zola, Leo Tolstoy, and Albert Einstein (Tamagne 2006). Although a parliamentary committee approved a repeal in 1929, it was never enacted by the full Parliament. Hirschfeld himself, like many other German homosexuals, did not sign these petitions because "coming out" publicly would have ended his career. In 1919 Hirschfeld appeared in the world's first film with a gay perspective, *Anders als die Andern* (*Different from the Others*), in which he argued directly for the decriminalization of same-sex sexual behavior.

Hirschfeld was motivated to form the Scientific Humanitarian Committee by one of his patients who committed suicide the night before his marriage to a woman. In his suicide note, the young man urged Hirschfeld to educate the public about "the fate and fortune of homosexuals" (Dose 2014, p. 41). Although the committee's primary function was to effect the repeal of Paragraph 175, it also worked to educate the professional and lay public about homosexuality. The committee's motto, *Per Scientiam ad Justitiam* (*Through Science to Justice*), expressed Hirschfeld's belief that the development of scientific knowledge about homosexuality, and dissemination of that knowledge to the public, would lead to enlightened social justice. In 1899, the committee began publishing an annual record, *Jahrbuch für sexuelle Zwischenstufen* (*Yearbook for Sexual Intermediacy*), with Hirschfeld as editor. And in 1908 Hirschfeld launched a professional journal, *Zeitschrift für Sexualwissenschaft* (*Journal for Sexology*), in association with the committee (Dose 2014).

In 1919, Hirschfeld founded the Institute for Sexual Science in Berlin. The institute was a center for academic research and training on sexuality. In addition, people from all over the world came to the institute for medical treatment of sexual problems, including venereal diseases and sexual dysfunction, and for gender-confirming surgery, which Hirschfeld pioneered. The public also came to the institute for its museum of sex, the world's first, and for the world's leading library on sexuality. By the 1920s, the institute was one of Berlin's major tourist attractions (Dose 2014).

Hirschfeld argued that same-sex sexuality was biologically based and entirely natural. Going well beyond the existing theory that homosexuals made up a "third sex," he developed a complex conceptual model of "sexual intermediacy" in which

we all began life as one asexual creature, then . . . develop various sexual characteristics after being exposed to hormones and physical maturation.

Everyone experiences this development in unique ways, though. Consequently, we all represent slightly different mixtures of the various sexual characteristics. In other words, we are all "sexual intermediaries." (Whisnant 2016, p. 28)

According to this model, people's physical, psychological, and sexual form could lie anywhere on a continuum between the theoretical extremes of "fully female" and "fully male." Hirschfeld estimated that more than 43 million individual types were possible, and thus he conceptualized normal human sexuality as being extraordinarily diverse (Beachy 2014).

Adolf Brand, 1874–1945

Although Magnus Hirschfeld was very influential in his time, not all same-sex-oriented men agreed with his biological-medical perspective on sexuality. Adolf Brand was a publisher who represented the "masculinist" construction of male same-sex desire. He published the world's first homosexual publication, *Der Eigene*, from 1898 to 1932. The title is hard to translate to English, but it refers to the right of people to their own individuality. In 1903, he cofounded a private club, *Die Gemeinschaft der Eigenen*, to support the publication, although it was more of an elitist literary salon than an organization or movement. Unlike Hirschfeld, Brand was open about his sexuality, and his publication activities landed him in jail on several occasions (Whisnant 2016). He also was an early proponent of "outing," which added to his periodic legal troubles (Schwules Museum Berlin and Sternweiler 2008).

The masculinists joined in the effort to repeal Paragraph 175 because its existence led to extortion and other violence against same-sex-oriented men and because they believed sexuality was private and should not be regulated by the state (Brand 1931/1991). As Brand wrote in 1925, "The right of self-determination over body and soul is the most important basis of all freedom" (Brand 1925/1991, p. 155). The masculinists rejected the idea of a "third sex" or "intermediacy," which suggested to them that men with same-sex desires were effeminate and not fully men. By contrast, they argued that a man's behavior and dress, which today we would call gender expression, had nothing to do with his sexual desires for other men (Whisnant 2016). They also rejected the medicalization of sexuality; because it was the

GERMANY IN THE LATE 19TH AND EARLY 20TH CENTURIES   17

role of medical doctors to treat illnesses, medicalization therefore associated same-sex sexuality with illness (Friedländer 1907/1991).

The construction of same-sex sexuality promoted by the masculinists was based on ancient Greek traditions in which an adult man provided mentorship to an adolescent boy through their intimate relationship; the sexual aspect of the relationship was expected to end when the boy entered adulthood (Reiffegg 1902/1991). Some of the masculinists also expressed misogynistic and nationalistic views.

Emma Trosse, 1863–1949

It is difficult to find any mention of women in the history of sexual and gender minorities in late 19th- and early 20th-century Germany despite the important contributions of some women. Emma Trosse was the first woman known to have published on the topic of same-sex sexuality among women. In monographs published in 1895 and 1897, she wrote that same-sex sexuality was innate and natural, much the same as Karl Heinrich Ulrichs had stated, and that it should not be considered pathological or criminal. She also wrote about asexuality. One reason that knowledge about Trosse has been limited is that her publications did not identify her clearly as the author; one of them listed only her initials, and the other listed only her last name (Taylor and Taylor 2017). It seems likely that her erasure from history is also due to both her being a woman and her focus on women's sexuality. Trosse's publications appeared in the midst of the first wave of feminism and public discussion about the nature of womanhood. Antifeminists argued that a woman's primary characteristics were maternalism, caring, and selflessness, and that women who did not express these characteristics (i.e., those pushing for expanded roles for women) were unnatural (Leng 2014). Thus, Trosse's exploration of sexuality among women represented an early argument that women should not be bound by patriarchal expectations about their nature.

Johanna Elberskirchen, 1864–1943

More is known about Johanna Elberskirchen, a feminist pioneer, socialist, and writer who was one of the few women in the leadership of the Scientific Humanitarian Committee, and who argued for the development of an alliance between the committee and the feminist movement. Elberskirchen

18 SEXUAL AND GENDER MINORITY HISTORY

studied medicine at the University of Bern and law at the University of Zürich. By 1912 she began dedicating herself to feminist politics, and in 1915 she moved to Berlin, where she lived openly as a lesbian with her partner Hildegard Moniac. In her 1904 book, *The Love of the Third Sex*, Elberskirchen wrote that same-sex sexuality was entirely natural, and that people are fundamentally bisexual (Whisnant 2016). In *What Has Man Made of Woman, Child, and Himself*, also published in 1904, she attacked patriarchal heterosexuality for subjugating women and bringing many ills to society. Thus, she considered same-sex sexuality to be morally superior and urged women to totally separate from men, especially in sexual matters (Leng 2013).

Theodora Ana Sprüngli, 1880–1953

Another important woman from this period was the journalist Theodora Anna Sprüngli, better known by her pseudonym Anna Rüling. Although she was a prolific writer, Rüling rarely addressed same-sex sexuality in her work. She is known primarily for the speech she gave in Berlin at the 1904 annual meeting of the Scientific Humanitarian Committee. In this speech she not only identified herself as a lesbian but also argued strongly for an alliance between the feminist movement and the homosexual movement, especially since many feminists were also lesbians. Because of the more public nature of a speech as compared to a publication, Rüling is credited with having broken the silence about same-sex sexuality among women (Leidinger 2004).

Summary

In the first part of this counter-narrative we can see that many of the questions and issues of concern to sexual and gender minorities today were first raised well over 100 years ago in Germany. For example, are sexual desire and gender identification related, or are they entirely different aspects of individual identity? Are sexual and gender minority people "born that way"? Does the argument of biological origin help or hinder the pursuit of social justice? This part of the counter-narrative illustrates the constructed nature of sexual minority identities, especially among men, given the popularity of three different constructions in late 19th- and early 20th-century Germany: the Uranian, the sexual intermediate, and the masculinist. For those of us in the United States, this part of the counter-narrative allows us to decenter in at least one important way. That is, sexual and gender minority identities are not American inventions. We also can see in this part of the counter-narrative the role of sexism and patriarchy in the oppression of sexual and gender minorities, most specifically for those who did not identify as men. And we can see that sexual minority men who focused solely on themselves and their own experiences were participants in maintaining the invisibility of sexual minority women.

Chapter 3
The Weimar Republic and National Socialism

Prior to the First World War, the empires of Great Britain, Austria-Hungary, Germany, France, Russia, and Turkey maintained a precarious balance of power through shifting alliances and periodic military conflicts that resulted in changes to national boundaries. This precarious balance was shattered in 1914 as the great powers went to war with each other, gradually drawing in countries from all over the world. The war was a catastrophe that left more than 20 million people dead by the time hostilities ended in 1918. One way to make sense of this catastrophe is to view it as the end of the "old order." By the end of the war, four of the world's most powerful monarchies collapsed, resulting in massive social, political, and economic dislocation and the implosion of their empires.

By the fall of 1918, as the German Empire faced certain defeat, a revolution spread within its borders. The emperor abdicated in early November, and the provisional German republic signed an armistice with the victorious powers of Great Britain, France, and the United States. The revolution raged throughout Germany; socialists and communists fought against right-wing factions not only politically but also violently in the streets. Following a constitutional convention in August 1919, the Weimar Republic was formally established (named for the city where the convention was held), followed by a cessation of violence. The collapse of the monarchy and establishment of a socialist-led democratic republic resulted in a remarkable period of experimentation.

The Weimar era generated an explosion of creativity, producing artistic works that remain surprisingly relevant and popular a century later. Films such as *The Cabinet of Dr. Caligari* (Wiene 1920), *Metropolis* (Lang 1927), and *M* (Lang 1931), classics of early cinema, examined anxiety and discontent in an era of dramatic social change. The slashing social criticism of the musical plays *The Threepenny Opera* (Brecht and Weill 1928) and *The Rise and Fall of the City of Mahagonny* (Brecht and Weill 1930) continue to

Sexual and Gender Minority History. James I. Martin, Oxford University Press. © Oxford University Press (2025). DOI: 10.1093/9780197765500.003.0003

thrill audiences throughout the world. The movement of New Objectivity in painting rejected romantic aspirations among artists and instead depicted real life coldly, without illusions. In architecture, Bauhaus introduced the clean lines and functionality of modernist design.

The Weimar Republic swept away the German Empire's strict censorship on stage performances. As a result, Weimar-era cabaret delivered biting political and social criticism in its music, and it dealt openly with sexuality. Some of the most prominent performers and songwriters were sexual minorities. Claire Waldoff was one of the most popular cabaret performers. The title of her 1926 song *Raus mit den Männern aus dem Reichstag* means "throw the men out of the Parliament," and the song lampooned men and patriarchal society. As part of a larger review, Waldoff sang this song from a chariot that she rode onto a stage set of the Roman Senate (Jelavich 1993). Waldoff was openly lesbian and lived in Berlin with her partner Olly von Roeder, although she tended to be coy about her sexuality when performing (Lareau 2005). Waldoff was famous for her purposefully coarse and direct style of singing, which was meant to represent working-class Berliners. In a 1928 revue, Marlene Dietrich, who later became one of Hollywood's greatest stars, performed *Wenn die beste Freundin mit der besten Freundin* (*When the Best Girlfriend with the Best Girlfriend*) with singer Margo Lion. In this song, two married women on a shopping trip express their dissatisfaction with their husbands and how much better their relationship is with each other. It became an unofficial anthem for German lesbians during the Weimar era (Jelavich 1993). The gay rights anthem *Das Lila Lied* (*The Lavender Song*), written by Mischa Spoliansky and Kurt Schwabach in 1920, was dedicated to Magnus Hirschfeld. Lareau (2005) claimed that it was rarely performed in its day, but the fact that it was written, recorded, and performed even sometimes is astonishing.

Weimar Berlin

By the time the Weimar Republic was established, there was already an international movement for the liberation of women and a well-established movement in Germany for the decriminalization of same-sex sexual behavior among men. According to Beachy (2014), Germany was the birthplace of the sexual minority identities we take for granted today, and during the Weimar era Berlin became the world's capital of sexual and gender diversity. Magnus Hirschfeld claimed there were as many as 100 nightspots throughout the city that catered to sexual minority men. They ranged from upscale nightclubs to plain and inexpensive hangouts, from places to sing along with a piano player to those where you could pick up a young sex worker. The elegant Eldorado, famous for its cross-dressing performers, was one of the most popular nightspots. In addition to drawing a mixed sexual and gender minority crowd, it was a popular destination for "artists, authors, celebrities, and tourists wanting to admire a piece of 'decadent' Berlin cr catch a glimpse of someone famous" (Whisnant 2016, p. 94).

Weimar Berlin was especially remarkable for its vibrant lesbian scene, with more than 50 bars, clubs, and cafes that offered the same kinds of variety as those catering to gay men (Whisnant 2016). In addition, social clubs sponsored dances and costume balls, lectures, recreation and sporting events, and excursions to the countryside (Siegessäule 2021). With so many options, you needed a guide to the city! Luckily, *Berlins Lesbische Frauen* (*Berlin's Lesbian Women*) was there to help. Published in 1928, it was written by Ruth Roellig with a foreword by Magnus Hirschfeld. Perhaps more important were the lesbian-oriented magazines that were published on a regular basis. Among them, *Die Freundin* (*The Girlfriend*) had the largest circulation. *Die Freundin* advertised lesbian-oriented books, films, nightclubs, and events, and it included editorials and personal stories about lesbians. Its personal advertisement section allowed women to find a partner or friend (Whisnant 2016). In addition, as many as 30 lesbian-themed novels were published during the Weimar years, as well as lesbian-themed plays such as *Mädchen in Uniform* (*Girls in Uniform*; Marhoefer 2015).

Numerous other regularly published magazines targeted sexual minority men, including *Die Freundschaft* (*Friendship*), *Die Insel* (*The Island*), and the previously mentioned *Der Eigene* (Whisnant 2016). *Die Freundschaft* had a more political bent, though it also included nonpolitical material, while *Die Insel* was more oriented toward literature and entertainment; both ran advertisements for places where men could meet and enjoy each other's company. These publications, like those for lesbians, were important contributors to the development of sexual minority identities among individuals who learned there were others like themselves. They also helped to develop a sense of community through the promotion of events and activities, as well as organizations, and the cultivation of attitudes and aspirations.

Weimar Berlin was a popular destination for sexual and gender minority tourists from Great Britain and the United States, including the British authors W. H. Auden and Christopher Isherwood, the American painter Marsden Hartley, and the American architect Philip Johnson. For many such tourists, one of the big draws was the flourishing and unusually open male sex work market. A broad range of young men engaged in sex work. While some of them did so by choice, others were driven by joblessness and poverty, especially during the hyperinflation of the early 1920s and the post-1929 Great Depression (Beachy 2014). In addition to the availability of sex workers, Berlin provided many opportunities for visiting and local men to meet each other for sex if not the possibility of an ongoing relationship. In addition to the numerous bars and cafes, some of the major shopping streets in central Berlin, such as Friedrichstrasse, were also well-known cruising grounds, as were many public toilets and certain parts of the Tiergarten park (Whisnant 2016).

Weimar Berlin was also known for its elaborate sexual and gender minority balls, although they originated in the 1880s, if not earlier. Prior to the Weimar era, the balls were not advertised openly, but advertisements abounded in the new era. Some of the balls were exclusively for lesbians and many others were attended by both men and women, but most of them were predominantly oriented toward men. In all cases, a large proportion of the hundreds of attendees dressed in full drag. Attending drag balls became part of the tourist circuit during the Weimar era (Beachy 2014).

Dancing on the Volcano's Edge

During a lecture about Weimar-era Berlin, a student once asked me what it was like for individual lesbians and gay men, specifically whether you could walk comfortably down the street hand in hand with your partner. I imagined the student was trying to determine how much the atmosphere was like today; perhaps they were wondering whether it was even better than today. I answered that even though the visibility of sexual and gender minorities was unprecedented, as was the development of sexual and gender minority culture and community, Paragraph 175 was still the law of the land and same-sex sexuality remained stigmatized in the larger society. Media censorship was less severe than in the United Kingdom or the United States, but it was not absent in Weimar Germany. Even in the go-go early 1920s, publications like *Die Freundin, Freundschaft*, and *Der Eigene* were periodically shut down and their publishers charged with distributing pornography. In 1926, the so-called Trash and Filth Writings law tightened restrictions on sexually oriented publications purportedly for the protection of youth. Police raids on bars were infrequent in Berlin but they did occur; more aggressive policing of sexual and gender minorities occurred in other parts of the country (Marhoefer 2015). Men who engaged the services of sex workers were often at risk of being blackmailed (Beachy 2014).

In addition, all of the social experimentation, creativity, openness, and hard partying of this era was occurring against a backdrop of severe political and economic instability. The German parliament consisted of elected representatives from numerous political parties, and it was highly unstable. The parties on the extreme left and extreme right did not support democratic government. Even the parties in the center had difficulty finding common ground on important issues. The composition of governing coalitions changed frequently based on elections and bickering between the various parties (Kolb 2005). The economic situation of the Weimar Republic was never good. Prior to the First World War, Germany had experienced rapid industrialization and urbanization that resulted in a high degree of social inequality. Like many other combatant countries, Germany experienced inflation and economic deprivation during the war. The reparations and other economic losses imposed on Germany upon its defeat added to the country's problems. Nevertheless, in its first years the Weimar government was successful in stimulating the country's economy through the use of expansionary monetary and fiscal policy (Storer 2013).

By 1922, however, the rate of inflation began to accelerate dramatically. According to Holtfrerich (1986), the cost of living increased 73% from January 1921 to January 1922; from January 1922 to January 1923, it increased nearly 5,400%; and from January to October 1923, the increase was more than 300 million percent. More concretely, Layton (2015) estimated that the cost of a pair of shoes increased from 12 German marks before the start of the war to 1 million marks in the summer of 1923, and to 32 trillion marks by November of that year. In the summer and fall of 1923 prices rose from one hour to the next. In such an environment, it made sense to spend money as quickly as possible, if one had any, and to live for the moment. Desperation caused by the collapse of the economy drove many working-class people to engage in petty crime and sex work, while tax evasion, fraud, and embezzlement became commonplace among those with greater means. The government was able to stabilize the currency by the beginning of 1924, but that did not end the hardship experienced by many people. Labor strikes

SEXUAL AND GENDER MINORITY HISTORY

and protests became increasingly widespread in the run-up to the hyperinflation, and during the worst of the inflation there were food riots. When the government introduced a new currency to bring inflation under control, many small businesses went bankrupt, and unemployment increased precipitously (Storer 2013). After the government succeeded in stabilizing the currency at the end of 1923, a period of relative calm occurred for several years even though the social and economic conditions were far from strong. It was during this period, often called the "Golden Twenties," that the social and cultural accomplishments of the Weimar Republic reached full flower.

The Party Ends

By the end of the First World War, the United States had the world's biggest and strongest economy. When the US stock market lost an unprecedented 23% of its value over the course of two days in late October 1929, it caused a chain reaction of events that reverberated throughout the American economy. As the American economy collapsed into the Great Depression, the rest of the world's leading economies fell with it. Since Germany's economic and political conditions were already shaky, the consequences there were especially severe. For example, industrial unemployment climbed to nearly 44% by 1932 (Crafts and Fearon 2013). Politically, the country had already begun shifting to the right, and when the centrist president died suddenly in 1925, a former war hero with political ties to the right was elected. With the onset of the Depression, the parliament became even more dysfunctional, and the president increasingly bypassed it in favor of an appointed "cabinet of experts" (Storer 2013, p. 175). As the people became disillusioned with democratic government, more and more of them voted for radical antidemocratic parties on the left (German Communist Party) and the right (National Socialist German Workers' Party). Political violence between the two extremes increased, with hundreds of people killed in paramilitary attacks and riots. With the election of November 1932, the National Socialists became the dominant party in parliament, and its leader, Adolf Hitler, was named chancellor of Germany in January 1933 (Storer 2013).

The National Socialist government immediately set out to liquidate all of its opponents and to marginalize racial and sexual and gender minorities. It outlawed all sexual and gender minority organizations. Beginning in

February 1933 with its Campaign for a Clean Reich, the government shut down all sexual and gender minority publications (including *Der Eigene* and *Die Freundin*) and most lesbian and gay clubs, most notably the Eldorado. By 1935 all of them were forcibly gone (Schwules Museum Berlin and Sternweiler 2008). On the morning of May 6, 1933, the Institute for Sexual Science was attacked and heavily vandalized by a large group of Nazi students who also looted its library, art collection, and medical files (Beachy 2014). The library's holdings, including all of Magnus Hirschfeld's writings, were destroyed on the night of May 10th at Berlin's Opera Plaza, where Nazi students burned tens of thousands of books that they considered un-German. Similar book burnings occurred in 70 cities and towns throughout the country, and they were followed by a policy of state censorship designed to prevent any variance from National Socialist ideas (Lewy 2016). Magnus Hirschfeld was in Switzerland when the Institute for Sexual Science was vandalized and looted and its books burned. He had left Germany on a worldwide speaking tour in 1930 and never returned. He attempted to start a new institute in Paris, but it never came to fruition. Hirschfeld died in 1935 while living in Nice, and he was buried there at the Cimitière de la Caucade (Dose 2014).

In a 1934 summer purge known as the Night of the Long Knives, rivals to Hitler's leadership within the Nazi Party were executed. Most notable among them was Ernst Röhm, the homosexual head of the Storm Troopers. Thereafter, the party engaged in a purge of homosexuals from its membership, and the government became more overtly hostile to sexual minorities. In June 1935, the government expanded Paragraph 175 to include virtually any expression of same-sex desire (Whisnant 2016). That is, "any sexual act between men as well as any fleeting touch or exchange of glances could be construed to take same sex loving men to trial or to send them to jail" (Hessisches Ministerium für Soziales und Integration n.d.). Persecution of sexual minority men and prosecutions under Paragraph 175 were conducted by the Reich Central Office for the Combat of Homosexuality and Abortion. The dual focus of this office reflected its racial purpose (Schwules Museum Berlin and Sternweiler 2008).

Racial superiority of the German people was a fundamental belief of National Socialism, and many of the government's laws and policies were intended to expand and strengthen the "German race" and safeguard the purity of its blood. National Socialists did not believe same-sex sexuality was inborn, and thus they did not consider sexual minority people to be a race. Sexual minority men were considered a threat to the pure German race mainly because they did not reproduce. That is, "every homosexual represented children lost to the nation" (Epstein 2015, p. 81). Moreover, National Socialists believed same-sex sexuality among men spread like an epidemic since sexual minority men "infected" other men (especially young men) by seducing them (Epstein 2015). Complementarily, abortion represented the destruction of potentially pure German children. Unlike Jews, whom the Nazi state sought to exterminate, sexual minorities were isolated from each other and forced into acceptable roles. An experimental program sought to find a cure for same-sex sexuality among men using hormone therapy, castration, and enslaved female sex workers. An estimated 100,000 men were arrested under Paragraph 175 during the 12 years of the Nazi era, of which about 50,000 were sentenced and approximately 15,000 were sent to concentration camps, where most of them died (Newton 2012).

Lesbians were not persecuted as directly as homosexual men. They were not criminalized by Paragraph 175, and there isn't evidence of lesbians being sent to concentration camps explicitly because of their sexuality. However, lesbians were persecuted in numerous indirect ways. For example, neighbors could denounce a lesbian adult to the police if they were suspicious about her living with another woman, not socializing with men, or dressing in a way they considered insufficiently feminine. The government rigidly enforced specific gender roles for German women that were designed to serve its racial agenda. Women were strongly encouraged to marry early and have many children. In general, they were not supposed to work outside the home. They were expected to be subservient to men. Those who deviated from these roles could be sent to a concentration camp or punished severely in other ways (Marhoefer 2016). There is scant evidence of lesbians in concentration camps. However, Nelly Mousset-Vos was imprisoned at the concentration camp Ravensbrück because of her activities with the Belgian resistance, as was Nadine Hwang for helping people escape occupied France. While imprisoned, the two women developed a deep love relationship with each other that survived the war and lasted for decades more (Gertten 2023).

Singer Claire Waldoff performed less and less after 1933 since the National Socialist government had no tolerance for public dissent or social criticism, and it closed down most of the Berlin cabarets. If she were not so popular, her life might have been in greater danger not only for her history of singing critical songs written by Jews but also for being a lesbian (Ring 2017). Waldoff and her partner left Berlin in 1939 and lived in the countryside in southern

Germany until their deaths in 1957 and 1963. Ruth Roellig's lesbian guide to Berlin was banned in 1938, by which time she had already stopped writing lesbian-oriented material. Her two novels published during the Nazi era contained nationalistic and antisemitic themes. She last published in 1937, although she survived the war and continued to live in Berlin until her death in 1969 (Pettis 2005).

The thousands of men who were sent to concentration camps for violating Paragraph 175 had to wear a pink triangle insignia during their incarceration. Between 1936 and 1945, about 1,000 of these men were sent to the concentration camp Sachsenhausen, near Berlin. The phrase *arbeit macht frei* on the camp's entrance gate meant "work sets you free," but most of the sexual minority men sent there were either sadistically worked to death in the camp's brickworks or murdered. Others died as subjects of unethical medical experiments, some of which were designed to change their sexual orientation. Before they were killed, many sexual minority men were forced to visit the camp brothel in another effort to make them straight; the women forced to work in the brothel were prisoners brought from the nearby camp Ravensbrück (Heger 1972; Morsch and Ley 2011; Plant 1986).

It is not known exactly how many sexual minority men died in concentration camps or how many survived incarceration. Unlike other survivors, sexual minority men were still considered criminals after the liberation and war's end. The Nazi-era version of Paragraph 175 was maintained in West German criminal law until 1969, when it was somewhat liberalized; it was not completely repealed until the reunification of West and East Germany in 1994. By then about 50,000 additional men had been arrested (Hessisches Ministerium für Soziales und Integration n.d.). For many years historians did not even acknowledge there were sexual minority victims of National Socialism. Nearly 30 years after the war's end, Josef Kohout shattered this silence by pseudonymously publishing his autobiographical account of imprisonment at Sachsenhausen, *The Men with the Pink Triangle* (Heger 1972). It would take until 2002 for the German government to officially acknowledge the sexual minority victims of National Socialism.

The first public memorial in Germany for sexual minority victims of National Socialism, the Rosa Winkel plaque, was installed on Berlin's Nollendorfplatz in 1989. The words on the triangle-shaped plaque say "Beaten to death, silenced to death: The homosexual victims of National Socialism." There are now many memorials to these victims throughout Germany, including the Frankfurter Engel, a statue of an angel with a broken neck installed in Frankfurt am Main in 1994, and one at the concentration camp Sachsenhausen. Public memorials to the sexual minority victims of National Socialism have been installed in several locations outside Germany as well, including Amsterdam, Sydney, and Tel Aviv. There were no such memorials in the United States until 2003, when Pink Triangle Park was dedicated in the Castro district of San Francisco. It remains the only one.

Summary

In this chapter, we can see clearly how people with the most power in society may construct and revise a national narrative according to their interests, imperiling those on the society's margins. In Germany, the narrative of a racially superior nation rationalized the marginalization and murder of millions of minoritized people. The concept of intersectionality is especially helpful in understanding the plight of marginalized people in this process. Lesbians, gay men, and other sexual minorities were more likely to run afoul of the National Socialist government if their gender expression transgressed traditional norms or if they were Jewish or had Jewish ancestors.

This counter-narrative of German history from a sexual and gender minority perspective provides two lessons that are especially powerful. First, sexual and gender minority people have an international, multigenerational history that has been erased from public memory. The erasure has been even more complete for those sexual and gender minority people who did not identify as men. Given the existence of this history, any freedoms that sexual and gender minority people experience today should be understood within the context of the struggles and sacrifices made by generations in the past. Second, social justice for minorities does not progress in an unbroken, irreversible manner. Progress can be, and often is, reversed. This part of the counter-narrative shows how an established minority community that developed slowly over the course of 60 years was quickly swept away. I have been astonished by the power of this lesson for many of my students, especially given the irregular and sometimes reversed progress of social justice for African Americans. Many students today have grown up during a period of unmistakable though sometimes illusory progress for sexual and gender minority people, and they have not imagined that it could be reversed.

Chapter 4
Foundations in the United States

Colonization of America

When European colonists set down roots in the land they called America, they encountered Indigenous inhabitants who exhibited patterns of gender and sexuality that horrified them. Because the Indigenous peoples of this land did not produce written records, the only records that do exist are those of the colonists, who generally did not integrate Indigenous oral histories into their written narratives. Many colonists' records describe Indigenous people who appeared biologically male but dressed and behaved as women, and others who appeared biologically female but dressed and behaved as men. There were hundreds of Indigenous names for such people (Rosario 2022), including the Shonone *tainna wa'ippe* and the Paiute *dubads* (Lang 2016); the Mescalero Apache *Nde'isdzan* and the Zuni *lha'mana* (Rosario 2022); and the Tewa Pueblo *kwidó*, the Lakota Sioux *winkte*, and the Navaho *nádleeh* (Jacobs et al. 1997). Although the roles these people played varied from culture to culture, the colonial narrative eventually referred to all of them as *berdaches*, an 18th-century French term for enslaved kept boys (Rosario 2022), a concept that was largely irrelevant to Indigenous cultures. This gross misunderstanding of the gender and sexual diversity among Indigenous cultures became a justification for the "brutal elimination of Indigenous practices and people" (Rosario 2022, p. 16).

European colonization of America was accompanied by the subjugation, removal, and genocide of Indigenous people, which opened more and more land for settlement (Beemyn 2006). For example, the fertile homelands of the Choctaw and Chickasaw, which made up most of what eventually became the state of Mississippi, were coveted for the highly lucrative and rapidly expanding cultivation of cotton (Saunt 2019). The Choctaw were forced to give up their land little by little in successive treaties with the United States during the first decades of the 19th century. Removal of Native inhabitants from their homelands was advanced in 1830 by the passage of the Indian Removal Act, which provided for the exchange of their coveted homelands

Sexual and Gender Minority History. James I. Martin, Oxford University Press. © Oxford University Press (2025). DOI: 10.1093/9780197765500.003.0004

32 SEXUAL AND GENDER MINORITY HISTORY

in the South for land in the territory now known as Oklahoma. That year, the Treaty of Dancing Rabbit Creek required the Choctaw to give up the remainder of their homeland and move to the new territory (Mississippi Band of Choctaw Indians 2016). Six thousand Choctaw set out in October 1831, but only about 4,000 survived the six-month journey marked by poor planning and incompetence among US officials, harsh weather, and disease. Additional removals of Choctaw occurred in 1832 and 1833 (Greenwood 2017), and in 1837 the Chickasaw traveled the same tragic path (The Chickasaw Nation 2023).

Regulation of Sexuality and Gender

Colonists imposed moral and legal codes they brought with them from Europe, including sodomy laws, on all the lands they settled (Beemyn 2006). British law was applied in all of the lands claimed by Britain; this included the Buggery Act of 1533, which made sexual behaviors between men and between women a capital crime. By the mid-17th century, the colonies began to enact their own laws. For example, Plymouth Colony enacted a sodomy law in 1636, as did the Massachusetts Bay Colony in 1641 and Connecticut in 1642 (Painter 1991–2005). In general, these laws called for the death penalty. Although executions for sodomy might have been rare, records indicate they occurred in British, Spanish (i.e., Florida), and Dutch (i.e., New Netherland) colonies. Sodomy laws enacted by the colonies generally did not apply to women, although the New Haven Colony was a notable exception. However, sexual behavior between women was sometimes punished according to laws criminalizing "lewd behavior" or "unseemly practices" (Beemyn 2006, p. 151). Among men and women, the severity of punishment for sodomy and other sexual infractions could vary according to their social class and race. For example, between 1700 and 1718 in Pennsylvania, the penalty for sodomy was life imprisonment if the offender was white, but death if the offender was black ("Sodomy Law: Pennsylvania, December 7, 1682" n.d.).

The last execution for sodomy in the American colonies occurred in Georgia in 1743. After independence, most of the 13 original states retained their laws against sodomy but abolished the death penalty for it by the end of the 18th century. However, punishment for sodomy remained quite severe. The laws in Connecticut and Georgia called for life imprisonment. In New

Hampshire and Massachusetts, they called for "solitary confinement and from one to ten years' hard labour" (Beemyn 2006, p. 152). In Rhode Island, a first offense called for imprisonment for three years or less, but a second offense called for the death penalty. North and South Carolina retained the death penalty for even a first offense (Beemyn 2006). New Jersey's law called for solitary confinement and hard labor for up to 21 years, and it applied to women as well as men.

Colonial laws also regulated gender expression in both men and women, especially through the criminalization of "cross-dressing" (Beemyn 2006, p. 151). Capers (2008) asserted that societal expectations regarding appearance and clothing have historically worked to reinforce social hierarchies regarding class, race, and sex. To illustrate, Capers described a 17th-century Massachusetts law prohibiting people with incomes less than £200 from wearing gold or silver. Also, the clothing that could be worn by enslaved Africans and their descendants in South Carolina was stringently regulated. In addition to their skin color, "their clothing had to mark them as subordinate" (p. 8).

Transgressing Gender Norms

Notwithstanding these laws, there are many accounts of Americans who transgressed gender norms in the 18th and 19th centuries. In a number of these cases, female-bodied individuals served in the Army by passing as men. Deborah Sampson enlisted in the Continental Army in 1782 under the name Robert Shurtleff and served for about a year in the Fourth Massachusetts Regiment without being discovered. Sampson later married a man and became popular throughout New England by speaking about her experience in the Army. Loreta Velasquez and Mary Ann Clark served in the Confederate Army during the Civil War, the former as Harry Buford and the latter as Henry Clark. Sarah Emma Edmonds served in the Union Army under the name Franklin Thompson. Jennie Hodgers enlisted in the Union Army in 1862 and served in the 95th Illinois Infantry as Albert Cashier (Bronski 2011).

Other female-bodied individuals transgressed gender norms in civilian environments, especially in the rural West. Charley Parkhurst was born female in 1812 but ran away from a Vermont orphanage as a young teenager and subsequently lived and dressed as a man. Parkhurst led a celebrated career as a fearless stagecoach driver in the mountain West until he retired to a ranch in California. He was especially renowned for his skill with a whip. It was said that "from 20 feet away he could slice open the end of an envelope or cut a cigar out of a man's mouth" (Elk Grove Historical Society n.d.). For bravery in repelling violent robbery attempts on his stagecoach, Parkhurst's employer, Wells Fargo, rewarded him with a solid gold watch and chain. Because Parkhurst voted in the national election of 1868, he is credited with being the first female-bodied American to vote. No one knew Parkhurst was female bodied until he died in 1879 and was being prepared for burial (Elk Grove Historical Society n.d.).

Stagecoach Mary Fields, who was enslaved from birth in the early 1830s, became the first African American stagecoach driver when she was over 60 years old. Mary was known to smoke and drink in saloons and to have a hot temper, but unlike Charley Parkhurst, there's no evidence that she lived full time as a man. After Emancipation, Mary migrated north to Ohio and eventually west to Montana. In both places she did gardening, laundry, and maintenance and repair work, as well as supply acquisition and delivery. In 1895, she became a Star Route Carrier (an independent contractor) for the US Post Office, for which she drove a stagecoach on a rural northern Montana route (Amspacher 2020). According to Amspacher, "Mary built a reputation of being fearless while working as a mail carrier. Mary's job was not only to deliver the mail but to also protect the mail from bandits, thieves, wolves and the weather as well." She was an expert in the use of both rifle and revolver, which she carried with her. After eight years as a Star Route Carrier, Mary retired to Cascade, Montana, where she started a laundry business and became so beloved by the community that she "drank in saloons for free and ate for free at local restaurants" (Amspacher 2020).

There are a variety of reasons American female-bodied individuals in the 18th and 19th centuries might have chosen to challenge the gender norms of their time. Some might have had an internal experience of being men, and if they lived today, they might consider themselves transgender. Others are likely to have found better financial opportunities by passing as men, since women generally were not allowed to have their own income and careers. Some women passed as men in order to fight side by side with their husbands in wartime. Still others might have been attracted by the greater freedom and excitement offered by men's social roles (Bronski 2011). As described by Stryker (2008),

> Imagine being a young female person in the 1850s who can't face a life of marriage and child rearing, who has no practical work skills outside of the home, and who dreams of adventure in the military, at sea, or in the mining towns of the mountainous and desert West. Donning your brother's clothes, you slip away in the night and head out to meet your fate. (p. 31)

Among male-bodied individuals, transgression of gender norms followed different patterns. Much of the frontier West consisted of all-male environments, including cowboy communities as well as mining, railroad, and logging camps. In these environments many men became devoted to each other emotionally and, in some cases, sexually (Beemyn 2006). Perhaps most dramatically, at the height of the Gold Rush of 1849, San Francisco was a booming frontier town of mostly single young men living in "rooming houses and cheap hotels, augmented by all-male public baths" (Bronski 2011, p. 46).

> With women and social restrictions both in short supply, men entertained each other in the city's saloons, gambling places and boarding houses. . . . A number of men at dances would wear a dress or wrap a bandana around their arm to indicate that they would assume the traditional women's part. (Beemyn 2006, p. 159)

Although there is little direct evidence of sexual behavior between men in the frontier West, Beemyn (2006) claimed that "sex between men was . . . an accepted fact of life in mining, logging, and railroad camps" (p. 159).

This frontier environment would largely end by the dawn of the 20th century. In an 1893 address to the American Historical Association, historian Frederick Jackson Turner drew from an official bulletin of the 1890 Census to report on the closing of the frontier. As Turner explained, it was no longer possible to ascertain a frontier of settlement because settled areas had since developed in virtually every part of the nation (Turner 1893/2023). The growing encroachment of settlement on the wilderness in which all-male communities thrived eventually extinguished the freedom to transgress gender norms in these areas, especially among men (Benemann 2006).

Walt Whitman and the Love of Comrades

During the second half of the 19th century, the writing of the great American poet Walt Whitman expressed a vision of a democratic America in which close relationships between men played an integral part. For example:

> I will plant companionship thick as trees along all the rivers of America, and along the shores of the great lakes, and all over the prairies,
> I will make inseparable cities with their arms about each other's necks,
> By the love of comrades,
> By the manly love of comrades.
>
> (Whitman 1855/2018, p. 195)

Whitman was born in 1819 in Huntington (Long Island), New York, and lived his entire life in the settled and "civilized" East. He first published his collection of poems, *Leaves of Grass*, in 1855 followed by several significantly revised editions until his death in 1892. Beginning with the 1860 edition, the frankly sexual content of many poems in the collection made his work controversial. In particular, the cluster of poems called *Children of Adam* celebrated sexual love between men and women, and the cluster called *Calamus* celebrated love between men. The former cluster was more explicit in its sexual language, and for many years it was the more controversial of the two. Boston banned the book in 1882 primarily due to its inclusion of these poems. The latter cluster became increasingly controversial as familiarity with the concept of homosexuality grew in late 19th-century America.

> And that night while all was still I heard the waters roll slowly continually up the shores,
> I heard the hissing rustle of the liquid and sands as directed to me
> whispering to congratulate me,
> For the one I love most lay sleeping by me under the same cover in the cool night,
> In the stillness in the autumn moonbeams his face was inclined toward me,

And his arm lay lightly around my breast—and that night I
was happy.

(Whitman 1855/2018, p. 195)

Relationships with other men played a central role in Whitman's life. During the course of the Civil War, in hospitals in Washington and New York, Whitman visited, attended to, cared for, and wrote about thousands of wounded young soldiers who came from all over the country to fight for the North and the South. Letters between him and many of these young men expressed great affection and love that was more than platonic (Shively 1989). Whitman's longest relationship was with Peter Doyle, an Irish immigrant who fought for the South. When they met in 1865, Whitman was in his mid-40s, and Doyle was a 21-year-old streetcar conductor in Brooklyn. Although they never lived together, their romantic bond lasted for the rest of Whitman's life. Nevertheless, he periodically established strong relationships with other young men, particularly Harry Stafford (Folsom and Price n.d.).

Whitman's close relationships with men recall the older man–younger man pattern of the German masculinists, described previously, a variation on ancient Greek traditions in which an adult man provided mentorship and love to a youth within the context of a sexual relationship. Such relationships are generally suspect today, even vilified as exploitative. In Whitman's case, his relationships were with young men (age 19 and older) rather than youths, but they were still quite unequal with respect to age, experience, education, and social class (Shively 1989). In the case of Harry Stafford, the relationship became less intimate when Stafford married a woman, but the friendship between the two men continued. This pattern most closely reflects the Greek tradition. By contrast, Peter Doyle never married.

Whitman's poetry was widely read, and he influenced a number of other important writers in the United States and beyond. The British authors John Addington Symonds and Edward Carpenter both met Whitman and were strongly influenced by him, and they became two of the earliest sexual minority rights activists in the English-speaking world. In 1883 Symonds published *A Problem in Greek Ethics*, a treatise on same-sex love in ancient Greece. Carpenter wrote a number of books on same-sex and other forms of sexuality beginning in the 1890s; his 1912 book *The Intermediate Sex* was based on Karl Heinrich Ulrichs's conceptualization of the third sex. Whitman's writing is also known to have had an influence on the British playwright and author Oscar Wilde, who, in one of his poems, referred to same-sex love as "the love that dare not speak its name." Wilde's trial and conviction for gross indecency in 1895 was widely publicized, bringing discussion about homosexuality into the public domain and strengthening demonization of same-sex-oriented men (Bronski et al. 2023). A German-language translation of *Leaves of Grass* was published in Switzerland in 1889, and it became popular and influential in Germany by the first decade of the 20th century, although not generally for its homoerotic content. However, the question of whether Whitman was a homosexual was openly discussed within the context of the homosexual liberation movement in Germany, and at least two articles on the subject were published in *Jahrbuch für Sexuelle Zwischenstufen*, the journal published by Magnus Hirschfeld's organization (Grünzweig 1995). Thus, Whitman and his writing had an influence on the development of modern sexual minority identities and communities, at least among men.

Romantic Friendships and Boston Marriages

While Walt Whitman's relationships with younger men represent one pattern of male same-sex relationship in 19th-century America, it was not the only pattern. Some young men engaged in long-lasting romantic friendships with other young men of the same class and similar age; these relationships usually ended with one or both of them marrying a woman. There is evidence that at least some of these relationships had a sexual component. Even after marrying, many men maintained intensely intimate friendships with other men, although these relationships were less likely to have a sexual component (Beemyn 2006).

More is known about "romantic friendships" among women during this era, which refer to passionately romantic relationships prior to the advent of publicly recognized lesbian identities (Faderman 1991). Long-lasting romantic friendships between two unmarried women who lived together have been called Boston marriages. Jane Addams, the mother of social work and winner of the 1931 Nobel Peace Prize, was in such a relationship. In Chicago, Addams opened Hull House in 1889, the first American settlement house, along with her close friend and likely romantic partner, Ellen Gates Starr. But Mary Rozet Smith, a wealthy heiress who arrived at Hull House in 1890, became Addams's life partner. In 1904, the two women bought a vacation home in Maine, and they lived together until Addams's death in 1934. Numerous passionate letters attest to the great importance they held for each other (Faderman 1999).

Relationships such as Addams and Smith's flourished during the first wave of feminism, as opportunities for middle-class white women to have lives outside of traditional marriage began to develop. This occurred in particular due to the growth of women's colleges; Mount Holyoke College opened in 1837, followed by the other "Seven Sisters" colleges over the next 50 years. For the first time, women could not only obtain a higher education but also have careers as educators and college administrators (Faderman 1991). At the same time, women developed new professions, most notably social work. Thus, it became possible for two middle-class women to support themselves without having to rely on marriage to a man. These relationships tended to be socially condoned as long as others believed they were not sexual in nature. There is evidence of romantic friendships among leaders of women's colleges, in particular Bryn Mawr and Mount Holyoke, and among some of the women's suffrage movement's leading activists (Faderman 1999). From a contemporary perspective, it's very hard to determine the extent to which Boston marriages or other romantic friendships had a physically sexual component since even the most passionately worded letters between partners, such as those between Addams and Smith, lack the kind of explicitly sexual language expected today as evidence.

The dearth of evidence of romantic friendships among nonwhite women during the 19th century might suggest the absence of such relationships were it not for the collection of letters between Addie Brown and Rebecca Primus. Written between 1859 and 1869, the letters from Brown to Primus and from Primus to her own family attest to a strong romantic, or erotic, relationship between the two women. Although Brown refers in her letters to correspondence from Primus, none of it survives. Nonetheless, Primus saved Brown's letters for 62 years until her death in 1932, perhaps indicating how important the relationship was to her. Both women were freeborn African Americans living in the North; Brown was an orphan from Philadelphia who had limited education and worked mainly as a domestic servant in New York and Connecticut, while Primus was a well-educated teacher from a prominent black family in Hartford. It's unknown how the two women met, but the earliest of Brown's letters indicate she was already enamored of Primus and involved with her family. Unlike the middle-class white women in Boston marriages, Brown and Primus did not live together; they were not even in

40 SEXUAL AND GENDER MINORITY HISTORY

the same city for most of the years of their correspondence. For example, Primus lived on the eastern shore of Maryland for four years, where she established and then taught in a school for formerly enslaved African Americans. However, the Primus family appeared to accept their relationship, as did the larger black community (Hansen 1995).

Differences in patterns of 19th-century romantic friendships described above reflect the impact of gender and race. For example, because he was a man, there was no question that Walt Whitman could aspire to a career and to live independently. No such options were available to women of the same era. Only with the advent of women's colleges and newly available careers in education and social work could women live independently from men. Consequently, middle-class white women in Boston marriages could support themselves (Faderman 1991). In addition, white and middle-class privilege inoculated them against suspicion about their sexuality. That is, the propriety of such women was considered beyond reproach (Beemyn 2006). In general, black women and working-class white women could not afford higher education, and well-paying jobs were not available to them. Accordingly, for such women to set up house together would have been financially out of reach. They were more likely to be embedded in a supportive network of kin and community. In such networks, strong and loving relationships between women may have been accepted as long as they did not preclude marriage to a man (Hansen 1995).

Pre-Gay Identities Among Men

In George Chauncey's (1994) landmark history of sexual and gender minority men in New York City prior to 1940, one of the earliest constructions described was similar to the Urnings of Karl Heinrich Ulrichs's conceptualization. As early as 1890, men who referred to themselves as *fairies* thought of themselves as women in men's bodies. Although they could not dress as women legally, they would make up their face, do their hair, and behave as women, specifically women prostitutes. Their romantic and sexual desire was for traditionally masculine men, especially sailors and laborers, which they called *trade*. Trade would engage with fairies sexually, but in doing so they were not considered by others or themselves anything other than normal men as long as their role in sex was as a *top*, in contemporary terms. This might be hard to understand today since the binarism of homosexuality/heterosexuality is such a fundamental assumption in American culture (even the third option of bisexuality is difficult for many people to understand). However, prior to the 1930s Americans tended not to categorize people's sexuality according to their sexual object choice; categorization according to one's gender role behavior was much more common, especially in working-class communities. Accordingly, this construction of fairies and trade was especially prevalent among working-class and immigrant men, and the constellation of saloons, resorts, and public spaces that supported fairies was entirely within working-class neighborhoods. Nevertheless, there were middle-class fairies as well. Such men had to live double lives since it was not possible for them to behave as fairies in middle-class home or work environments. Respectability and privacy were dominant values in such communities, and anyone who dared to violate them risked losing everything.

Men who considered themselves *queer*, a construction that arose in the 1910s, experienced their desire for other men as separate from their gender, a construction that recalls the German masculinists since they rejected any association of femininity with their desire for other men. These men, who were more likely than fairies to be middle class, avoided displays of difference in public, and they developed ways to signal their "queerness" that only other queers would recognize. As long as the general public was unfamiliar with homosexuality, especially the middle-class public, queers could function in relative safety (Chauncey 1994).

However, the first decades of the 20th century were a time of substantial social change that was relevant to this order. Throughout the 1910s, women (at least those who were considered white) gained the right to vote in an increasing number of states, and the ratification of the 19th Amendment to the US Constitution in 1920 extended this right to all states. During the 1920s, women, particularly those who were unmarried, entered the workforce in unprecedented numbers. During these two decades, mixed-sex socializing became sanctioned and increasingly common. At the same time, medical discourse about sexuality gained significant power in middle-class society. In this discourse, sexual object choice was considered a fundamental component of individual identity, and it no longer mattered what gender role one played; any same-sex sexual behavior marked one as a homosexual. As the concept of homosexual identity gained acceptance, so too did the opposite concept of heterosexual identity. However, the concept of gender inversion, as exemplified by fairies, did not yet disappear. Fairies were thought to be an intermediate (or third) sex, sometimes called *inverts* due to their inverted gender. Trade and queers were considered *perverts* because they were normal men who perverted their natural sexual instincts. Such men became especially vilified by middle-class society. But among more marginalized segments of society, especially in working-class and immigrant communities, this medicalized discourse gained much less traction (Chauncey 1994).

One reason for the greater acceptance of sexual and gender diversity in lower-class communities in the late 19th and early 20th centuries was the preponderance of single young men living in them. For example, 40% of men over 15 years of age living in Manhattan in 1900 were unmarried (Chauncey 1994). New York and San Francisco in particular drew huge numbers of young male immigrants from Europe, Latin America, and Asia. Many of these men intended to work in the United States for a few years before returning to their home countries, and others worked until they could afford to bring their families to join them (Boyd 2003; Chauncey 1994). These men lived, worked, and played in a virtually all-male world, not unlike men in the cowboy communities and railroad, mining, and logging camps of the frontier West.

Summary

The first part of this counter-narrative of American history describes constructions of gender and sexual difference among Indigenous inhabitants, descendants of European colonizers, and immigrants to the United States until the first decades of the 20th century, all of which are generally erased from the public history most people learn. Those who experienced and demonstrated gender or sexual difference during these years did so before the concepts of homosexuality and heterosexuality were developed and popularized. Accordingly, sexual object choice was not an important determinant of identity or social difference. Instead, difference was determined by one's gender role in sexual and social behavior and, presumably, one's internal experience of gender. Within the context of the eradication of Indigenous patterns of gender diversity, and despite the importation from Europe of rigid standards for gendered behavior, transgression of gender norms occurred among men and women in a variety of ways. Men developed devoted and sometimes sexual relationships in the all-male cowboy, railroad, mining, and logging communities of the frontier West before encroaching settlement extinguished their freedom to do so. Many women escaped their prescribed gender role by dressing and behaving as men in military service or by living independently in the rural West.

There is much evidence of passionate relationships between men and between women in 19th-century America. Walt Whitman, one of the most important American poets, had romantic relationships with other men throughout his lifetime, and his published vision for a democratic America was based on the love of comrades. The development of women's colleges in the second half of the century provided the opportunity for higher education and entrance to newly available professions among white, middle-class women. Freed from the necessity to depend on men, many such women chose to live together in long-lasting romantic relationships, among them the mother of social work, Jane Addams.

In this material, we also see that erasure of gender and sexual variance from the American historical narrative is more complete for nonwhites and those who were not middle class. For example, there is no written record by Indigenous people about their gender-diverse members, and a single set of letters provides the only evidence of romantic relationships among 19th-century working-class black women as compared to the many examples of such relationships among middle-class white women.

Finally, patterns of marginalized gender among men emerged in New York City at the end of the 19th century that were similar to those found in Germany during the same era. Fairies resembled the Urnings described by Karl Heinrich Ulrichs, while queers were more similar to Adolf Brand's masculinists. In both countries, pre-gay constructions of identity either claimed or rejected feminine gender as an explanation for men's same-sex desires. Among masculinists and queers, the desire for other men was entirely separate from their gender, which they considered thoroughly masculine.

Chapter 5
The Jazz Age

As they did in Germany, the 1920s brought expanded opportunities for self-expression and connection among sexual and gender minority people in the United States. One reason was the growth of American cities; by 1920, more people lived in urban areas than rural areas. The Northeast had become majority urban decades earlier, but by 1920 this trend extended to the Midwest and West; only the South remained majority rural. Detroit's population grew by 53% in the 1910s, and Chicago grew by 19%; New York and Philadelphia both grew by 15%. Urban growth continued in the 1920s, with Los Angeles increasing its population by 53%, Detroit by 37%, Chicago by 20%, and New York by 19%. Explosive growth in manufacturing, especially in the Midwest; immigration from Europe; and the first Great Migration of African Americans from the South were the main contributors to the growth of American cities during this era, with the latter two factors also increasing cities' racial and ethnic diversity. The burgeoning film industry was a major contributor to the growth of Los Angeles.

The First World War contributed to the development of sexual and gender minority identities and communities leading up to the 1920s. The United States was engaged in the war for less than two years, but by its end in late 1918 more than four million men either volunteered or were drafted for military service. They came from every part of the country and all walks of life; most of them embarked for and returned from Europe through the port of New York, which abounded in opportunities to encounter gender- and sexually diverse men. In addition, while they were mobilized in Europe, American men were exposed to less puritanical cultures with respect to sex. In New York and the major cities of Europe, and in the all-male military environment, many men who experienced same-sex desires first encountered others with similar desires. Some of those men chose to remain in New York at the end of their deployment rather than return to the small towns and rural areas where their families lived (Chauncey 1994). Although American women were not allowed in either the Army or Navy during the First World War, millions of them participated actively in the war effort as nurses,

Sexual and Gender Minority History. James I. Martin, Oxford University Press. © Oxford University Press (2025).
DOI: 10.1093/9780197765500.003.0005

Red Cross volunteers, motor pool drivers and mechanics, and switchboard operators. On the home front, many women took up jobs on farms and in factories that were usually held by men. Their contributions to the war effort added new momentum to the decades-long suffrage movement, and in 1920 the 19th Amendment to the US Constitution finally guaranteed women's right to vote ("Women in World War I" 2022). The more active participation of women in public life represented a significant change to traditional gender roles, especially among the middle class, and it allowed many women to imagine new possibilities for their personal lives as well.

The 18th Amendment, which was ratified in 1919, prohibited the manufacture, sale, or transport of alcohol in the United States, and surprisingly, it became another contributor to the development of sexual and gender minority communities during the 1920s. As Chauncey (1994) claimed, "Prohibition was designed to reduce the cultural influence of immigrants" (p. 307), especially the Catholic Germans, Italians, and Irish. These groups not only represented the brewers, distillers, and winemakers in the United States but also were associated with saloons, brothels, and other lower-class entertainment venues the reformers strongly condemned. Not coincidentally, these were also the places where cross-dressing entertainers, male prostitutes, fairies, and trade could be found (Boyd 2003; Chauncey 1994). In major cities like New York, Chicago, and San Francisco, the public was generally opposed to Prohibition and openly violated it. San Francisco was so extraordinarily anti-Prohibition that its board of supervisors actually reprimanded police in 1921 for enforcing the law (Boyd 2003).

While restaurants and nightclubs patronized by middle- and upper-class people closed down without the ability to sell alcohol, thousands of illegal speakeasies opened with bootlegged alcohol sold through organized crime networks. According to one estimate, at least 5,000 speakeasies could be found in the borough of Manhattan by 1927. Speakeasies were often innovative. For example, unlike drinking establishments of earlier times, women were welcome, even those who were white and affluent. Especially since speakeasies were often located in racial and ethnic minority neighborhoods, they also allowed for limited interracial and interclass mixing. The inherent illegality of speakeasies added to their excitement (McGirr 2016).

> The speakeasies eroded the boundaries between respectability and criminality, public and private, and between commercial space and home life, for the hosts welcomed patrons into their basement hideaways as if into

their homes, and encouraged them to mingle with the other guests and to spurn the conventions that normally governed their public behavior. . . . It was in this context that the flamboyant gay men known as fairies . . . began to play a more prominent role in the culture and reputation of [New York]. (Chauncey 1994, p. 308)

The Harlem Renaissance

The Harlem Renaissance, a period of extraordinary creativity and innovation in African American culture, occurred within the context of this environment. A less well-known aspect of the Harlem Renaissance was its central importance in the development of sexual and gender minority identities and communities. During the first wave of the Great Migration, African Americans moved in large numbers from the rural South to the major cities of the East and Midwest. In New York City, African Americans moved increasingly to Harlem, in northern Manhattan. In 1920, they made up about one-third of the population of central Harlem; by 1930 the neighborhood was more than 70% African American. Among this burgeoning population were artists, writers, and musicians who "produced one of the most significant eras of cultural expression in the nation's history" ("A New African American Identity: The Harlem Renaissance" n.d.). Many of them were sexual minorities, including the writers Countee Cullen, Langston Hughes, Zora Neale Hurston, and Richard Bruce Nugent and the blues singers Gladys Bentley, Lucille Bogan, Alberta Hunter, and Ma Rainey.

The work produced by the artists, writers, and performers of the Harlem Renaissance generally focused on the lived experience of African Americans and on racism and black identity. Sexual or gender minority themes were not usually expressed openly, and in most cases the people mentioned above were not publicly open about their same-sex relationships; Richard Bruce Nugent and Gladys Bentley were notable exceptions. Nugent's 1926 short story "Smoke, Lilies, and Jade" described same-sex love and desire among men. Gladys Bentley typically performed in men's clothes, sang raunchy lyrics, and flirted with women in the audience. Bentley was also openly lesbian and even claimed to have married a woman. Sexual and gender minority themes appeared in a number of blues songs. For example, in Lucille Bogan's 1935 song "B.D. Woman Blues," B.D. referred to "bulldagger," slang for a butch woman:

> Comin' a time, B.D. women ain't gonna need no men.
> Comin' a time, B.D. women ain't gonna need no men.
> Oh the way they treat us is a lowdown and dirty sin.
> B.D. women, you sure can't understand.
> B.D. women, you sure can't understand.
> They got a head like a sweet angel and they walk just like a
> natural man.

Ma Rainey's 1928 song "Prove It on Me" expressed same-sex love among women a little more directly:

> They said I do it, ain't nobody caught me.
> Sure got to prove it on me.
> Went out last night with a crowd of my friends.
> They must've been women, 'cause I don't like no men.

The decade of the 1920s is often called the Jazz Age. During the years of Prohibition, racial boundaries in New York and some other major cities became slightly less rigid, which allowed white people to gain greater exposure to African American culture than they would previously. It became especially fashionable for middle-class and affluent white people to visit Harlem to experience its vibrant nightlife and exciting music. Some of the more lavish nightclubs, such as the Cotton Club, catered specifically to white audiences; black people were restricted from entering unless they were employees or performers. Other clubs, including the Savoy Ballroom, Small's Paradise, and Harry Hansberry's Clam House, were racially mixed but predominantly black (Chauncey 1994). Jazz exploded out of Harlem, New Orleans, and Chicago, with the great talents of Duke Ellington, Louis Armstrong, Fats Waller, and others, to become the popular music of the day. Jazz-based dances such as the Charleston, Black Bottom, and Lindy Hop swept the country. Even symphonic music became strongly influenced by jazz, with George Gershwin's work the best example.

It was within this context that sexual and gender minority people, both black and white, began to find a sense of community. A crucial step in the development of any sexual or gender minority identity is the awareness that there are others like oneself, others who have similar sexual or romantic yearnings, or similar experiences of gender. The presence of similar others thus allows for the rise of a shared identity. The work produced by sexual and gender minority writers and musicians of the Harlem Renaissance provided evidence to anyone who understood the clues. In addition, there were many venues in Harlem where sexual and gender minority people could gather in relative safety. A number of nightclubs and speakeasies welcomed sexual and gender minority patrons, including Harry Hansberry's Clam House, Small's Paradise, and the Hot Cha. Sexual minority men also could meet at the Mount Morris Baths. In addition, many rent parties and buffet flats attracted sexual and gender minority participants. At rent parties, which were thrown by residents to raise money for their rent, you paid a small cover charge and could buy alcohol and homemade food while you enjoyed singing and dancing to live music (Hurewitz 1997). Buffet flats were entertainment venues inside private homes, either houses or larger apartments. They functioned as virtual speakeasies where you could drink alcohol, dance, and enjoy entertainment that might even include gambling, prostitution, and live sex shows (Robertson et al. 2012). Rent parties and buffet flats provided a showcase for many talented musicians, singers, and dancers. For example, Fats Waller and Gladys Bentley got their start in this environment; the Charleston and other dance crazes originated there as well (Wilson 2010).

Drag Balls

Chauncey (1994) asserted that the drag balls were even more important for the development of sexual and gender minority identities, especially since they brought together in one place the largest number of sexual and gender minority people: "It was at the drag balls, more than any place else, that the gay world saw itself, celebrated itself, and affirmed itself" (p. 299). Masquerade events and balls had been popular throughout 19th-century America, and although they might have appealed especially to sexual and gender minority people for the opportunities they gave to transgress gender norms for dress and behavior, they generally were not intended for that purpose. However, in the last decade of the century, sexual and gender minority people in New York began to appropriate this tradition with private balls for same-sex dancing. Ironically, since it was illegal for two men or two women to dance together, couples could avoid arrest by having one partner dress as the other sex. These drag balls became increasingly popular in the first decades of the 20th century, reaching their height in the 1920s and 1930s. At least a half-dozen large, high-profile balls were held annually in New York;

drag balls were also held in Baltimore, Chicago, and New Orleans (Beemyn 2014; Chauncey 1994).

Drag balls held in African American communities were among the most popular. The Hamilton Lodge Ball, held in February at Harlem's Rockland Palace, was the biggest of them all. Previously known as the Masquerade and Civic Ball, which had been held annually since the end of the Civil War, it became known as the Faggots Ball when sexual and gender minority people appropriated it in 1923 and, sometimes, the Dance of the Fairies. By the early 1930s, the ball was regularly attended by white onlookers who included many celebrities, and it was enthusiastically covered in the African American press. Even as the ball grew in popularity and increasingly drew white and middle-class black people, the participants remained mostly working-class African Americans. At its height, the ball drew participants from hundreds of miles away; a reported 8,000 people attended the 1937 Hamilton Lodge Ball. Many attendees wore extravagant costumes, and the evening's highlight was the "parade of the fairies" and costume competition. Although the Hamilton Lodge Ball attracted an interracial crowd, it barely transcended the racial boundaries that existed in society at that time. White sexual and gender minority people were among the costumed participants, but the large crowds of white onlookers in attendance were frequently "slumming," as they were in Harlem's jazz clubs, enjoying the spectacle from a distance while confirming their racial, gender, and sexual prejudices. In addition, not all African Americans were comfortable with white people attending "their" ball. Racial hierarchy was especially evident in the costume competition, which white contestants won each year until 1931 (Chauncey 1994).

Greenwich Village

Sexual and gender identities also developed outside the context of Harlem and other African American communities. In New York, Greenwich Village was another important focal point. The Village had been attracting sexual and gender minority people since the late 19th century when notorious fairy "resorts" were located on Bleecker Street. By the first decades of the 20th century, artists, writers, and other "bohemians" moved into the area, which was largely populated by working-class Italian immigrants, and they established a major capital of social, political, cultural, and sexual nonconformity (Hurewitz 1997). After the First World War, the Village became an important tourist and entertainment destination due to its numerous Italian restaurants and shops, winding streets, and charming atmosphere; the existence of many speakeasies and clubs accelerated this development. During the 1920s, the Village gained a reputation as a center of sexual and gender minority life as well, as sexual and gender minority people moved into the neighborhood, with many restaurants, tearooms, and clubs catering to them. Some of these venues were opened by sexual and gender minority people themselves. For example, Eve Addams opened a tearoom on MacDougal Street with this sign on its front door: "Men are admitted but not welcome" (Chauncey 1994, p. 240). However, not everyone who lived in the Village approved of these developments; Addams's tearoom was shut down by the police in 1926, and Addams (a Jewish immigrant) was deported to France. Despite opposition from some Villagers, sexual and gender minority people continued to expand their presence in the neighborhood (Chauncey 1994).

Los Angeles

During Prohibition, the coast of Southern California was the site of large alcohol smuggling operations, and an expansive system of underground tunnels in downtown Los Angeles was used to transport bootleg liquor to an estimated 30,000 speakeasies operating in the area (Bradner 2019). As it did in New York, Prohibition glamorized illegality and social marginality in Los Angeles. Meanwhile, the movie industry took root in Hollywood during the first decades of the 20th century, and by the 1920s it had become one of the country's most lucrative industries. Many of the early writers, directors, set and costume designers, and actors came from Europe or the New York stage, where they were accustomed to a "bohemian" lifestyle of nonmonogamy and fluid gender and sexuality. While they kept these aspects of their lives out of the awareness of the general public, in private they built an extensive sexual and gender minority community (Faderman and Timmons 2006). The directors Dorothy Arzner and F. W. Murnau and the actors William Haines, Nita Naldi, Alla Nazimova, Pola Negri, and Ramon Novarro were among those who were sexual minorities during the silent film era of the 1920s (Slide 1999). Actors transgressing sexual and gender norms were shown in a number of silent films. For example, the male actor Julian Eltinge dressed and performed as a woman in several films (and on stage as well), and women caressing each other in a café and military men in women's dress

San Francisco

When it came to resisting Prohibition and puritanical middle-class values in the early 20th century, San Francisco was in a class by itself. With its history as a 19th-century boom town of mostly single young men in search of riches in the Sierra gold rush and Nevada silver rush, drinking, gambling, same- and other-sex prostitution, and other forms of risqué entertainment were central aspects of the city's economy. The social purity and moral reform movements that swept the rest of the country prior to the 1920s faced opposition from its civic and business leaders, and temperance found very little popular support there. During Prohibition, wine and liquor were not only smuggled in but also openly produced in the city. While female impersonators (men masquerading as women) had always been popular entertainers in San Francisco, during the 1920s drag (cross-dressing by sexual or gender minority individuals) became increasingly visible in the city both on the stage and in the streets (Boyd 2003).

The Pansy Craze

Transgression of gender norms became more visible in American culture during the second half of the Prohibition era. This period is called the Pansy Craze since flamboyantly effeminate men of this era self-identified as "pansies," replacing the earlier "fairies." Drag performances gained popularity in nightclubs and on the legitimate stage, effeminate men became stock characters in films, same-sex themes appeared in novels, and gender flexibility even showed up in popular music. Gene Malin was the most famous of the pansy performers, climbing the ladder from New York drag ball contestant to Greenwich Village club performer and emcee to marquee act at an elegant theater district speakeasy; he later opened his own club in Hollywood and acted in a few films. Malin differentiated himself from the many female impersonators that preceded him with his campy repartee and overtly queer persona. His success led to a proliferation of pansy performers in major cities. Speakeasies and clubs featuring pansy performers became known as "pansy clubs," including the Club New Yorker and

Jimmy's Backyard in Hollywood, and Club Abbey and the Pansy Club in New York (Chauncey 1994). In Chicago, pansy clubs were located mainly in Bronzeville, an African American neighborhood on the South Side that was a center of culture and nightlife. Chicago also had some clubs on the mainly white North Side, like Diamond Lil's and the Ballyhoo Club (De La Croix 2012). Novels with sexual and gender minority themes published during these years include *Strange Brother* by Blair Niles (1931) and *Twilight Men* by Andre Tellier (1931). The most important of these novels, *The Well of Loneliness*, by British author Radclyffe Hall (1928), had a lesbian theme (Chauncey 1994). In their popular 1925 song, "Masculine Women Feminine Men," Edgar Leslie and James Monaco colorfully portrayed the Pansy Craze era:

> Masculine Women, Feminine Men,
> Which is the rooster which is the hen?
> It's hard to tell 'em apart today.
> And say . . .
> Sister is busy learning to shave,
> Brother just loves his permanent wave,
> It's hard to tell 'em apart today.
> Hey! Hey!
> Girls were girls and boys were boys when I was a tot,
> Now we don't know who is who or even what's what.
> Knickers and trousers, baggy and wide,
> Nobody knows who's walking inside.
> Those Masculine Women, Feminine Men.

Henry Gerber and the Society for Human Rights

The 1920s also marked the first step in advocacy for sexual and gender minority rights in the United States, with Henry Gerber establishing the first American sexual and gender minority rights organization in Chicago in 1924. Gerber was born in Germany in 1892 and immigrated with his family to the United States in 1913, settling in Chicago. In 1919 he enlisted in the Army and was mobilized to Germany for three years as part of the occupation of the Rhineland. He became familiar with the homosexual rights movement while stationed there, visiting Berlin several times

54 SEXUAL AND GENDER MINORITY HISTORY

and subscribing to German homosexual publications. Upon his return to Chicago, Gerber set out to establish a movement for the rights of American homosexuals (De La Croix 2012). He started by envisioning an organization that he named the Society for Human Rights, a direct translation of the German *Bund für Menschenrecht*. However, he had difficulty persuading more than a handful of men to join in his effort. He was particularly interested in gaining the support of medical professionals, as was the case in the German movement, but no such support materialized. The three other men who agreed to join Gerber as officers of the society were poor or working class: an African American preacher, a railroad worker, and an "indigent laundry queen" (Gerber 1962, p. 7). They decided to focus their efforts on repealing the Illinois sodomy law. In 1924 their application to the state of Illinois for a charter as a nonprofit organization was approved, apparently due to a lack of investigation into the society's purpose. Soon after, Gerber initiated the first American homosexual publication, a newsletter that he named *Friendship and Freedom* (Gerber 1962). The name was a translation of *Freundschaft und Freiheit*, the subtitle of Adolf Brand's publication *Der Eigene*.

Unfortunately, the "indigent laundry queen" had concealed that he was married with children; when his wife discovered his involvement in the society, she reported it to a social worker, who in turn informed the police. The arrest on trumped-up charges, inflammatory newspaper coverage, and trials of Gerber and the other officers led to the society's demise less than a year after receiving its state charter. The case against the four men was eventually dismissed because the police never had a warrant for their arrest, but Gerber lost his job with the post office and was financially ruined. After this experience, he took a job in New York as a proofreader that he obtained through an old friend and eventually re-enlisted in the Army, where he served as a proofreader and editor for 17 years until his honorable discharge in 1945 (De La Croix 2012; Gerber 1962).

Summary

Economic expansion and urbanization, wartime mobilization, immigration of Eastern and Southern Europeans and migration of African Americans, and social changes due to Prohibition and women's suffrage combined to make the Jazz Age a turbulent yet highly creative period. It was also a foundational period for the development of sexual and gender minority identities and communities in the United States. Previously isolated sexual and gender minority individuals who served in the military during the First World War found there were others like them, as did those who moved to the rapidly growing urban areas. Shared identities developed among the drag balls, speakeasies, rent parties, and buffet flats of Harlem and Chicago; in the clubs and "bohemian" enclaves of Greenwich Village; in the early moviemaking community of Hollywood; and in the risqué entertainment venues of San Francisco. In many ways, these developments paralleled those in 1920s Germany, although Prohibition, which provided the fertile environment for sexual and gender minority community growth, was a uniquely American experience. However, there was virtually no movement in the United States to advance sexual and gender minority rights other than a small, short-lived effort in Chicago that was inspired by the movement in Germany.

However, the advances made by sexual and gender minorities during this era occurred within the context of a society that largely disapproved of the social changes happening in the country. In 1920, the US population was nearly 90% white, the vast majority of which claimed parentage that was not "foreign born." Slightly less than half of the population lived in rural areas (US Census Bureau 2021). As national policy, Prohibition was intended to restrict the social and cultural influence of the growing foreign-born, especially Catholic, population in urban environments. Five years after Prohibition was ratified, Congress severely restricted immigration, especially for those who were not Northern or Western Europeans; Asians were entirely disallowed from immigrating. At the same time, racial hierarchy and segregation were widespread and rigidly enforced, and the migration of African Americans from southern states was met with hostility and, not infrequently, violence. The middle-class and affluent white people who went "slumming" in Harlem and Greenwich Village during the 1920s did not necessarily approve of what they saw there. Among the working-class or poor African Americans and immigrants who led the visibility and growth of sexual and gender minority communities during the Jazz Age, sexual difference continued to be defined by one's gender role behavior. White, middle-class men and women, however, began to define their sexual identity in terms of their sexual object choice.

Chapter 6
The 1930s and the Great Depression

The end of the 1920s also marked the end of a long period of economic expansion and optimism. The crash of the US stock market in late 1929 heralded a collapse of the nation's economy over the course of the next four years that encompassed severe price deflation, widespread business bankruptcies, bank failures, and high unemployment. By 1932, overall unemployment reached nearly 23%, with industrial unemployment more than 31%, this at a time when there was no publicly funded social safety net (Crafts and Fearon 2013). In addition, many businesses reduced their remaining employees' hours such that by 1932 only about 59% of workers had full-time jobs. Unemployment was especially high among African Americans. The suffering was enormous among the poor, many of whom were previously working class or even middle class. People stood in long lines at charity-run soup kitchens. Older children left home and tried to survive on their own rather than continuing to burden their families. Large, makeshift shantytowns full of destitute people appeared in cities throughout the country, and as many as two million hoboes hitched rides on the road or railroad, picking up odd jobs here and there. Many rural families lost their farms, and on the Southern Plains the Dust Bowl destroyed whatever chance they might have had to eke out a living (Rauchway 2008). As portrayed by John Steinbeck's 1939 novel, *The Grapes of Wrath*, hundreds of thousands migrated to California, hoping for a better life. Yip Harbug and Jay Gorney's popular song from 1932, "Brother Can You Spare a Dime," captured the despair of these years:

> They used to tell me I was building a dream, and so I followed the mob,
> When there was earth to plow, or guns to bear, I was always there right on the job.
> They used to tell me I was building a dream, with peace and glory ahead,
> Why should I be standing in line, just waiting for bread?

Sexual and Gender Minority History. James I. Martin, Oxford University Press. © Oxford University Press (2025).
DOI: 10.1093/9780197765500.003.0006

> Once I built a railroad, made it run,
> Made it race against time.
> Once I built a railroad, now it's done.
> Brother can you spare a dime?

In the depths of the Depression, the 1932 election dealt a crushing blow to the previously dominant Republican Party, sweeping in Democrat Franklin D. Roosevelt as president as well as large Democratic majorities in both houses of Congress. The new administration launched an ambitious set of programs and reforms, the New Deal, to put Americans back to work and restore the nation's economy. While the New Deal was effective in decreasing unemployment and reversing the country's economic decline, it also represented a significant increase in government power and reach that was stridently opposed by conservative business leaders.

One of the more popular initiatives of the New Deal was the repeal of the 18th Amendment. By this time, Americans were fed up with Prohibition. Although many had been opposed to the policy from the beginning, others were dismayed by the rampant criminality and violence it brought. In particular, although warfare between rival crime organizations over the wealth generated by bootleg liquor most famously occurred in Chicago, it also raged in other major cities. Bribery and other forms of corruption were widespread among city officials. Still other Americans were distressed by the Pansy Craze and breakdown in traditional gender and sexual norms described previously, which they believed Prohibition had wrought. In 1931, New York police shut down Club Abbey and the Pansy Club along with drag balls outside of Harlem. However, a stronger push to reverse the visibility of sexual and gender minority life came after Prohibition's repeal (Chauncey 1994).

The 21st Amendment to the US Constitution, ratified in 1933, repealed Prohibition and gave each state the authority to regulate the sale of alcohol. Although most states chose to allow the sale and consumption of alcohol, some counties or municipalities within those states decided to remain "dry." In New York and many other states, an alcohol control agency was established to set and enforce regulations, which it did through cooperation with local authorities. California relegated these responsibilities to its existing state tax board, and it prohibited local control over these matters (Boyd 2003). These differences had significant implications for sexual and gender minority people.

Remarginalization of Sexual and Gender Minorities in New York

Repeal of Prohibition allowed state governments to take back from organized crime the profits from the sale of alcohol, and it also provided them with the opportunity to define the limits of allowable social life. The New York State Liquor Authority (SLA) was empowered to make sure places where alcohol was consumed did not become "disorderly," a term that was left purposefully vague. In New York City, the mere presence of sexual and gender minority people could result in an establishment being considered disorderly. During the 1930s, New York City police made hundreds of reports of violations of SLA regulations, which generally involved observation or suspicion that homosexuals were patrons of the establishment. If the violation was confirmed by a visit of an SLA undercover agent, the establishment would lose its liquor license. Ironically, this contributed to the rise of gay bars, since the owners of many bars with mixed clientele made sexual minority patrons feel increasingly unwelcome. As increasing numbers of these patrons moved elsewhere, the new establishments became dependent on their business. Gay bars often had short lives, but their owners discovered it was nevertheless possible to turn a profit with them. When one gay bar closed down, another would open (Chauncey 1994). Eventually, these bars became owned and operated by crime organizations that would pay off the police in order to continue operating.

The New York World's Fair, billed as "The World of Tomorrow," opened in April 1939, and the SLA targeted sexual and gender minority–oriented bars for closure in the preceding months. The fair involved massive public and private sector investments, and there was a purposeful campaign to "clean up the city" (Chauncey 1994, p. 342) before the expected millions of tourists would visit from all over the world. The area around Times Square was a particular focus of this campaign since it was a primary area for tourism; it also had become a location where many sexual and gender minority–oriented bars were located. In one example, a bar named Gloria's was warned by the SLA that it would lose its license if it did not "ban homosexuals from the premises" (p. 338). The owner of the bar took the SLA to court after he refused to follow the order; he lost the case, and the license was revoked (Chauncey 1994).

Some mixed establishments survived without expelling their sexual minority patrons; these tended to be very upscale clubs that operated with

60 SEXUAL AND GENDER MINORITY HISTORY

specific rules. For example, the Astor Hotel Bar allowed sexual minority men to gather only on one side of the bar, and they had to act very discretely. Dressing flamboyantly or behaving in ways that were "too gay" would get them ejected. Other similar establishments were the Plaza Hotel's Oak Room and the Rainbow Room at Rockefeller Center (Chauncey 1994).

White people continued to travel to Harlem for its nightlife for a few years after the repeal of Prohibition. Gladys Bentley was at the height of her career in the first half of the 1930s. She headlined at the Ubangi Club for several years until it closed in 1937, but by that time her act had lost its popularity. Since unemployment was disproportionately high among African Americans during the Depression, Harlem was in especially bad economic shape. The frustration and despair of its residents contributed to the Harlem riot of 1935 in which three people died and hundreds were injured (Wilson 2010). The Cotton Club, which featured black entertainers for white audiences, closed the following year and then moved to midtown Manhattan. Harlem's drag balls continued to increase in popularity through the 1930s, with the Hamilton Lodge Ball drawing as many as 8,000 participants in 1937. However, New York City police arrested 15 participants for "offering to commit lewd acts" at the 1938 ball (Ray 1938), which proved to be the final year for this event.

Chicago

In May 1933, Chicago opened the doors to the Century of Progress International Exposition, which encouraged people to look beyond the devastation of the Depression and celebrate the future. The two-year World's Fair drew 48 million visitors. Only two months before it began, the city's popular mayor was shot to death in Miami while shaking hands with newly elected but not yet inaugurated President Roosevelt. The mayor's successor, autocratic Edward Kelly, built the most powerful and corrupt political machine in the country. As mayor, Kelly allowed organized crime to thrive as long as it benefited the machine (Biles 1981). In particular, pansy clubs continued to flourish in Bronzeville, where organized crime worked hand in hand with Kelly's machine. The Annex Buffet and Cabin Inn were particularly popular clubs where the Sepia Gloria Swanson and the Sepia Mae West and other black drag artists performed. Two large drag balls were allowed to continue each year throughout the 1930s. However, Kelly did not tolerate visible sexual and gender minority life in white sections of the city. For example, he prevented Lillian Hellman's lesbian-themed play *The Children's Hour* from being performed. He also shut down the K-9 Club, a popular Northside pansy club, and orchestrated raids on the Northside lesbian venues Roselle Inn and Twelve-Thirty Club. While there were other bars and bathhouses where white sexual minority men could meet during the 1930s, they had to exist below the level of awareness of the general public to avoid being raided by police (De La Croix 2012).

San Francisco

Because California law gave its tax board total control of alcohol distribution and sales and prevented local authorities from having any power in these matters, the ability to enforce liquor laws throughout the state was weak. The post-Prohibition law allowed alcoholic beverages other than beer to be served only in establishments that also had substantial food sales (e.g., restaurants and hotels); bars and saloons were allowed to serve only beer (Gill 1950), which was far less lucrative. Nightclubs were an in-between venue type that became successful in this environment. In San Francisco's North Beach, nightclubs such as Mona's and Finocchio's featured drag performers (drag kings at Mona's, drag queens at Finocchio's) and added to the city's ongoing reputation as an exotic, exciting destination for tourists. In 1936 Finocchio's relocated to a much larger space and expanded its gender-transgressive floor show; it drew large tourist crowds (mainly heterosexual) for decades (Boyd 2003). Mona's was a women's club, drawing mostly young, working-class women who adopted butch and femme roles as well as occasional middle-class women tourists (Faderman 1991).

Los Angeles

The impact of California's lax control over the post-Prohibition distribution and sale of alcohol was even more pronounced in Los Angeles because of the city's patchwork geography. In the first decades of the 20th century, Los Angeles grew exponentially by annexing surrounding areas, including the previously independent city of Hollywood. Although access to the Los Angeles water supply induced many other cities toward annexation, the highly restricted and affluent city of Beverly Hills, only a couple miles west of Hollywood, chose to remain independent. Between Beverly Hills and Hollywood lay an unincorporated area of less than two square miles that, in 1925, adopted the name West Hollywood. West Hollywood was outside the jurisdiction of the City of Los Angeles police, and it did not have a police force of its own; law enforcement was provided by the Los Angeles County Sheriff, which was stretched quite thin over more than 4,000 square miles. Not surprisingly, West Hollywood became a popular location for illegal speakeasies during the Prohibition era. In the 1930s, it was the Las Vegas of its time, with nightclubs and casinos all along the Sunset Boulevard "Strip" (West Hollywood Marketing Corporation 2024). Being beyond the reach of the Los Angeles police, West Hollywood also became an important destination for sexual and gender minorities. Officially, unaccompanied single patrons and same-sex couples were not allowed in the most exclusive clubs on the Strip, but many sexual minority women and men, including famous actors, attended with other-sex dates of convenience (Gierach 2003).

Several of the best-known Hollywood stars during this era were sexual and gender minorities. The androgynous style of female stars Tallulah Bankhead, Marlene Dietrich, Greta Garbo, and Kathryn Hepburn played an important role in their popularity, but their careers would have imploded if the public knew they had same-sex relationships. In the 1930 film *Morocco*, Dietrich kissed a woman while wearing a man's tuxedo; in the 1933 film *Queen Christina*, Garbo also dressed in men's clothes, and she kissed a woman twice, once on the lips. In neither film are the kisses given any sexual meaning. However, Dietrich's and Garbo's performances resonated strongly with women struggling with their own same-sex attractions. By contrast, male sexual minority actors such as Cary Grant, William Haines, and Randolph Scott could not afford the slightest hint on screen that they might be less than fully heterosexual or cisgender. There were many sexual minority actors, writers, and directors in Hollywood who privately maintained what might have been the most "gay-friendly" place in the country in the 1930s, but their public images were increasingly guarded to avoid any suspicion (Faderman and Timmons 2006; Roots of Equality 2011).

The movie industry was not immune to the Depression, though, and in the early 1930s it faced serious economic headwinds. Consequently, the industry was vulnerable to social conservatives who threatened its bottom line through government-imposed censorship and boycotts of theaters showing movies they considered offensive. To avoid censorship imposed by government, the industry set up a system of self-censorship in 1930 called the Production Code, which set out three main principles (Morgan 2018): Movies "should not lower the moral standards of moviegoers by manifesting sympathy for crime, wrongdoing and sin; they should uphold correct standards of life; and they should not ridicule law, natural or human" (p. 17). However, enforcement was initially lax. In 1934, the studios agreed to more stringent enforcement of the code; after this date, no movie could be made without its script receiving prior approval from the Production Code Administration (Morgan 2018). The code required movies to adhere to conservative Christian values; noncisgender or sexually diverse characters, nudity, and even heterosexual passion were strictly disallowed. In addition, movies risked failure at the box office if their stars were perceived to be immoral, so any evidence of noncisgender or "unstraight" behavior among them was stringently hidden from the public.

Nevertheless, Hollywood continued to be a major draw for sexual and gender minority people who worked behind the scenes, such as set and costume designers, whose sexual or gender identities were not on the public radar (Consulting GPA 2023). They contributed to the development of a large sexual and gender minority community in Los Angeles whose members congregated in more than one area. Downtown Los Angeles was an important gathering place for sexual and gender minority men, although it was less safe than West Hollywood. Pershing Square had been a popular cruising ground since at least the 1920s. By the 1930s, it anchored several blocks of Fifth Street that became known as "the run," where coffee shops, bars, and cafes increasingly became hangouts for working-class sexual and gender minority men; more affluent men frequented the upscale lounge at the Biltmore Hotel, across the street from the square. Everyone had to be extremely discreet because of the ever-present danger of harassment and arrest by the police (Consulting GPA 2023).

Pathologizing Sexual Difference

In 1937, several factors contributed to a national panic about "deviant" sexuality, with grave consequences for sexual and gender minorities. First, four female children were sexually abused and murdered in New York City during the summer, which followed by several months the well-publicized abduction and murder of a 10-year-old boy in Tacoma, Washington. Second, newspapers across the country stoked public hysteria about sexual predation at least in part because it increased their sales (Sutherland 1950). Third, leaders in law enforcement pushed for crackdowns on "sexual psychopaths" (Bronski 2011). Fourth, psychoanalysis moved to a position of dominance in American psychiatry around this time (Ruffalo 2018), and the public became much more familiar with psychoanalytic theory (Samuel 2013). Psychiatrists exerted increasing influence on explanations of and responses to "deviant" sexuality (Sutherland 1950).

The leading law enforcement authority in the late 1930s was J. Edgar Hoover, director of the newly formed Federal Bureau of Investigation. In 1937, he published an article in the *New York Herald* titled "War on the Sex Criminal," in which he claimed American women and children were at risk of predation by sex perverts (code for male homosexuals).

> The "harmless" pervert of today can be and often is the loathsome mutilator and murderer of tomorrow.... Sex criminality is a serious matter which can affect any parent and any home. It is a matter that can be eradicated only by a high state of public vigilance and indignation, plus adequate study and the framing of laws designed especially for the handling of such cases. (Hoover 1937, p. SM 23)

In 1937, within the context of a campaign to recall him based on charges of political corruption and immorality, the mayor of Los Angeles proposed a Sex Bureau for the purpose of controlling "degenerates," a derogatory term used at that time for sexual and gender minority people. The bureau was established in 1938, and it predated state "sexual psychopath" laws by requiring individuals charged with a sexual offense to be evaluated by a psychiatrist prior to their court appearance before a judge, who would be provided with a copy of the evaluation. At the same time, the city established a registry for sex offenders; persons living in Los Angeles who were convicted of a sexual offense within the previous 20 years anywhere in the United States were required to provide the registry with "their name, address, history and fingerprints" (Hurewitz 2007, p. 139). Although the public was particularly inflamed about sensationalized sex-murder crimes, "sexual offenses" also included "lewd and lascivious contact," "lewd vagrancy," and "sex perversion," which nearly always were made against sexual minority men. These were the charges that dominated the activities of the Sex Bureau and the city's police (Hurewitz 2007).

Within the next three years, California, Illinois, Michigan, and Minnesota passed "sexual psychopath" laws, beginning a wave of similar state laws over the next few decades. In general, these laws called for involuntary commitment of offenders for an indeterminate time to inpatient psychiatric treatment, a victory for psychiatry over competing formulations involving harsher criminal penalties or medical-surgical intervention (e.g., castration). However, the laws were often surprisingly vague; those passed in the 1930s did not even require the criminal offense to be sexual in nature, and only the California law required a conviction. In other words, people who were suspected but not convicted of a crime, any crime, could be committed if a psychiatric evaluation found them to be sexual psychopaths, even though there were no specific diagnostic criteria. In California, 435 people were committed under the state's sexual psychopath law in its first 10 years; in Minnesota, over 200 were committed during the same time period; and in Michigan, 99 were committed in the first four years of its law (Lave 2009).

Lesbians in the 1930s

Although sexual minority women were not targeted by law enforcement as directly as men during the late 1930s, it was a difficult time for them as well. As mentioned previously, there were a few women's bars scattered around the country, such as the Chicago establishments Roselle Inn and Twelve-Thirty Club, which endured police raids, and the safer Mona's in San Francisco. all of which were patronized mainly by working-class women. Sexual minority women also could go to mixed establishments with sexual minority men, but those places were even more likely to be raided by police. Middle-class sexual minority women were much less likely to go to bars at all, and there were very few ways for them to meet each other. Using today's language, many of them lived their lives deep in the closet. A main challenge they faced was the dire economic environment. While women in the booming 1920s were employed outside the home in increasing numbers, those gains were reversed during the Depression. Even more than the evaporation of available jobs, there was strong sentiment during these years that working women took jobs away from men. In other words, they were scapegoated for the bad economic times. Thus, it became economically unfeasible for women to live together independently unless they were wealthy. and without a means to support themselves, they had few options other than marriage to a man. Economic circumstance was not the only factor working against sexual minority women. As American psychoanalysts differentiated themselves from their European roots in the 1930s, their highly pathologizing views of sexual and gender variance among men and women gained increasing power in society. Sexual minority women were portrayed as either pathetic or dangerous in newspapers and novels; portrayals in movies were not allowed at all. In this environment, some women with same-sex desires married men but maintained relationships with women on the side. Such arrangements added to the pressure for them to keep their desires secret (Faderman 1991). More than sexual minority men of this era, sexual minority women too often were forced into isolation from others with whom they might have been able to develop a sense of group identity.

Summary

The Great Depression was a worldwide calamity that had far-reaching impacts on sexual and gender minorities in the United States. Historically high unemployment, business bankruptcies, and bank failures led to widespread privation among Americans. The optimism and social experimentation of the 1920s were replaced with pessimism and social retrenchment. Social conservatives took advantage of the movie industry's economic vulnerability and forced it to adopt conservative Christian values, ending depiction on screen of sexual and gender variance. J. Edgar Hoover, director of the Federal Bureau of Investigation, exhorted the public to get behind law enforcement efforts to criminalize sexual minorities, whom he scapegoated in response to a series of well-publicized and violent sex crimes. First in Los Angeles, and then in states across the country, sexual minority men were criminalized and committed to involuntary psychiatric treatment, testament to psychiatry's rising influence and the increasing sway of American psychoanalytic ideas.

Many people celebrated when Prohibition was repealed as part of the Roosevelt administration's New Deal, but since the 21st Amendment gave state governments control of alcohol distribution and sales, the implications varied from state to state. Some states chose to prohibit the sale of alcohol. In California, the state's alcohol beverage control board was not allowed to partner with local police departments in carrying out its responsibilities, which led to lax enforcement. Unpoliced West Hollywood became a center of nightlife and a magnet for sexual and gender minorities, while the city of Los Angeles became a national leader in efforts to criminalize them. New York's SLA sought to redefine appropriate socializing, which involved harassment and closure of establishments it considered "disorderly," defined all too often as tolerating the presence of sexual minority patrons. This was part of a larger effort in New York City to make sexual minorities invisible from tourists and disapproving others. Throughout the country, sexual minority women were forced into isolation by the bleak economic circumstances and conservative social pressures. In Harlem, the disproportionately negative impacts of the Depression on African Americans led to a decline in its famous nightlife and an end to the optimistic and creative Harlem Renaissance.

Nevertheless, sexual and gender minority life managed to continue in Hollywood behind the prying eyes of the public, in upscale hotel bars in New York and Los Angeles, in areas of Chicago where the mayor's political machine collaborated with organized crime to maintain diverse nightlife, and in underpoliced West Hollywood. Even in spite of the oppressive efforts of city governments and police departments, establishments catering to sexual minority men, in particular, would continue to open even if they didn't last long, and men would continue to find each other in parks, in coffee shops, and on the streets of Times Square and downtown Los Angeles. And although it might have been all but impossible for most sexual minority women to live together independently, or even to acknowledge their desires, some women managed to maintain relationships with other women outside of their marriage to a man. And for those women lucky enough to live in San Francisco, Mona's was a haven and home.

Chapter 7
The World at War

After its involvement in the First World War, the United States rapidly demobilized its military and turned its back on the world. Throughout the 1930s, Congress and the American public were strongly isolationist, and government maintained noninterventionist policies (Office of the Historian n.d.). The military was underfunded, out of date, and unprepared for any remobilization (Bérubé 2010). Meanwhile, there was increasing danger throughout the world. Rapid industrialization and modernization in Japan had made it the dominant country in East Asia, and in the first decades of the 20th century it was the victor in a series of wars that made Korea, Taiwan, and several South Pacific islands its colonies. Throughout the 1930s Japan waged war against China, which had been weakened by nearly a decade of civil war between the Nationalist government and Communist Party forces. In the Soviet Union, famine that was largely the result of the Communist government's policies killed at least five million people. General Secretary Joseph Stalin removed all those in government and military leadership who opposed him or his policies, and then he unleashed a brutal purge in which an estimated one million people were executed and millions more died in prison camps

At the other end of the political spectrum, fascism had emerged in Italy under Prime Minister Benito Mussolini only a few years after the end of the First World War, and by the 1930s the country had become a police state. The Spanish Civil War raged for three years until the right-wing Nationalists emerged victorious in 1939; their leader, Francisco Franco, became the country's brutal dictator. In 1933, National Socialist Party leader Adolf Hitler became chancellor of Germany and immediately liquidated political and social opposition. Through the rest of the decade, the German government built a system of concentration camps for political prisoners and, increasingly, "undesirable" populations that included petty criminals, homosexuals, and especially Jews. German Jews were progressively segregated from the rest of society, and they experienced escalating violence and loss of legal rights. Contrary to the terms of the armistice that ended

Sexual and Gender Minority History. James I. Martin, Oxford University Press. © Oxford University Press (2025).
DOI: 10.1093/9780197765500.003.0007

70 SEXUAL AND GENDER MINORITY HISTORY

the First World War, Germany rapidly rebuilt its military. It annexed Austria in 1938, followed by the German-speaking regions of Czechoslovakia (modern-day Slovakia and Czech Republic) several months later. In early September 1939, Germany invaded Poland from the west, triggering the Second World War, with Great Britain and France declaring war on Germany. Two weeks later, the Soviet Union invaded Poland from the east, and by the end of the month Poland ceased to exist as an independent nation.

The American public remained unconvinced that these events concerned them. American society was highly segregated, and not only with respect to African Americans. The small Japanese American population lived almost entirely on the West Coast, and in the Los Angeles area, where most of them resided, they were kept separate from whites through segregationist policies and practices (Daniels 2011). Chinese people had been in the United States since the mid-19th century, but the Chinese Exclusion Act of 1882 prohibited additional immigration from China. The Chinese American population experienced widespread prejudice and discrimination throughout the country (Wong 2005). Jews, who were concentrated in major cities, were restricted from living in many neighborhoods, going to certain schools, and entering certain professions. Charles Coughlin, a Catholic priest, preached hatred of Jews in his weekly radio broadcasts that had an estimated audience of 30 million ("Antisemitism in the 1920s and 1930s" 2024). Thus, it is not surprising that so many Americans cared little for what was happening to the Jews in Europe or to anyone in Asia.

By 1940, war was expanding in both Europe and the Pacific. The Soviet Union occupied the Baltic countries, while Germany overran Scandinavia, the Low Countries, and France. By 1941, Great Britain stood alone against Germany, and German planes were bombing London. Italy allied itself with Germany and invaded northern Africa. In the Pacific, Japan invaded Indochina (modern-day Vietnam). In response to the expanding war, American public opinion evolved to support aid to Great Britain but not direct involvement (US Holocaust Memorial Museum n.d.). In addition, by 1940 Congress had been persuaded to pass the Selective Service and Training Act, the first peacetime draft, in recognition that the country should prepare for the possibility of war. All men between ages 18 and 45 were required to register for the draft.

Opposition to American involvement in the war evaporated when Japan attacked the American naval base at Pearl Harbor on December 7, 1941.

US forces were totally unprepared for the attack, which killed more than 2,400 Americans. President Roosevelt appeared before Congress the following day to ask for a declaration of war on Japan, which was quickly given. On December 11th, Japan's allies Germany and Italy declared war on the United States, and the United States responded quickly with a declaration of war against them (US National Archives and Records Administration 2001). Several days later, an opinion poll showed that 91% of Americans were in favor of the war declarations (US Holocaust Memorial Museum, n.d.), an astounding turnaround in sentiment.

Americans Go to War

From 1941 to 1945, about 10 million American men were drafted into military service and 6 million more enlisted voluntarily. With so many men serving in the armed forces, women took their places in industry, which experienced tremendous growth to win the war effort (Bronski 2011). In the suddenly booming economy, great numbers of women from small towns and rural areas moved to large cities for factory jobs that previously would have been held by men (Faderman 1991), recruited by the government-sponsored "Rosie the Riveter" campaign. And beginning in 1942, women were invited to volunteer for military service; more than 350,000 served during the war (Martin 2020).

The massive deployment of men and women into military service and movement of women into industrial jobs had enormous consequences for sexual and gender minorities. Great numbers of sexual minority men served in the military even though they were officially considered unfit for service. Attempts to screen them out were quite lax during wartime; out of 18 million men screened by draft boards and induction centers, less than 5,000 were rejected on the grounds of being homosexual (Loughery 1998). As in the First World War but on a considerably larger scale, men who previously thought they alone had same-sex desires now found they were one of many. Some sexual minority men in military service, especially those from major cities, had experience to share about sexual minority subculture, bars, and other hangouts. On weekends New York, Chicago, San Francisco, and Los Angeles were flooded with soldiers and sailors looking for a good time, many of them gaining firsthand experience with the sexual minority subculture in those cities.

72   SEXUAL AND GENDER MINORITY HISTORY

By all accounts, a high proportion of women in the military during the war were sexual minorities. One reason was that screening for sexual minority status was especially lax for women; there were virtually no standards. Also, since women were not subject to the draft, recruiters were under pressure to enlist as many of them as possible (Bérubé 2010). In addition, sexual minority women were attracted by the prospect of adventure and professional work in all-woman environments such as those provided by the Women's Army Corps, Women Accepted for Volunteer Emergency Service (Navy), Marine Corps Women's Reserve, and Coast Guard Women's Reserve (Faderman 1991). Although women were not allowed combat roles, they served as nurses and clerical workers as well as air traffic controllers, weather forecasters, and communications directors, professional roles that never before had been available to them (Bronski 2011).

A Dangerous Environment

Even though the screening procedures were lax, the military was not a welcoming institution for sexual and gender minorities. During the course of the war, the Army and Navy increasingly viewed their presence as a problem that went beyond prohibited (or in the case of men, unlawful) behavior. Women or men who thought of themselves as lesbians or homosexuals, had same-sex attractions, or exhibited transgressive gender patterns came to be considered undesirable for military service. In other words, the military began to define sexual and gender minority individuals as a class of person rather than those who engaged in particular behaviors. As this development was guided by psychiatrists working with the military, sexual and gender minority status came to be understood as a mental illness. At the beginning of the war, men who engaged in same-sex sexual behavior could find themselves court martialed and imprisoned, although this was relatively rare. By 1943, the greater risk to sexual and gender minorities was being exposed publicly, even if they had been celibate, and then discharged from the military. An extensive surveillance system was constructed for the broader purpose of regulating the private lives of soldiers and sailors, but it was used more narrowly to ensnare and punish sexual and gender minorities (Bérubé 2010).

In 1941, Congress passed the May Act for the ostensible purpose of protecting the health of the troops by controlling prostitution near military bases. It gave the military the power to close businesses in these areas if the cities where they were located did not do so on their own. Facing an erosion of their own control, hundreds of cities shut down their red-light districts. In addition, alcohol-serving establishments had to abide by military regulations regarding its personnel, easily identifiable by the uniforms they were required to wear on leave. For example, military personnel were not allowed to become intoxicated, and those who were underage could not be served at all. Establishments caught violating these regulations could have their license revoked. The Army and Navy also surveilled establishments for other signs of "vice" that they believed would jeopardize the health and wellness of the troops, including contact between military personnel and sexual or gender minority civilians. During their surveillance rounds, military police would note places where they saw people believed to be sexual or gender minorities, and these businesses or public places would become off limits for military personnel. In San Francisco, Finocchio's was declared off limits, as were other establishments featuring drag performances in cities across the country. In cooperation with the military, waves of police raids on bars occurred in San Francisco, New York, Washington, and other cities (Bérubé 2010).

During periodic witch hunts that occurred on military bases both overseas and in the United States, suspected homosexuals were seized by military police without warning and placed in hospital psychiatric wards, or in stockades where they experienced public humiliation and abuse by guards. Suspects were commonly interrogated about their sexual lives and pressured to divulge the names of other homosexuals (Bérubé 2010; Bronski 2011). They became suspects in a variety of ways, not only when found in the presence of sexual or gender minority civilians. For example, some were named by other suspects during the course of interrogation. Others were reported by medical personnel who betrayed the confidentiality of their patients' personal information. These traumatic experiences ended with less-than-honorable discharge from the armed forces for approximately 10,000 soldiers and sailors, mostly men. "Blue" discharges, as they were called because they were printed on blue paper, were neither honorable nor dishonorable (which required a legal process and the commission of a crime). Instead, the blue discharge was an administrative separation from the military without any legal process or possibility of appeal (Bérubé 2010). The Veterans' Administration made the independent determination that recipients of blue discharges were not eligible for veteran benefits,

74 SEXUAL AND GENDER MINORITY HISTORY

including healthcare at Veterans' Administration facilities, college tuition, or occupational training. Employers were reluctant to hire veterans with blue discharges (Bronski 2011).

Blue discharges were issued for alleged "undesirable habits and traits of character" ("Blue and 'Other than Honorable' Discharges" n.d.), which was vague enough to allow for a variety of subjective determinations based on prejudice. For example, although only 6.5% of Army personnel were African Americans, they received more than 22% of the approximately 47,000 blue discharges from the Army (Petrick 2019). Thus, African Americans who were sexual or gender minorities were especially hard hit. In 1945, the *Pittsburgh Courier*, an African American newspaper, waged a public campaign against the blue discharge, accusing both the Army and the Veterans' Administration of actions based on outright prejudice. A flood of letters from veterans supported the inquiry and told their own stories of trauma. The newspaper's campaign was picked up by the House Committee on Military Affairs, and the committee's 1946 report strongly condemned the injustice. In the midst of this campaign, the Navy quietly began to upgrade discharges to "honorable" upon appeal, but the Army refused to do so (Bérubé 2010). In its 2019 review and upgrade of the blue discharge issued to one African American veteran in 1945, the Army Review Board for Correction of Military Records acknowledged this one review represented "thousands of disenfranchised veterans who were unable to avail themselves of the rewards that should have followed their years in the military" (Burnie 2019).

The example of blue discharges illustrates how injustices based on sexual and gender minority status overlapped with other minority-based injustices. Racial and ethnic minority men and women faced considerable prejudice and discrimination in the military, as they did on the home front. For instance, all branches of the military were racially segregated until the late 1940s, and African Americans were not allowed to serve in combat roles at first. In spite of these obstacles, minority soldiers and sailors served with honor and distinction. The highly decorated Tuskegee Airmen, an African American unit of the Army Air Corps, flew more than 1,500 successful missions over Europe and North Africa ("Congressional Gold Medal to the Tuskegee Airmen" 2006). Japanese Americans were prohibited from military service until 1943, when the 442nd Infantry Regiment was established. Despite the fact that these infantrymen, along with their families, had been removed from their homes by presidential order and sent to remote internment camps for the duration of the war, the all-Japanese American 442nd eventually became the most highly decorated unit of the entire Army (Brown 2021). The 158th Infantry, a unit of the Arizona National Guard that was primarily Mexican American and Native American, fought treacherous battles in the Pacific; General Douglas MacArthur showered it with praise, stating, "No greater fighting team has ever deployed for battle" (Magee 2003, p. 85). This was despite a lengthy and continuing history of discrimination and violence against Mexican Americans. While the 158th fought and gave their lives in the Pacific war, white sailors attacked and assaulted young, working-class Mexican Americans on the streets of Los Angeles in the Zoot Suit Riots of June 1943 (del Castillo 2000). Native Americans had the highest rate of voluntary enlistment of all racial/ethnic groups despite the genocide perpetrated against them by the American government. Without the invaluable skills of the Navaho Code Talkers, the United States and its allies might not have won the war (Magee 2003).

But It Wasn't All Bad

Countless sexual and gender minority soldiers and sailors transcended mistreatment with honor and acts of bravery, but unlike racial and ethnic minorities, opportunities for collective heroism were never provided to them. Nevertheless, military service provided many positive experiences. Among the millions of men who served during the war, nearly half were between 18 and 25 years old (Smith 1947); women had to be at least 21 to enlist, but those who served were also young (Bellafaire 2005). Those who were sexual and gender minorities learned there were others like themselves and that welcoming subcultures existed in large cities around the country. Many of these young men and women had their first same-sex sexual experiences during wartime, and some of them established devoted love relationships. Many others found meaningful companionship with buddies and friends. For sexual minority women in particular, the single-sex environment was extraordinarily positive since it allowed them to be independent of men, both economically and socially, and to develop a sense of sisterhood with each other (Bronski 2011). Even butch women and femme men, whose gender expression transgressed the rigid norms of the day, were able to find their place within the military environment. For example, many butch women attended motor transport training, where they learned how to operate, maintain, and repair a wide variety of military vehicles. Men could

76 SEXUAL AND GENDER MINORITY HISTORY

work as secretaries, typists, chaplain's assistants, or nurses. For both women and men, camaraderie developed among those who worked together in these roles (Bérubé 2010).

Sexual and gender minority men also found themselves appreciated for their contributions to variety shows and other efforts to maintain troop morale. The Army and Navy devoted great efforts to supporting their troops by providing recreational and social activities on base, opportunities for leave, and live performances that featured famous entertainers and movie stars. The best known of these presentations were offered by the United Service Organizations, but the Army's Special Services Branch presented many all-soldier shows.

> Male GIs wrote and produced soldier shows for each other wherever American troops were stationed. These were particularly important in basic-training camps, in remote areas where no local civilian entertainment was available, and later in occupied enemy countries where fraternization with the local population was forbidden. . . . Because the armed forces were racially segregated, black soldiers had to put on their own shows. (Bérubé 2010, p. 79)

These performances featured male soldiers in drag, often intended to be comical. The most famous of them was *This Is the Army*, written by Broadway veteran Irving Berlin, which moved from Army bases to Broadway to a national tour and, in 1943, to a successful screen adaptation. These shows provided sexual and gender minority men with opportunities to express themselves and use their special skills as both performers and behind-the-scenes crew (Bérubé 2010).

On the Homefront

More than 3 million troops sailed to the war in Europe from the New York Port of Embarkation, and about 1.6 million sailed to the war in the Pacific from the San Francisco Port of Embarkation. Other ports of embarkation included Seattle, Los Angeles, and Boston. Troops spent anywhere from a week to two weeks near the port before their departure into the darkness of battle, with time off for leave in the city. Since this tremendous movement of men and women continued regularly throughout the war, the market in these cities for entertainment and relaxation expanded considerably.

In particular, bars that welcomed, or at least tolerated, sexual and gender minority men and women multiplied in all of the port cities (Bérubé 2010; Faderman 1991). Even though they were usually off limits for military personnel, there were ways to evade the military police and shore patrol. Some changed into civilian clothes and hoped they wouldn't be recognized. Others went to places they heard about that were not yet on the off-limits list. In addition to military personnel, these cities also saw an influx of civilians, including those hoping to hook up with young military men and women (Bérubé 2010).

Millions of women were recruited to fill the jobs of men who went to war, and the explosive development of war-related industries, such as aircraft manufacturing, created many new areas of work. Women took jobs as welders, aircraft assembly workers, and mechanics (Vergun 2020), which otherwise would have been reserved for men; more than a million others filled clerical positions in the nation's capital. To take these positions, many women moved away from their families of origin and lived on their own or with roommates. Like women who enlisted for military service, so many women on the home front were now economically and socially independent (Bronski 2011), and a significant number of them were sexual and gender minorities (Faderman and Timmons 2006).

Chicago

With the wartime influx of soldiers and sailors on weekend leave, business boomed in Chicago's Northside bars catering to sexual and gender minorities. Locker clubs provided military personnel the opportunity to check their uniforms and rent civilian clothes so they could evade the military police and shore patrol. Many of the bars were dives such as Benny the Bums, which featured a drag show on Sundays. Chicago also had several piano bars that were popular with sexual minority men, including the Primrose Path, the Carousel, and the Town and Country bar in the Palmer House Hotel. Piano bars featured resident chanteuses; singer Joy Page entertained the audience at the Primrose Path with bawdy songs and jokes. The Twelve Thirty Club, on the city's Southside, featured entertainment by female jazz musicians and singers, and it was popular among sexual minority women. In general, these venues were owned or protected by organized crime families that paid off police and other local officials to stay open (De La Croix 2012).

Washington

The population of the nation's capital increased more than 20% during the 1940s. Much of the increase was war related, with many federal agencies doubling their need for workers to meet the expanded military and domestic needs. The majority of those who migrated to Washington for these jobs were women, including sexual minority women. In addition, a high number of military personnel were stationed in or near Washington during the war, many of whom were sexual and gender minorities. As with other major cities, the number of welcoming bars increased to meet the expanded market. And since so many sexual and gender minority people who came to Washington during wartime chose to stay, this trend continued even after the war ended. In addition to the bars, men cruised for other men in Lafayette Park and other public spaces, and house parties and drag events provided additional opportunities to socialize. However, Washington was strictly segregated until the 1950s, and most of the bars were for white men only. The Showboat was popular among white sexual minority women. The Cozy Corner and the Nob Hill were popular among African American sexual minority men. Sexual minority women who were African American were more likely to congregate at local bars that were mixed with respect to sexuality. Many women and men who were African American preferred to socialize at house parties where same-sex dancing was possible, since it was prohibited in the bars (Beemyn 2014).

San Francisco

In addition to the huge numbers of military personnel that flowed through the Port of San Francisco, there was a significant civilian migration to the Bay Area. The area's shipyards alone recruited tens of thousands of employees as they strove to meet the wartime needs of the Navy. The variety of sexual and gender minority–oriented bars increased considerably in San Francisco's North Beach neighborhood, especially after the end of the war. They included the Silver Dollar, the Black Cat, and, for women, Mona's and Tommy's Joint. Other bars were located in the Tenderloin, including the Brass Rail and the Old Adobe, where patrons could enjoy African American drag performances (D. Boyd 2010; N. Boyd 2003). City police worked with the Armed Forces Disciplinary Control Board to harass and close establishments like these during wartime; this cooperation continued after the war ended and into the next decade. In spite of the oppression, large numbers of sexual and gender minority veterans and civilians chose to settle in San Francisco in the postwar years. In 1949, California's tax board suspended the liquor license of the Black Cat because it was "a hangout for persons of homosexual tendencies." However, the owner appealed the suspension all the way to the state's supreme court on the grounds that "homosexuals had the right to assemble in bars and restaurants." The case was not decided until 1951, but the court's decision was momentous; it affirmed that homosexuals did, in fact, have a right to public assembly (Boyd 2003).

Los Angeles

A massive influx of defense spending to Los Angeles during wartime helped transform the city into an industrial giant and the leading metropolis of the American West (Verge 1994). Hundreds of thousands of women and men migrated for work opportunities in the city's aircraft factories and shipbuilding facilities. In addition, an estimated 250,000 veterans moved to Los Angeles after the war. By the end of the decade, it was home to more veterans than any other city in the country (McWilliams 1949). The large numbers of sexual and gender minorities that were part of this war migration built a thriving community. One migrant to Los Angeles in 1945 was Edythe Eyde. Within a year after moving, she self-identified as a lesbian, and by 1947 she was distributing *Vice Versa*, the first lesbian publication in the United States. Using the pseudonym Lisa Ben (an anagram of "lesbian"), she wrote and hand-typed multiple copies of each issue while working as a secretary at RKO Studios and distributed them to friends with the request that they pass them on to their friends (Faderman and Timmons 2006). Each 9- to 20-page issue of *Vice Versa* contained opinion pieces, short stories, poems, film and book reviews, and letters from readers. Ben later estimated that "several dozen" women read each issue. One of the remarkable aspects of *Vice Versa* was its positive viewpoint; Ben encouraged readers to develop a positive self-image about being lesbians. Unfortunately, the magazine lasted for only a year; when Ben's job changed, she no longer had the time to continue producing it (Streitmatter 1998).

Los Angeles's thriving sexual and gender minority community included two welcoming beaches, one just north of Santa Monica at Will Rogers State Beach, and the other, Crystal Beach, several blocks south of the Santa

Monica Pier. While Will Rogers (later nicknamed Ginger Rogers) attracted mostly men, Crystal Beach drew both men and women who also enjoyed the lively bars that fronted the beach (Faderman and Timmons 2006). About three blocks north was the Inkwell Beach, which was African American, and between the Inkwell and the pier was the original Muscle Beach where gymnasts, acrobats, movie stunt people, and weightlifters exercised amid admiring crowds. Among them was Bob Mizer, a young photographer who started providing photos of bodybuilders that they could use for competitions. Mizer had identified as gay when he was in high school, and he often would hang out with his friends at Pershing Square. After graduation, he apprenticed in the Hollywood studio of Frederick Kovert, a former female impersonator who produced nude male physique photos. In 1945, Mizer established his own studio, the Athletic Model Guild, in his mother's house near downtown Los Angeles where he and his older brother lived. In 1946, he started building a mail-order business for his physique photos, which were not nude, by advertising in the nationally distributed magazine *Strength & Health*. The business quickly became successful enough for Mizer to employ both his mother and his brother. As we will see in the next chapter, the Athletic Model Guild went on to become one of the most influential sexual minority organizations of the mid-20th century (D. Johnson 2019).

Summary

The Second World War had enormous impact on the United States both economically and socially. The massive wartime economy effectively ended the Great Depression. Great numbers of people migrated to major cities for industrial jobs. More women than ever before were economically and socially independent. The country emerged from the war as an economic and political superpower, while much of the rest of the world was devastated by the conflict. However, this dominant narrative erases the important effects of the war on sexual and gender and other minorities.

Across multiple marginalized groups, including women, sexual and gender minorities, and racial and ethnic minorities, wartime and its aftermath fomented a strong sense of injustice as their members fought and gave their lives for a country that treated them as second-class citizens. Members of racial and ethnic minorities had long-standing group-based identities, while this was not the case for sexual and gender minorities before the war.

But through the influence of psychiatry, the military increasingly advanced an understanding of sexual minorities as constituting a people, as opposed to those who merely engaged in proscribed behaviors, and persecuted and punished them based on this understanding.

However, the military also brought together great numbers of sexual and gender minority individuals, which allowed them to develop a sense of community despite the ongoing risks. In Los Angeles, San Francisco, New York, and other major cities, underground sexual and gender minority subcultures grew substantially during wartime with the tremendous influx of military personnel and civilians migrating for industrial jobs. Many sexual and gender minority people chose to live in these cities upon discharge from military service, where they contributed to the building of vibrant communities.

Across the country, existing sodomy and cross-dressing laws had provided a basis for the persecution of sexual and gender minorities through the criminal justice system, but beginning in the 1940s, psychiatry advanced the increasingly influential formulation that they were mentally ill. In spite of these oppressive forces, sexual and gender minority people found ways to connect; at bars, cafeterias, bathhouses, beaches, parks, and house parties, mostly off the radar of the general population, they found sexual release, support, camaraderie, and love. And in a state supreme court decision, on the typewritten pages of a hand-delivered magazine, and through the mail-order business of a young photographer there appeared the kernels of a movement yet to be born.

Chapter 8
The 1950s and the Homophile Movement

The postwar period is often remembered as a period of complacency, conformity, and rising affluence, a narrative largely constructed by television, which became the most influential of the mass media in the postwar era. Prior to the war, few Americans owned a television; by 1955 half of all homes had one, growing to 90% by the end of the decade (Kim 2022). *Father Knows Best*, *Leave It to Beaver*, and *The Adventures of Ozzie and Harriet*, which depicted life among happy, white, middle-class suburban families, were some of the most watched shows in the 1950s and early 1960s. People of color were largely absent from the narrative constructed by shows of this period except for their appearance in marginalized, subservient roles; sexual and gender minorities were entirely absent. These shows did reflect some real aspects of American life in the 1950s, such as the postwar marriage and baby boom, increased affluence and consumerism, and mass movement of white families to new suburban homes, but the reality of the postwar era was considerably more complex than what they portrayed.

Red Scare

By the beginning of 1950, the world was largely divided between the capitalist United States and its allies and the communist Soviet Union and its allies. The Cold War between these two superpowers would dominate world events for another 40 years, and with it the ever-present danger of nuclear annihilation. Through its bombing of Hiroshima and Nagasaki in 1945, the United States demonstrated the terrifying destructiveness of nuclear weapons. By the early 1950s, the two superpowers were engaged in an arms race to build the largest arsenal of increasingly powerful weapons aimed at each other, according to a defense strategy known as "mutually assured destruction." Proliferation of nuclear weapons occurred by the end of the decade, as Great Britain and France joined the club. In schools throughout the United States, air raid drills were held regularly in which children

Sexual and Gender Minority History. James I. Martin, Oxford University Press. © Oxford University Press (2025). DOI: 10.1093/9780197765500.003.0008

were instructed to duck under their desks and cover their heads to protect themselves from a nuclear blast (Pruitt 2019). The Federal Civil Defense Administration encouraged families to build fallout shelters in order to survive an attack (Bishop 2022). It also organized Operation Alert, an annual defense drill in which citizens in hundreds of cities were told to evacuate to bomb shelters for 15 minutes, and mock news coverage reported on the devastation inflicted by a fictitious attack ("Operation Alert, Los Angeles, 1957" 2013).

Fear of Soviet imperialism and communist subversion pervaded American society. The House of Representatives' Committee on Un-American Activities (HUAC) investigated Americans in positions of influence who were suspected of being communists. In late 1947 the committee subpoenaed more than 40 witnesses for several days of hearings on suspected communist influence in the entertainment industry. Some were considered friendly to the committee's investigation, including studio heads Walt Disney, Louis B. Mayer, and Jack Warner; many were targets of the investigation, including writers Bertolt Brecht and Dalton Trumbo. Soon afterward, Hollywood studio executives publicized their decision not to employ anyone with a current or previous connection to the Communist Party. Also in 1947, Congress passed the Taft-Hartley Act, which placed limits on union activities. One result was the requirement for Screen Actors Guild and other union members to sign a loyalty oath and swear their opposition to communism. Anyone who refused or was found to have present or previous connection to the Communist Party was blacklisted from employment in Hollywood. The HUAC investigations resumed in 1950, with targets being pressured to name others with communist sympathies; an estimated 500 names were provided to the committee. Those who expressed concern about the committee's methods were also blacklisted, as were those who supported progressive organizations ("The Blacklist and the Greylist" 1955).

Concurrently, Senator Joseph McCarthy became a media darling when he claimed to have a list of "known communists" in the US State Department. By 1953, he had become the chair of the Senate Committee on Government Operations as well as its Subcommittee on Investigations, from which he launched a year and a half of inflammatory hearings, often televised, on suspected subversives in various government agencies. Authors and university faculty were also investigated regarding their political beliefs. McCarthy subpoenaed more than 500 witnesses whom he typically intimidated through baseless accusations, innuendo, and threats. Although these investigations found little evidence of actual subversion, they destroyed the lives of many witnesses ("Portraits in Oversight: Joe McCarthy's Oversight Abuses" 2024).

Lavender Scare

The Red Scare described above was accompanied by a Lavender Scare that, although not as well known, was no less destructive. A 1950 Senate subcommittee investigation into suspected homosexuals in government agencies promoted the argument that homosexuals were security risks, since their need for secrecy made them vulnerable to extortion by communist agents. The subcommittee recommended the removal of all homosexuals from government employment in spite of finding no evidence to support the recommendation. It also called for the Federal Bureau of Investigation (FBI) to collect information about homosexuals. In 1953, President Dwight Eisenhower signed Executive Order 10450, which made "sexual perversion" grounds for firing from, and denying employment in any agency of the federal government, and it required all federal employees to sign "moral purity" oaths. By mid-decade, state and local governments across the country adopted similar policies and oaths (Bérubé 2010).

As a result of these policies, sexual and gender minority people in civil service, especially those working in the nation's capital, risked encountering some form of the following in their required security interview: "[We have] information that you are an admitted homosexual. What comment do you wish to make regarding this matter?" (Johnson 2004, p. 48). If the interviewee denied the accusation, the interviewer might ask more specific questions based on information already gained about them by the FBI. "Have you ever gone to the [x bar]?" "Do you know [x person]?" "Do you enjoy having sex with [x person]?" Surveillance by the FBI could be initiated by coworkers, supervisors, or supervisees voicing concern about one's appearance or behavior on or off the job. In such an environment, it was foolhardy to trust anyone. Thousands of sexual and gender minority employees lost their jobs through this process, most by choosing to resign, and they had difficulty finding new employment after that. Many were forced to move to another city. Some committed suicide. The Lavender Scare was not limited to government employees since security clearance also was required for employees of private sector companies with government contracts. Screening out or getting rid of suspected homosexuals spread well beyond government agencies to businesses throughout the country (Johnson 2004).

Under the direction of J. Edgar Hoover, the FBI established the Sex Deviates Program in 1950 with the ostensible purpose of providing to Congress information about people considered to be a threat to the nation's security. Under the program, fingerprints and other personal information about individuals arrested by local authorities for "sex deviate" charges were compiled by the FBI. Individuals' files also contained unsubstantiated accusations and allegations. The FBI used this information to destroy the careers of individuals employed by the federal government who were thought to be sexual or gender minorities. Although the program's primary focus was on government employees, Hoover expanded it substantially through the 1950s and 1960s to encompass private citizens who were suspected of being "sex deviates" even in the absence of an arrest record (Charles 2015). The FBI maintained an extensive surveillance program in collaboration with local police forces, the Civil Service Commission, and the Postal Service. Postal inspectors often worked undercover to locate homosexuals throughout the country (D'Emilio 1983). For example, they monitored physique magazines and other materials oriented toward homosexuals that were sent through the mail. They "subscribed to pen pal clubs, initiated correspondence with men whom they believed might be homosexual, and, if their suspicions were confirmed, placed tracers on victims' mail in order to locate other homosexuals" (p. 47). This program was maintained until the early 1970s (Charles 2015).

By the 1950s, the general public was no longer unaware of the existence of sexual and gender minorities. A major contributor to this change was the publication in 1948 of Alfred Kinsey's blockbuster book *Sexual Behavior in the Human Male*, which shocked the public with its findings that 37% of adult men in the United States had at least one same-sex sexual experience to the point of orgasm, and about 10% had mostly same-sex experiences. Kinsey's 1953 book *Sexual Behavior in the Human Female* reported at least one same-sex sexual experience to orgasm among 13% of adult women in the United States, with as many as 6% having mostly same-sex experiences. J. Edgar Hoover engaged in a campaign to convince the public that sexual and gender minorities were dangerous, especially since (like other subversives) they operated in the shadows of society. For example, he published an article in 1957 that argued for compulsory quarantining and forced treatment of "sex deviates" to protect the public, especially children, from people "who are criminals in spite of themselves" (Charles 2015, p. 111).

Hoover's public relations campaign helped to inflame a growing national panic about sexual and gender minorities. Two years before he published the article mentioned above, a witch hunt in Boise, Idaho, began in the wake of a rumor that 100 high school boys were having sex with local adult men. Hysteria was whipped up by the city's newspaper, and national coverage of the scandal ensued. A two-year investigation involved questioning of about 1,500 people and resulted in convictions of 15 men, most for having consensual sex with another adult man. One of the men was sentenced to life imprisonment, and two received 15-year sentences (Gerassi 1966). Police sweeps of public parks and spaces where sexual and gender minority people congregated were common in Los Angeles (Faderman and Timmons 2006), Philadelphia (Stein 2004), San Francisco (Boyd 2003), and Washington (Beemyn 2014). Bars were raided frequently in New York, especially in the run-up to mayoral elections. Police sweeps in New York and other cities were often preceded by newspaper articles announcing police action against "nests of deviates" (D'Emilio 1983, p. 49). After a bar raid, it was common for newspapers to list the names of those arrested in addition to their address and the name of their employer (D'Emilio 1983).

Self-Identification and Building Networks

Within this extremely oppressive context, there were several attempts to encourage self-identification and the building of networks among sexual minority people. As described previously, Lisa Ben produced a few issues of *Vice Versa* and distributed them to other sexual minority women in Los Angeles during the late 1940s. The first edition of *A Gay Girls' Guide*, a campily titled guide to bars and cruising spots, was produced by an anonymous author in 1949 and circulated among sexual minority men in New York. Although the guide focused on New York City, it included information about bars and other places to go in several cities. It also contained a "gayese-English dictionary" and sections on "types of trade" and "sex techniques."

Bob Mizer, the Los Angeles photographer who established the Athletic Model Guild, began publishing the magazine *Physique Pictorial* in 1951, the first photo magazine oriented toward sexual minority men. Mizer's success in marketing his physique photos over the previous few years resulted in an impressive mailing list of subscribers throughout the United States and in many other countries. Within a few years, *Physique Pictorial* appeared on newsstands in large American cities. The athletic young men appearing on the magazine's pages were scantily clad, not nude, but the publication's homoerotic intent was pretty clear. As such, it ran the risk of seizure by postal authorities, and its subscribers risked arrest and exposure as "deviants." In 1954, the appearance of *Physique Pictorial* on some Los Angeles newsstands led to a newspaper campaign against Mizer and his eventual conviction for distributing obscene material. However, the conviction was overturned by an appellate court, and the magazine continued publishing until 1990. For decades, and for untold numbers of sexual minority men who thought they were alone in the world, seeing this magazine on a newsstand brought their first awareness of being gay and the realization that they were not the only one (D. Johnson 2019).

A similar role for sexual minority women was filled by paperback "pulp" novels, which first appeared in 1950 with Tereska Torres's *Women's Barracks.* These inexpensive paperback books could be found in dime stores, drugstores, and bus and train stations in every city. Their cover artwork depicted fully dressed women in suggestive poses, with lurid and sometimes condemnatory titles that indicated "dangerous" sexuality. The novels described romantic and sexual encounters between women, but they often had unhappy endings (Forrest 2005).

> Back in those days, when the vast majority of lesbians were like isolated islands with no territory other than risky lesbian bars to call our own, and no way of finding more than a few of one another, we were in every way susceptible to accepting and even agreeing with the larger culture's condemnation of us. We despairingly hoped that stories in the original paperbacks would not end badly but realized that in the view of the larger society, "perversion" could have no reward. (Forrest 2005, p. xiv)

With the success of Torres's novel, the publisher Fawcett Gold Medal Books continued to develop the market. Next came Vin Packer's *Spring Fire* in 1952. Ann Bannon wrote a series of pulp novels between 1957 and 1962 featuring the character Beebo Brinker, a butch lesbian. Another important contributor to the genre was Paula Christian, who wrote six pulp novels between 1959 and 1965. All of the author names mentioned here are pseudonyms; it was much too dangerous to use one's real name in association with such transgressive material (Forrest 2005). "Ann Bannon" was actually Ann Weldy, who lived in the Chicago area and began writing to deal with her sexual feelings for other women and her unhappy marriage to a man. "Paula Christian" was Yvonne MacManus, a Mexican American woman originally from Los Angeles. "Vin Packer" was one of several pseudonyms for Marijane Meaker from upstate New York. In spite of the oppressive social context of the era, their writing helped sexual minority women to identify who they were and to realize they were not alone.

The first actual support group for sexual minority men, the Veterans Benevolent Association, was established in 1945 in New York and incorporated in 1947. The association, which remained in existence until 1954, provided social networking opportunities for sexual minority veterans through regularly scheduled meetings and discussion groups, and legal advice for recipients of blue discharges (Bérubé 2010). Between 1949 and 1951 (accounts vary), Merton Bird, an African American lawyer, and W. Dorr Legg, his white partner, established the Knights of the Clocks, a mutual support group in Los Angeles for interracial sexual minority couples like themselves (Bronski 2011; Loughery 1998).

Mattachine Society

A broader and more enduring impact was made by the Mattachine Society, an educational, support, and advocacy organization for sexual minorities that was established in Los Angeles in 1950 by Harry Hay, Rudi Gernreich, Bob Hull, Chuck Rowland, and Dale Jennings. Two years earlier, Hay had conceptualized the idea that homosexuals made up a minority group, and he began to envision a movement that would lead to their liberation. These ideas were inspired by the 19th-century British author Edward Carpenter, who in turn was influenced by Walt Whitman and Karl Heinrich Ulrichs. In addition, Hay had heard from one of his first lovers about the 1924 Society for Human Rights. Hay was also inspired to organize homosexuals by his active involvement in the American Communist Party and in the contradiction between the party's social justice ideals and its hostility toward same-sex sexuality. Hay wrote up his ideas about an organization for homosexuals and, over the course of two years, showed them to a number of people he thought might be interested. However, he found no one who was willing to join him until he met Rudi Gernreich. Gernreich, a young Jewish dancer and aspiring fashion designer, fled Austria after its annexation by Nazi Germany in 1938, and he was familiar with the German homosexual rights movement. Hay and Gernreich became lovers soon after they met, and together they found the three other men mentioned above (Timmons 1990).

The Mattachine Society's originally stated purposes included unifying homosexuals who were isolated from each other, educating the public about same-sex sexuality, advocating for positive legislation, and leading a movement for the betterment of homosexuals. The organization's name referred to French medieval masked societies of unmarried men who performed dances and satirized social injustice. Harry Hay thought that homosexual life was akin to wearing a mask and that, like the medieval performers, homosexuals had the potential for speaking truth to power. In a conscious effort to avoid the medical baggage that "homosexual" had acquired, the steering committee decided on "homophile" as the name of the movement they hoped to start (Timmons 1990); this term continues to be used to describe the sexual minority movement of the 1950s and 1960s. During its first couple of years, Mattachine sponsored semipublic discussion groups about same-sex sexuality. Among the attendees, men or women who appeared to be sexual minorities were privately invited to join the organization, but those who were "flamboyant" or transgressed gender were not invited (Faderman and Timmons 2006). However, even those who were invited to join did not know who the organization's leaders were; secrecy was a dominant feature of Mattachine's organizational structure (Timmons 1990).

When Dale Jennings was entrapped by police in a public restroom in 1952 and charged with "lewd and dissolute conduct," Mattachine's steering committee made the radical decision to fight the charge in court. Jennings's lawyer, an Arab American, was successful in getting the charge dropped. Although mainstream newspapers did not report on the trial, Mattachine generated its own publicity and disseminated information about ways sexual minorities could protect themselves in the event of arrest. Interest in the organization skyrocketed; soon there were enough interested people to fill several discussion groups, and new chapters sprung up in cities throughout California (Timmons 1990).

Meanwhile, expansion of Mattachine's membership brought diversification of viewpoints about goals and strategies. At its constitutional convention in 1953, some members voiced discomfort and suspicion about the steering committee's secrecy. Some even demanded to know whether there were subversive elements among the leadership, and a proposal was advanced to require members to sign a loyalty oath. One member threatened to give the FBI a list of Mattachine's members if the organization failed to disavow "leftist sympathies." Given these views, Harry Hay and Chuck Rowland feared their past membership in the Communist Party would be detrimental to the organization's future, and all of the founders stepped down from their leadership roles. Delegates to the convention decided to make the organization more traditional in its structure, with an elected board and open membership. The new leaders were politically conservative; under their direction Mattachine focused on helping homosexuals to integrate into mainstream society and no longer conceived of them as an oppressed minority group. With these changes, most of the discussion groups in Los Angeles evaporated, and the small number of women members dwindled; the organization's headquarters eventually moved to San Francisco (Loughery 1998). While Mattachine's influence declined, it spurred independent though similarly named offshoots in other cities, especially New York and Washington, that later would have greater impact. The Mattachine Society was investigated extensively by the FBI between 1953 and 1956.

Nevertheless, the Mattachine Society played an important role in a landmark mid-1950s study that challenged psychiatric wisdom about same-sex sexuality. Psychologist Evelyn Hooker administered projective tests to 30 men who reported their sexual behavior to be exclusively same-sex oriented, most of whom were members of the Los Angeles chapter of Mattachine, and compared them to 30 men who reported exclusively other-sex-oriented behavior after matching for age, education, and intelligence. A panel of expert psychologists was unable to distinguish the two groups of men on personality structure and overall adjustment (Hooker 1957). This study provided the first empirical evidence that homosexuality was not a mental illness, but it would take more than a decade for the mental health professions to reach this conclusion.

ONE Inc

Late in 1952, at a Mattachine discussion group in West Hollywood, conversation focused increasingly on the idea of publishing a magazine. The original idea might have been Harry Hay's, but Dale Jennings and others wanted the project to be independent of him. To advance the publication project, Jennings joined with Martin Block, Don Slater and his partner Tony Reyes, Bailey Whittaker, John Nojima, and Knights of the Clocks founders Merton Bird and Dorr Legg to form a nonprofit organization named ONE Inc. The founding members were remarkably diverse, with Bird and Whittaker African Americans, Nojima Japanese American, Reyes Mexican American, and Block Jewish American. The organization's name was suggested by Whittaker, referring to an aphorism by 19th-century British author Thomas Carlyle, "a mystic bond of brotherhood makes all men one" (Faderman and Timmons 2006; Timmons 1990). The first issue of *ONE Magazine* appeared in 1953, and it continued publishing until 1967. Although women were not among the founders of ONE Inc., some who joined early on were integral to the magazine's production. Joan Corbin was the art director for 10 years, and Irma Wolf was one of the first editors. With Corbin and Wolf in leadership positions, a number of other women joined as writers and artists, and as officers of ONE Inc. (Legg 1994). By the end of its first year, *ONE Magazine* added the phrase "the homosexual magazine" to its title, later changing it to "the homosexual viewpoint." Each issue contained articles, fiction, poetry, book reviews, and letters to and from the editors. The covers often had striking, original artwork. During the 1950s, some of the cover stories were "Are Homosexuals Neurotic?," "Is Your Child a Homosexual?," and "I Am Glad I Am Homosexual."

ONE Magazine quickly drew the attention of law enforcement. Even though everyone involved with the magazine used pseudonyms, the FBI determined their real identities and harassed them. The Postal Service also took an interest and sent agents to the organization's office in August 1953 to confiscate copies of the magazine's latest issue. Although that seizure resulted in no charges, a second seizure in October 1954 led to ONE Inc. being charged with violating the federal Comstock Act of 1873, which criminalized use of the Postal Service to distribute "obscene" material. The postmaster of Los Angeles considered three items in the October 1954 issue obscene: a story about lesbians, a poem that referred to homosexuality in British history, and an advertisement for the Swiss homophile magazine *Der Kreis*. It's unclear why these particular items elicited the ire of the postmaster, but the federal district court hearing the case in 1956 declared them obscene, a decision that was upheld by the Ninth Circuit Court of Appeals in 1957. Since the American Civil Liberties Union had refused to defend ONE Inc. in court, the organization turned to a young lawyer named Eric Julber for its defense. After the failure of the appeal, Julber made the audacious decision to take the case to the US Supreme Court. It was the first case having to do with same-sex sexuality ever brought before the court. To everyone's surprise, the court decided the standards used by the Postal Service to judge homosexual content were discriminatory since they were more stringent than those used to judge nonhomosexual content. In January 1958 the court struck down the lower court decisions, which meant that publications could no longer be considered obscene simply because of their homosexual content (Faderman and Timmons 2006).

Meanwhile, ONE Inc. grew beyond its original singular focus on publishing a magazine. First, it established a Social Service Division that provided peer counseling for sexual and gender minorities. In 1956, it established ONE Institute, which offered courses in homophile studies in Los Angeles. Courses examined same-sex sexuality with respect to many fields, including anthropology, history, literature, medicine, psychology, and sociology. Extension courses were offered in San Francisco and, in the 1960s, Chicago, Detroit, and New York. From 1958 until 1970, ONE Inc. published the *ONE Institute Quarterly of Homophile Studies*, a journal of scholarly articles. And in 1981, the ONE Institute Graduate School received authorization from the California State Department of Education to offer MA and PhD degrees in Homophile Studies (Legg 1994).

Daughters of Bilitis

The first national lesbian organization, Daughters of Bilitis, was established by four couples in San Francisco in 1955. A Filipina American woman named Rose Bamberger had conceived of a social club for lesbians as an alternative to the bars, where same-sex dancing was prohibited and being caught in a vice squad raid was always a risk. Rose envisioned a club in which lesbians could meet, dance with each other, and socialize in the safety of each other's homes. Those joining Rose and her partner Rosemary Slieper at a planning meeting were Del Martin and her partner Phyllis Lyon, Noni Frey and her partner Mary (last name unknown), and Marcia Foster and her partner June (last name unknown). Mary was a Mexican American woman, but besides her and Rose, the others were white. The name of the organization was deliberately obscure, referring to *Songs of Bilitis*, erotic poems about the ancient Greek poet Sappho that were included in the collected works of 19th-century French author Pierre Louÿs. At their first meeting, the women chose Del Martin to be the organization's president, Noni Frey as vice president, Phyllis Lyon as secretary, and Marcia Foster as trustee. They decided that new members had to be "a gay girl of good moral character" (Gallo 2007, p. 4) and at least 21 years old. Men were not allowed to attend events unless they were invited.

As more women joined Daughters of Bilitis, conflicts arose regarding members' gender expression and the purpose of the organization. Within a few months, the founders established a rule that prohibited members from wearing masculine attire, ostensibly because doing so risked police intervention. Also, butch and femme roles were primarily working-class patterns at that time, and they made the middle-class members feel uncomfortable. By the end of the organization's first year, its expanded membership expressed interest in engaging in activities in the public sphere and less interest in continuing as a private social club. Meanwhile, Del Martin and Phyllis Lyon had come in contact with ONE Inc. and the Mattachine Society, and this led Daughters of Bilitis to sponsor public discussion groups on lesbian issues. With the organization's change in focus, Rose Bamberger and other working-class members lost interest (Gallo 2007; Lo 2021).

The issues of concern to women who joined Daughters of Bilitis were not the same as those concerning sexual minority men. Sexual minority women and men were both targets of the oppressive Lavender Scare, and in bars both risked harassment and arrest by police. Those who violated the rigid rules for gendered dress were especially vulnerable. However, unlike men, women did not cruise for other women in public places, and they were not targets of entrapment by police. Thus, the major issue that animated the homophile-era politics of sexual minority men held little importance for them. On the other hand, sexual minority women experienced sexist oppression, which they shared with other women. For example,

> many lesbians had been, or still were, married; exposure would mean losing custody of their children. As single women in the workforce, lesbians also faced pressure to earn a living while having fewer job opportunities, being paid less than men, and dealing with sexual harassment. (Bronski 2011, p. 181)

However, participating in Daughters of Bilitis was at least as risky for women as participating in the Mattachine Society or ONE Inc. was for men. Members were fearful of being discovered and exposed by police, and much effort was devoted to ensuring their privacy. Although it was not known at the time, the FBI was investigating the organization as early as 1956 (Charles 2015).

In late 1956, Daughters of Bilitis began the first nationally distributed lesbian publication, *The Ladder*, which continued until 1972. Each issue presented the organization's main purpose as fostering "the integration of the homosexual into society." Issues included reports about the organization's meetings as well as other articles, poetry, etiquette advice, and letters from readers. By its second year, *The Ladder* had hundreds of subscribers. It also could be found at newsstands in a few major cities (Martin 2016). As sexual minority women outside of San Francisco learned about Daughters of Bilitis, often by reading *The Ladder*, they began chapters in Los Angeles, New York, and Chicago (Gallo 2007).

Trans Visibility

Gender minority identities began to emerge during the 1950s. In 1952, Virginia Prince, a heterosexual man in Los Angeles who secretly dressed in women's clothes, produced and distributed to other cross-dressing men a couple of issues of a newsletter called *Transvestia: The Journal of the American Society for Equality in Dress*. At the time, such men referred to themselves as transvestites, the English translation of a term invented by Magnus Hirschfeld more than 40 years earlier. Transvestites dressed in women's clothes for their own identity needs, not for entertainment, which differentiated them from female impersonators and drag artists. However, their lack of desire for genital transformation also differentiated them from transsexuals, an identity label also invented by Hirschfeld. In 1953, Danish American Christine Jorgensen, who had served in the Army as a man, attained instant celebrity as the first widely known transsexual in the United States after receiving hormone treatment and gender-confirming surgery in Denmark. Jorgensen shrewdly used her celebrity status to foster a successful career as a nightclub entertainer and to promote greater understanding about gender minorities (Stryker 2008). At the same time, gender variance among middle-class sexual minority men became increasingly unacceptable. With their strong desire for social acceptability, such men feared and resented the old stereotypes represented by "swishes," as fairies and pansies came to be known in the 1950s (Loftin 2007).

Summary

Following the extreme social upheaval of the previous two decades, the 1950s brought intense focus on stability and "normality." The dominant narrative of this era, as disseminated by the entertainment industry, erases the corrosive impact of the preoccupation with communist subversion and the violent suppression of all those considered a threat to the security of American society. Sexual and gender minorities were considered among the gravest of those threats. Reversing the relaxation of rules for gender roles and sexuality that occurred during wartime, the 1950s saw glorification of "traditional" gender roles and heterosexual families. In addition, the limited gains in equality made by racial and ethnic minority soldiers who fought in the Second World War were never extended to civilians, and minority veterans encountered the same segregation and white supremacy as they had before the war.

Nevertheless, this era saw the establishment of foundational sexual minority organizations. Awareness among many sexual minority men that there were others like themselves came with the newsstand appearance of magazines like *Physique Pictorial*; for sexual minority women it was the appearance of pulp novels. Building on the military and psychiatric conceptualization of homosexuals as "a people" rather than just individuals who engaged in prohibited behaviors, Harry Hay conceived of them as an oppressed minority. Prior to the purge of its founding leaders, the Mattachine Society disseminated this revolutionary idea among its members, particularly in California. Even though the Mattachine Society discarded this idea after the purge, and other homophile organizations never adopted it, the idea could not help but germinate. ONE Inc. and Daughters of Bilitis more successfully engaged sexual minority men and women throughout the country and instilled in them a sense of group identification and common cause, especially through their publications *ONE Magazine* and *The Ladder*. This advance was especially important for sexual minority women, who were even more isolated than sexual minority men. Racial and ethnic minority men and women played important roles in the establishment of ONE Inc.

and Daughters of Bilitis, but these organizations did not make the specific concerns of nonwhite sexual minorities, or those who were not middle class, a focus of their efforts. In addition, bifurcation of sexual and gender minority identities occurred increasingly as middle-class sexual minorities aspired to social acceptability, and greater self-awareness and group identification began to develop among gender minorities.

Chapter 9
A Rising Tide of Resistance

By the mid-1950s, cracks began to occur in America's rigidly segregated and racially hierarchical social structure. In *Brown v. Board of Education* (1954), the US Supreme Court declared segregated public education unconstitutional. Nevertheless, school systems throughout the South refused to desegregate. In 1957, nine African American students attempted to start the school year at white-only Little Rock (Arkansas) Central High School but were stopped by a violent mob. Not dissuaded, they tried to attend two more times, finally succeeding after President Eisenhower ordered the Army to enforce a court order allowing their attendance. However, the students endured continued harassment and threats of violence from white students throughout their high school experience (National Park Service 2021).

Following the arrest of 15-year-old Claudette Colvin in 1955 for not giving up her seat on a public bus to a white man in Montgomery, Alabama, African Americans organized against segregated public transportation. Later that year, Rosa Parks, an officer for the local chapter of the National Association for the Advancement of Colored People, precipitated the Montgomery Bus Boycott when she refused to move from her seat in the white-only section of a city bus. In the face of fire bombings and other forms of violence from enraged whites, African Americans maintained the boycott for 13 months. Rosa Parks's conviction for disorderly conduct was eventually overturned by a federal district court, and in 1956 the US Supreme Court declared Montgomery's segregated busses unconstitutional (Burns 1997). Regardless, segregation in public transport remained widespread throughout the South.

In 1961, the Congress of Racial Equality organized a Freedom Ride to challenge this situation; two buses of African Americans and whites departed Washington, DC, for New Orleans. Upon arrival in a South Carolina bus terminal, one of the Freedom Riders, 21-year-old John Lewis, a future member of the House of Representatives, was assaulted when he tried to enter the white-only waiting room. When the first bus reached Anniston, Alabama, a violent white mob attacked with iron bars and firebombed it.

Sexual and Gender Minority History. James I. Martin, Oxford University Press. © Oxford University Press (2025). DOI: 10.1093/9780197765500.003.0009

100 SEXUAL AND GENDER MINORITY HISTORY

The remaining bus went on to Birmingham, where the violence continued. Unable to continue further by bus, the Freedom Riders completed their journey by air. Freedom Rides expanded in the following months, with northern whites riding with African Americans to Mississippi and Alabama. The Interstate Commerce Commission eventually ordered interstate buses and bus terminals to desegregate (Peck 1962).

In 1960, four African American college students sat down at the white-only lunch counter at F. W. Woolworth's in Greensboro, North Carolina, and asked to be served. When they were refused, they remained at the counter for the rest of the day. In what became known as a sit-in, the students returned the next day with 25 others, and even more on successive days. Sit-ins spread to other segregated lunch counters in Greensboro and, over the next couple of weeks, to other southern cities. After six months, Woolworth's agreed to desegregate (Chafe 1981). The nonviolent tactic of the sit-in was used in hundreds of other locations during the 1960s. Nonviolence highlighted the moral high ground of opposition to Jim Crow–era white supremacy, a brutal reality exemplified by the 1963 bombing of Birmingham, Alabama's Sixteenth Street Baptist Church that resulted in the deaths of four African American young women.

The civil rights movement expanded through the 1960s, as did the backlash to it. In August 1963, the March on Washington for Jobs and Freedom drew an estimated quarter-million participants to protest racial discrimination and rally for passage of civil rights legislation. The march is especially remembered for Dr. Martin Luther King's "I Have a Dream" speech. In June, a civil rights bill proposed by the Kennedy administration had been introduced in both houses of Congress, but it encountered strong opposition. Five months later, President Kennedy was assassinated in Dallas, and Lyndon Johnson, Kennedy's vice president, was sworn in as president alongside the grieving Mrs. Kennedy. In the wake of the assassination, President Johnson exerted tremendous pressure on Congress to pass the stalled legislation and he signed the Civil Rights Act of 1964 into law at the beginning of July (John F. Kennedy Presidential Library and Museum n.d.). As the Civil Rights Act was nearing passage, hundreds of college students from all over the country traveled to Mississippi to help register African Americans to vote and expose the racial hatred and violent intimidation that marked everyday life for the state's African American residents. The 10-week-long Freedom Summer drew the attention of the national news media, especially when one

African American and two white volunteer participants were murdered by members of the Ku Klux Klan (Edmonds 2014).

Even after the passage of the Civil Rights Act, efforts to register African Americans to vote encountered deadly violence. In Alabama, Jimmie Lee Jackson, a 26-year-old African American man, was shot and killed by a state trooper in 1965 following his participation in a voting rights march. A Selma-to-Montgomery March was organized in the aftermath of this tragedy. One week after Jackson's death, on Bloody Sunday, about 600 participants began the 50-mile march from Selma, led by Rev. Hosea Williams and John Lewis. However, a phalanx of armed state and county police confronted them as they reached the crest of the Edmund Pettus Bridge, and they ordered the march to disperse. When the marchers refused, the police charged into the crowd on horseback and attacked with batons, bullwhips, and tear gas. Among the many injuries, John Lewis sustained a fractured skull. The entire episode was shown on national television, and it horrified much of the public outside the South; demonstrations were held throughout the country. A little more than two weeks later, after a federal court supported the right to march and President Johnson ordered the Army and federal agents to provide protection, Dr. King led thousands of marchers across the bridge to Montgomery. Four months later, President Johnson signed the Voting Rights Act of 1965, which outlawed many of the obstacles that southern states employed to prevent African Americans from voting (Lewis 1998).

However, by the mid-1960s, racial discrimination and aggressive policing of impoverished and disempowered black communities in northern and western cities led to increasing violence. In July 1964, rioting occurred in Harlem and Rochester, New York, and in August, in Philadelphia. Only days after the Voting Rights Act of 1965 was signed into law, six days of rioting in the Watts neighborhood of Los Angeles resulted in 34 deaths and more than 1,000 injuries. In July 1966, rioting broke out in Cleveland and Chicago. These events foreshadowed the "long, hot summer" of 1967, when civil disorder erupted in black communities from coast to coast. Among them, the most catastrophic were six-day paroxysms of gunfire, arson, and looting in Detroit and Newark. Forty-three people died in Detroit and 26 in Newark, most of them African Americans. Enormous damage was done to the urban core of these cities, and many African Americans were traumatized by the mayhem and destruction to and military occupation of their neighborhoods (Balkin 2017; Rojas and Atkinson 2017).

The last years of the 1960s were awash with civil disorder and strife. In April 1968, Dr. King was assassinated in Memphis, where he had gone to support a sanitary workers strike. By then he was recognized as one of the leaders of the civil rights movement, if not the primary leader. His murder ignited rioting in 172 cities, with white-owned businesses and other symbols of white supremacy the targets of grief and rage, especially among poor and disenfranchised young men (Jeffries 2018). Two months later, Senator Robert F. Kennedy, President Kennedy's younger brother, was assassinated in Los Angeles while campaigning for the presidency.

Meanwhile, the Vietnam War had become a major source of dissention across the country. Although the United States had been involved militarily in Southeast Asia since the mid-1950s, President Johnson significantly escalated its involvement. In 1965, the United States committed ground troops to the war, and by 1968 more than a half million were serving in what was viewed by an increasing number of Americans to be an unwinnable and immoral quagmire. Antiwar protests, student strikes, and sit-ins roiled a growing number of university campuses, and as more of the general population became opposed to the war, massive demonstrations occurred repeatedly in Washington and other cities. The 1968 Democratic National Convention in Chicago was highly divisive, with pandemonium breaking out among prowar and antiwar delegates and thousands of protestors clashing outside with more than 20,000 police and National Guardsmen. On August 28th, with national news cameras rolling, protesters chanted, "The whole world is watching" as they were attacked and beaten by police, resulting in hundreds of injuries (Achenbach 2018).

However, the 1960s also saw the rise of the second wave of feminism. In 1961, President Kennedy appointed the Commission on the Status of Women, whose final report, issued two years later, criticized the unequal status of women in American society (President's Commission on the Status of Women 1963). In 1963, Betty Friedan published the bestseller *The Feminine Mystique*, which described unhappiness among white, middle-class married women and critiqued the widespread belief that being a homemaker was the pinnacle of American womanhood. Two years after the passage of the Civil Rights Act of 1964, which prohibited discrimination based on sex as well as race, color, religion, and national origin, many women were dismayed that sex discrimination in employment continued unabated. In response, Friedan and dozens of other women formed the National Organization for Women (NOW). In 1968, NOW issued a bill of rights that called for an end to discrimination against women and advocated for women's reproductive freedom (National Organization for Women 1970).

Out of the Shadows and Into the Streets

Throughout the 1960s, sexual and gender minorities continued to be widely disapproved by American society, and the Federal Bureau of Investigation's (FBI) campaign against them remained firmly in place. Homophile organizations and sexual minority entertainers and artists were investigated by the FBI, as were leaders of the African American civil rights and Black Power movements. In many localities, harassment and persecution of sexual and gender minorities by police occurred in bars, coffee shops, and other social gathering spots. News media encouraged vilification of sexual and gender minorities by referring to them as perverts and degenerates. When police bar raids occurred, the media divulged names, addresses, and places of employment of arrested patrons, inviting discrimination against them. Otherwise, most media outlets considered sexual or gender variance to be unmentionable. However, two notable exceptions occurred in the first half of the decade. In 1962, *Greater Philadelphia* ran an article, "The Furtive Fraternity," which reported on Philadelphia's leading sexual minority rights organization and included a tour of bars, coffee shops, and cruising grounds that served the city's growing sexual minority community (Stein 2004). Even more impactful was the 1964 article in *Life*, one of the country's most widely distributed magazines, titled "Homosexuality in America." The article focused on gay men and described their world as "sad and often sordid" (Welch 1964). However, it also told sexual minorities everywhere that gay life could be found in major cities, especially San Francisco, which it declared "the gay capital."

In May 1959, the first rebellion of sexual and gender minorities against police harassment occurred in downtown Los Angeles at Cooper Do-nuts, a 24-hour donut shop that was a popular nighttime hangout, especially among gender minorities. One night in May, police officers attempted to arrest five patrons, which led to others throwing coffee cups, stirring sticks, and anything else they could find. The officers had to call for backup, and the street was cordoned off for the rest of the night (Faderman and Timmons 2006). Rebellions against harassment occurred in other cities over the next few years. On an April evening in 1965, three sexual minority youths refused to leave Dewey's, a downtown Philadelphia restaurant, when told to do so by the management because they were wearing "non-conformist clothing." Although Dewey's had been a hangout for sexual and gender minority Philadelphians since the 1940s, during the 1960s its employees became unhappy with "rowdy" youth wearing transgressive attire who adopted it as a hangout. The action taken by the three youths followed the harassment and expulsion of more than 150 others. Police arrested the three, but that led to a five-day "protest demonstration" and another sit-in, and Dewey's eventually relented (Stein 2004, pp. 245–246).

On a July night in 1966, in San Francisco's Tenderloin district, sexual and gender minority street youth picketed Compton's Cafeteria to protest their harassment by management. Compton's was a popular hangout for the "queens," hustlers, and street youth who populated the Tenderloin. Although the picket was shown on local television, it had no effect on Compton's management. One month later, when a police officer attempted to eject a gender minority woman from the restaurant, she threw coffee in his face. This began a riot, with sugar shakers, dishes, and silverware thrown at officers. In the melee, the restaurant's windows were shattered. The following day, a crowd of Tenderloin residents picketed their exclusion from the restaurant, and when the windows were replaced, they were smashed again (Members of the Gay and Lesbian Historical Society of Northern California 1998).

And in 1967, a Los Angeles Vice Squad raid at the Black Cat led to several days of protest outside the bar and the dissemination of thousands of information sheets to passing motorists. During the raid, numerous officers assaulted patrons and destroyed property. The raid resulted in the conviction of six men for kissing other men on their lips. Their case was eventually appealed to the US Supreme Court, which declined to hear it (Faderman and Timmons 2006).

New Organizations Develop

These actions were supported by a growing number of local homophile organizations around the country. Daughters of Bilitis branched out from San Francisco, with chapters in New York, Los Angeles, and Chicago, among other cities. And although the Mattachine Society ceased to be a national organization in 1961 due to "financial and administrative problems" (Stein 2004, p. 207), independent chapters opened in Philadelphia, New York

Chicago, and Washington. The Philadelphia chapter opened shortly before the national organization imploded, and its leaders chose to rename it the Janus Society. When the raid on Dewey's occurred, the Janus Society organized a five-day protest that ended with a reprised sit-in (Stein 2004). In Los Angeles, joining the older homophile groups was the new organization Personal Rights in Defense and Education (PRIDE), formed in 1966. PRIDE organized the protest against police harassment in the wake of the Black Cat raid (Faderman and Timmons 2006). In San Francisco, Glide Memorial United Methodist Church was particularly important. It organized the ecumenical Council on Religion and the Homosexual in 1964 along with the leaders of Daughters of Bilitis and ministers from several Protestant denominations. Glide ministers helped to establish the street youth organization Vanguard in 1966, and in the wake of the Compton's Cafeteria riot, the church supported the formation of Conversion Our Goal, the first American transsexual peer support group, by providing meeting space and printing facilities. Conversion Our Goal published a newsletter that listed healthcare services for gender minority people, among which the Center for Special Problems at the San Francisco Public Health Department was particularly important (Stryker 2008). In the wake of the riot, San Francisco's Society for Individual Rights started the country's first gay community center.

In Chicago, Mattachine Midwest was established in 1965, and local chapters of Daughters of Bilitis and ONE Inc. opened within a few years. Mattachine Midwest was more integrated with respect to women and men than other homophile organizations, and it also evinced stronger concerns about social injustice facing nonwhite and working-class people. However, police harassment of sexual and gender minorities was as problematic in Chicago as in other large cities. In 1961, Illinois became the first American state to repeal its sodomy law, part of a total overhaul of its criminal laws based on recommendations made by the American Law Institute. But at the same time, the city of Chicago passed a law allowing for easier closure of "undesirable" bars, which actually tightened the noose around sexual and gender minority life in the city despite the liberalization of state law (Stewart-Winter 2016).

The Mattachine Society of Washington was established in 1961 by 36-year-old Frank Kameny, an astronomer fired from federal employment as part of the Lavender Scare purge, and Jack Nichols, a 23-year-old man who had come out as gay years earlier. The new chapter took a more activist path than most homophile organizations. For example, it wrote to President

106 SEXUAL AND GENDER MINORITY HISTORY

Kennedy about the injustices experienced by homosexuals, and it looked beyond the local situation for sexual minorities by forging a regional confederation, East Coast Homophile Organizations (ECHO), with the Janus Society, the Mattachine Society of New York, and Daughters of Bilitis. ECHO held its first conference in Philadelphia in 1963, but divergent concerns of lesbians and gay men, and the power imbalances between them, stymied its growth (Stein 2004).

The Mattachine Society of New York was established in 1955, but until the mid-1960s, it was a conservative, nonconfrontational organization. The main instigator of its change was Craig Rodwell, who had been a sexually active hell-raising teenager in his native Chicago before moving to New York after graduating high school in 1958. Even though he found Mattachine to be overly conservative, he volunteered in its office until he turned 21, when he became old enough to join. Around the same time, he had a short relationship with future gay political leader Harvey Milk, 10 years his senior, which ended largely because Milk wasn't ready to accept the sexual openness and desire for activism that Rodwell embodied (Loughery 1998). Rodwell set out to bring more young people into Mattachine by establishing Mattachine Young Adults. The effort was highly successful; although it led to the departure of some older members, the greater number of new ones caused the organization to grow substantially (Duberman 1993). In September 1964, Rodwell joined young firebrand Randy Wicker in picketing Manhattan's Whitehall Induction Center over military policies that discriminated against and mistreated homosexuals. Although it was not covered by the press and virtually no one saw it, the picket was the first direct action against a federal government entity by American sexual minorities (Loughery 1998). Meanwhile, Rodwell enticed Dick Leitsch, another of his lovers, to attend Mattachine meetings; by late 1965, Leitsch was elected president, and Rodwell vice president.

Direct Action Begins

Based on the example of African Americans fighting for their civil rights, Randy Wicker believed that homosexuals should do so as well through direct action. Shortly after the Whitehall picket, he suggested a picket of the FBI building in Washington, but Frank Kameny's chapter did not support the idea. However, when news broke in 1965 about revolutionary Cuba sending homosexuals to prison camps, young activists in both New York and Washington leaped into action. On one weekend in April, Jack Nichols led a 10-person picket at the White House, with Randy Wicker and Craig Rodwell leading 20 others in a picket at the United Nations (Loughery 1998). Kameny saw the light after that even though the mainstream middle-class homophile movement was averse to such tactics. In May, Mattachine of Washington held a second picket at the White House, and in October a third White House picket drew 65 participants. In the second half of 1965, the organization picketed the Pentagon, the State Department, and the Civil Service Commission ("The Gay Civil Rights Movement Turns to Public Picketing" n.d.). Meanwhile, despite its challenges, ECHO managed to stage a demonstration at Philadelphia's Independence Hall on July 4, 1965, apparently on the suggestion of Craig Rodwell. Among the participants was Barbara Gittings, who had served as president of the New York chapter of Daughters of Bilitis and as editor of *The Ladder*, although the national organization disapproved of the demonstration. Kay Lahusen, a photographer and former art director for *The Ladder* as well as Gittings's lover, also participated along with eight other women and 34 men.

Rodwell's initial idea was for July 4th to become a sort of homosexual national holiday, with demonstrations each year at Independence Hall; it was to be called the Annual Reminder (Duberman 1993). As explained by Kay Lahusen, using the pen name Kay Tobin (1965),

> Systematically and unrelentingly, [the homosexual] is placed into and kept in the category of a second-class citizen. That the homosexual American citizen is a homosexual is always noted; that he [*sic*] is also an American citizen, with all that goes with that status, is always forgotten.... The homosexual American citizen, upon savage penalty of law and upon pain of loss of livelihood and other severe disadvantage, is denied the proper pursuit of harmless happiness open to other citizens.... Every other possible lesser means of remedy for an intolerable situation having been tried without success, we now try to bring our case directly before the public, before our fellow citizens, on a day and at a place which are singularly appropriate. (pp. 6–8)

At Frank Kameny's insistence, women demonstrators had to wear skirts and heels, with men in jackets and ties, to show they were upstanding citizens. Although some people chafed at these requirements, the Annual Reminder occurred every July 4th until the end of the decade, each time increasing the number of participants and even garnering mainstream media coverage by 1967.

In New York, Dick Leitsch worked directly with Mayor John Lindsay in early 1966 to end the police department's harassment and mistreatment of homosexuals through the practice of entrapment following a five-part newspaper exposé on corruption among the city's police. The New York Civil Liberties Union joined Mattachine in lobbying on this issue, and in April both the mayor and the new police commissioner agreed to order an end to the practice ("Entrapment Attacked" 1966). Around the same time, Leitsch was joined by Craig Rodwell and John Timmons, another Mattachine member, in seeking a challenge to the New York State Liquor Authority's long-standing prohibition on serving alcohol to homosexuals. Inspired by civil rights sit-ins, Leitsch and the others planned to clearly identify themselves as homosexuals as they attempted to order drinks at a bar, accompanied by a *Village Voice* photographer. Following three abortive attempts at other locations, the bartender at Julius's, a gay bar in Greenwich Village that had recently been raided, refused to serve them, claiming he was following the law. Upon being refused, which was captured in a now-famous photograph, Leitsch issued a complaint to the State Liquor Authority, whose chairman subsequently claimed the refusal-of-service policy did not exist (Johnson 1966). State courts ruled the following year that the mere presence of homosexuals did not make a bar disorderly (McFadden 2018).

Gay Is Good

Continuing his efforts to expand interest in the homophile movement among young people, Craig Rodwell tried convincing Mattachine to open a storefront in Manhattan. Failing at that, he struck out on his own in 1967 to open the Oscar Wilde Memorial Bookshop in Greenwich Village. The store featured positive homophile works, the first such store in the United States, but pointedly no sexually oriented materials. The store was revolutionary in its openness, proclaiming "A Bookstore of the Homophile Movement" in its front window (Marotta 2004). As difficult as this level of openness was for some members of the homophile movement, sexually suggestive gay materials like the Athletic Model Guild's publications and other physique magazines were considered a greater threat to their aspirations for middle-class respectability. Philadelphia-based *Drum* was the most widely distributed gay-oriented publication in the country during the 1960s, combining news and opinion pieces with nearly nude male photography and sexually oriented cartoons. Clark Polak created *Drum* from the Janus Society's newsletter when he served as the organization's president, but his vision of sexual liberation for gay men alienated lesbians, as did his apparent misogyny. He was eventually forced from the Janus Society's leadership, and he was shunned by other homophile leaders (Stein 2004).

Homophile organizations proliferated across the country, and in 1966 representatives from many of them met in Kansas City with the idea of forming a national organization. However, lesbians, primarily represented by Daughters of Bilitis, didn't want to subordinate themselves to a national agenda dominated by gay men, and other organizations refused to give up their independence. As a result, at a meeting in San Francisco six months later, they formed a confederation along the lines of ECHO. Named the North American Conference of Homophile Organizations (NACHO), it had several national meetings over the next few years. The most notable one occurred in 1968 in Chicago, shortly after the Democratic National Convention, when it adopted a Homophile Bill of Rights that called for the decriminalization of same-sex sexual behavior and an end to discrimination against homosexuals and harassment by police. NACHO also adopted the slogan "Gay Is Good" based on "Black Is Beautiful," which had been coined a few years earlier (Loughery 1998). A more assertive stance was taken by the Homophile Action League, formed by Philadelphia women after a police raid on a lesbian bar in 1968. The group's first newsletter proclaimed,

> We are *not* a social group. We do *not* intend to concentrate our energies on "uplifting" the homosexual community, for such efforts would be sadly misplaced. It our firm conviction that it is the heterosexual community which is badly in need of uplifting. (Stein 2004, p. 277)

African American Sexual Minorities in the 1960s

Although black identity and the fight for civil rights took precedence over sexual and gender minority concerns for many African Americans during the 1960s, several influential contributors to African American culture and politics were sexual minority individuals. Lorraine Hansberry's *A Raisin in the Sun* was the first play by a black woman to be produced on Broadway when it opened in 1959. It portrayed the harrowing experiences of an African American family after moving into a previously white-only neighborhood of Chicago. Proclaimed the best play of 1959 by the New York Drama Critics, *A Raisin in the Sun* was subsequently adapted for film, which was released in 1961. Although it was not publicly known, Hansberry identified as a lesbian by this time. Upon separation from her husband of four years, she initiated contact with Daughters of Bilitis and contributed letters to *The Ladder*. Hansberry died an untimely death from cancer in 1965, after which her former husband donated her papers to the New York Public Library with the stipulation that anything having to do with her sexual minority interests or status would remain hidden from public view (Mumford 2016).

Among Hansberry's close friends were several other important sexual minority African Americans. For example, the great singer-songwriter Nina Simone had sexual relationships with both men and women (Tillet 2015). She wrote the song "Young, Gifted, and Black" about Hansberry, and her searing indictment of racial segregation and violence, "Mississippi Goddam," is an iconic song of the civil rights era. Another close friend was James Baldwin, a towering figure in African American literature. Baldwin wrote about white racism and black identity, and the struggle of having intersecting sexual and racial minority identities. Because he was widely known to be gay, and since some of his novels dealt with same-sex sexuality, he was not accepted by most leaders of the civil rights and Black Power movements (Timberg 2017). And although he was a leading spokesman about racism, he was not an invited speaker at the 1963 March on Washington for Jobs and Freedom ("Boots on the Ground" n.d.).

Lorraine Hansberry also counted Bayard Rustin among her friends. Rustin was Dr. King's main advisor on the strategy of nonviolent protest (Eig 2023), and he was the primary architect of the March on Washington. However, some civil rights leaders disliked him because he was unabashedly leftist, pacifist, and, especially, gay. Rustin was arrested multiple times during the 1940s and 1950s in police sweeps of homosexuals; an arrest in California led to a 60-day jail sentence for "lewd vagrancy." The FBI provided information about Rustin's sexuality, and his jail record, to segregationist Senator Strom Thurmond in 1963, who subsequently tried to discredit the upcoming March on Washington based on that information. Despite threats from political rivals, Rustin refused to withdraw from organizing the march, but he refrained from taking a prominent speaking role (D'Emilio 2023).

A Trans Movement Begins

In 1960, Virginia Prince began publishing the magazine *Transvestia*, a more ambitious version of the newsletter she distributed several years earlier. Published multiple times a year for more than 20 years, it included "social commentary, educational outreach, self-help advice, and autobiographical vignettes" (Stryker 2008, p. 54) for its cross-dressing readership. In 1961, Prince convened a group of *Transvestia* subscribers in Los Angeles to form the Hose and Heels Club, which subsequently met on a regular basis. By the following year, Prince turned the club into a national organization, the Foundation for Personality Expression, which opened a number of chapters around the country. Membership was open only to married, heterosexual men, mainly white and middle class, who liked to dress in women's clothing for their personal enjoyment. By 1968, Prince began living full time as a woman (Stryker 2008).

Meanwhile, Reed Erickson, who inherited a large family fortune in Louisiana, entered treatment with Dr. Harry Benjamin in 1962 for the purpose of masculinizing his female body. Dr. Benjamin was a German-born colleague of Magnus Hirschfeld who had immigrated to the United States. With his transition fully underway in 1964, Erickson used his inheritance to establish the Erickson Educational Foundation to support Dr. Benjamin's work and the Institute for the Study of Human Resources to provide funding for other academic and medical research. In 1966, with Erickson's financial support, Dr. Benjamin published *The Transsexual Phenomenon*, a groundbreaking book that explained the difference between transsexualism and transvestism and outlined affirmative treatment for transsexuals. Erickson was also a major funder of the National Transsexual Counseling Unit in San Francisco. Through his many efforts, which included direct supportive work with gender minority individuals and sensitivity training with police, Erickson helped put San Francisco on the map as the "hub of the transgender movement in the United States" (Stryker 2008, p. 81).

Summary

During the 1960s, massive social and political changes roiled the American landscape, led by the movement to challenge widespread and long-standing injustices against African Americans in the Jim Crow South and in cities throughout the North and West. In addition, the divisive Vietnam War led the country into increasing political turmoil and civil unrest. Within this context, sexual and gender minorities began to defy and organize against the oppressive forces arrayed against them. These efforts occurred in two different ways. Working-class, nonwhite, and gender minority people began to rebel openly against police harassment and mistreatment in the bars, restaurants, and other public places where they gathered. Meanwhile, homophile organizations of mainly middle-class, white, sexual minority people proliferated, confederated, and began to engage in orderly, direct action. In several cities, homophile organizations supported the street-based rebellions with pickets, dissemination of information, and legal action. While older homophile organization members tended to avoid direct action and openness about their identities, younger members pushed the organizations in those directions.

In addition to generational differences, middle-class sexual minorities also varied with respect to sexual liberation among men. The popularity of *Drum* and homoerotic physique magazines reflected just how important sexuality was to a growing collective gay identity. This should not be surprising, since it was gay men's sexual desire for other men that was the basis for sodomy laws, discriminatory alcohol control regulations, and police repression, especially with respect to entrapment tactics. Nevertheless, these desires also conflicted with aspirations for respectability among many gay men and were a significant obstacle to cooperation with lesbians.

The rising women's movement was a potent competitor for the attention of white lesbians, whose concerns about employment discrimination and reproductive and parental rights were shared with other women but were not on the radar of most homophile organizations. Similarly, the failure of the homophile movement to acknowledge how racism impacted nonwhite sexual minorities was a main reason for the continued whiteness of these organizations. And while earlier identity constructions combined elements of gender and sexuality, sexual and gender identities began to diverge during the 1960s. Specific gender minority identities emerged, as did a growing number of organizations that provided information, support, and health services for them, particularly in San Francisco.

Chapter 10
Stonewall and Its Aftermath

American society fractured along increasingly stark lines in the last years of the 1960s. A counterculture movement among American youth combined left-wing politics and rejection of materialist mainstream culture with marijuana and psychedelic drug use, sexual openness, and rock music. As many as 100,000 young people converged on San Francisco in the 1967 Summer of Love to participate in what they hoped would be a cultural revolution. Two years later, nearly a half million participated in a legendary, drug-saturated three-day rock music festival in Woodstock, New York. Increasingly large protests against the Vietnam War and the draft occurred regularly throughout the country. The militant political group Weather Underground, which advocated the overthrow of the US government and capitalism, conducted bombings in New York, Chicago, and Washington between 1969 and 1972, causing property damage but no injuries except to its own members.

There was increasing impatience among African Americans with the slow progress of the civil rights movement. In 1966, Bobby Seale and Huey Newton, college students in Oakland, California, founded the Black Panther Party, a Black Power movement focused on community empowerment and self-defense; chapters were soon established in many other cities. The Young Lords, initially a Chicago street gang, became a left-wing community empowerment and social justice movement among Puerto Ricans, with chapters in cities on both coasts and the Midwest. Both of these movements promoted armed resistance to violence against their communities. The Federal Bureau of Investigation considered them grave threats to the country and worked to destroy them through assassinations and sabotage, and vilification in the mainstream press. Meanwhile, opposition to the civil rights movement, especially among working-class whites, found a spokesman in Alabama governor George Wallace, whose third-party race for the presidency in 1968 won five states and about 10 million votes. Wallace remained a political force throughout the 1970s, campaigning for the Democratic Party's nomination for president in 1972 and 1976.

Sexual and Gender Minority History. James I. Martin, Oxford University Press. © Oxford University Press (2025). DOI: 10.1093/9780197765500.003.0010

114   SEXUAL AND GENDER MINORITY HISTORY

At the height of the Vietnam War, President Nixon appealed for support from conservatives, whom he called "the great silent majority of my fellow Americans." Meanwhile, Vice President Agnew made caustic attacks on the press and on student protestors and liberal universities. In May 1970, Ohio National Guardsmen opened fire on Kent State University students engaging in a peaceful protest, killing four and injuring nine. Eleven days later, Mississippi State Police fired on Jackson State University student protesters, killing 2 and injuring 12. Between these two tragic events, hundreds of construction workers in New York attacked a crowd of college students protesting the war. The popular film *Joe* (Avildsen 1970), released two months later, dramatized the societal fragmentation; in it, a man inadvertently kills his own daughter in a rage-filled murder spree against counterculture young people.

In 1971, the *New York Times* and *Washington Post* published articles based on the Pentagon Papers, a large trove of leaked documents indicating the federal government had lied to the public for many years about its conduct of the Vietnam War. Evidence of the extent to which the public had been deceived by both Republican and Democratic administrations fueled a growing lack of trust in the government. The Watergate scandal, in which President Nixon engaged in illegal activities during his re-election campaign, added to the mistrust. Facing certain impeachment and removal from office, the president announced his resignation on national television in 1974. By then, the United States had negotiated an end to its participation in the war. However, soldiers were not always welcomed or supported after returning home, as antiwar activists denigrated their service and others wanted to forget the war completely. In 1975, the capital of South Vietnam was captured by the North Vietnamese army, bringing the war to an end. Twenty years of American involvement, more than 58,000 American lives, and hundreds of billions of dollars failed to prevent the communist victory.

Defeat in Vietnam was only one of the ways in which American dominance in the world seemed to falter. Throughout the 1970s, the country experienced stagflation, a combination of high inflation and unemployment. In 1973, the oil-producing countries of the Middle East, amid war with Israel, imposed a five-month embargo on imports to the United States and its allies. The price of oil quadrupled, and gasoline shortages occurred throughout the country.

At the same time, rising activism by women resulted in significant gains through legislation and judicial decisions. Title IX of the Educational Amendments of 1972 and the Women's Educational Equity Act of 1974 prevented sex discrimination in educational programs and activities. The Equal Rights Amendment to the US Constitution was passed by both houses of Congress in 1972 and sent to the states for ratification. In 1973, the US Supreme Court ruled in *Roe v. Wade* that women had a constitutional right to obtain an abortion, and the Pregnancy Discrimination Act of 1978 prohibited discrimination based on pregnancy status.

Ethnic minority activism increased in the late 1960s and 1970s. Young Mexican Americans adopted Chicano/a as a new identity based on ethnic pride. Thousands of Chicano/a high school students in East Los Angeles walked out of classes in March 1968 to protest systemic discrimination against them by the Los Angeles school district, and student walkouts spread to other cities in the Southwest. In Denver, more than 1,000 young Chicanos/as attended the seminal 1969 National Chicano Youth Liberation Conference, which produced a vision for Chicano/a national identity. The Brown Berets, a paramilitary organization like the Black Panthers, was founded in Los Angeles in 1967 to fight aggressive policing of Chicano/a communities; within two years it had 29 chapters in seven states (Estrada 2006; Muñoz 2018).

Descendants of immigrants from disparate Asian countries began to develop a shared identity. Yuji Ichioka and Emma Gee, graduate students at the University of California, Berkeley, invented the self-identifier "Asian American" in 1968 and founded the Asian American Political Alliance, which advanced the idea that experiences of marginalization and racism were common to all Asian Americans. Asian American students participated in the Third World Liberation Front strikes that resulted in the establishment of ethnic studies departments at the University of California, Berkeley and San Francisco State University. Asian American neighborhood activists in Los Angeles, San Francisco, Seattle, and New York advocated for the preservation of their communities in the face of gentrification and established programs that provided essential services (Maeda 2016).

Between November 1969 and June 1971, the activist group Indians of All Tribes occupied Alcatraz Island, the site of a decommissioned federal prison in San Francisco Bay, to protest the dispossession of Aboriginal lands and destruction of Indigenous cultures (T. Johnson 2019). For more than two months in 1973, 200 Oglala Lakota occupied Wounded Knee, South Dakota, the site of a horrific massacre perpetrated by the Army in 1890, to protest the government's treatment of Native American people. These actions were part of a Red Power movement that spurred legislation

Road to Stonewall

By the late 1960s, sexual and gender minorities in most American cities could gather in bars that either welcomed or tolerated their business. These bars were usually invisible to mainstream society, as they kept a low profile in undesirable locations. Nevertheless, local police often targeted them for periodic raids. San Francisco was a notable exception. By then, the California Supreme Court had established that sexual minorities had a constitutional right to assemble and receive service in alcohol-serving establishments, and San Francisco's police department had been chastised in court for its corrupt payoff schemes involving gay bars. An openly gay man, José Sarria, had already run for the San Francisco Board of Supervisors, although he did not win. Gay bar owners formed the Tavern Guild of San Francisco in 1962, which provided mutual support for member establishments and led to more welcoming environments for bar patrons. By the end of the decade, the Tavern Guild was one of the city's most important sexual and gender minority institutions, as it sponsored many fundraising events and contributed financially to the development of several community organizations (Boyd 2003).

Other important developments occurred in Los Angeles, where the police department continued to harass bars serving sexual and gender minorities despite the state supreme court's decision. *The Advocate*, a local gay newspaper, began publishing monthly in 1967, providing news that mainstream publications ignored or distorted. *The Advocate* quickly adopted a national focus, but its impact on Los Angeles was especially significant. At least as important was the 1968 founding of the Metropolitan Community Church by Troy Perry. The church grew rapidly, providing social services and a strong sense of community as it tended to its members' spiritual needs; it quickly became one of the largest sexual and gender minority organizations in Los Angeles. And by decade's end, sexual and gender minority Angelenos demonstrated that they were a voting bloc that could influence local elections (Faderman and Timmons 2006).

By contrast, the environment in New York, the city with the largest sexual and gender minority population, was particularly repressive. The New York

STONEWALL AND ITS AFTERMATH   117

State Liquor Authority had made it so difficult for bars to serve this population legally that organized crime families came to dominate the business. Mob bar owners commonly paid off local police to avoid arrest for violation of liquor and health laws. And despite ending the practice of entrapment in 1966, the city's police continued to harass bar patrons through periodic raids. Patrons who transgressed gender norms were especially at risk during a raid, as police interpreted the wearing of fewer than three articles of clothing considered appropriate for one's biological sex to be a violation of state law. If a person's biological sex was not easily identifiable, police conducted a strip search to examine their genitals (Carter 2004).

Nevertheless, New York continued to be a magnet for sexual and gender minority individuals seeking to reinvent their lives. Among them were youths from unaccepting or abusive families who, with few resources, lived on the streets or in flophouses, often supporting themselves through sex work. The Stonewall Inn, a bar on Christopher Street in Greenwich Village, was where they met friends, blew off steam, and danced. In 1969, the Stonewall Inn was the most popular bar in the Village, technically a private club, although it cost only a nominal fee to join. It was a cash cow for its organized crime owners; the liquor was bootlegged and watered down, drinks were served in unwashed glasses since there were no washing facilities, and the contact information more affluent customers gave to join was sometimes used to extort them (Carter 2004). Its customers were mostly gay men and "queens," as gender-diverse gay men called themselves; according to guides published in 1969, it was especially known for its young crowd that loved to dance (Stein 2019, pp. 114–123).

The Stonewall Riots

Shortly after 1:00 a.m. on Saturday, June 28th, the Public Morals Squad of the New York City Police Department, Lower Manhattan Division, initiated a raid on the Stonewall Inn. Deputy Inspector Pine, who led the division, obtained a warrant to "search the premises, seize alcohol, and have the bars cut up and removed along with the Stonewall's vending equipment" (Carter 2004, p. 131). The ostensible purpose of the raid was to shut down the establishment due to its owners' illegal activities. Many customers were irritated because it was the second raid within a few days. As the police examined each customer's identification and dress to determine who should be arrested, a

118 SEXUAL AND GENDER MINORITY HISTORY

contingent of "transvestites" was particularly uncooperative, as were some lesbians who complained about being frisked. Eventually, customers not chosen for arrest were allowed to exit the bar. However, they did not leave the area; instead, they milled around on the street in front of the bar, some waiting for their friends to be released and others wanting to see what would happen next. Since it was a hot summer night, the streets of the Village were crowded, and as the numbers outside the Stonewall Inn grew to the hundreds, customers began to camp it up and play to the crowd as they emerged from inside (Carter 2004).

When police started loading customers chosen for arrest into a paddy wagon, jeers and shouts came from the crowd. A "transvestite" customer smacked a police officer over the head with her purse as she was loaded into the paddy wagon. As the crowd continued to grow, police were pelted with pennies and showered with insults. A butch lesbian refused to stay in the paddy wagon and fought with police after they manhandled her. According to some accounts, she yelled to the crowd to do something. Fights with police broke out, especially among the street youths. As loose change, beer cans, and bottles were thrown, the outnumbered police took refuge inside the bar and barricaded the door, which further incited the crowd. With the street youths leading the melee, anything that could be found was hurled at the building, including trash cans, cobblestones, bricks, and garbage. By this time, the crowd included many middle-class gay men in addition to "queens," hustlers, and other Village denizens. At the riot's height, a parking meter was uprooted from the ground and used as a battering ram against the bar's barricaded door, and Molotov cocktails and flaming trash cans were thrown through the building's smashed windows. After local officers and the city's Tactical Patrol Force finally arrived, the barricaded police were freed, but the riot continued in the surrounding streets. While street youths taunted the police, trash cans were set on fire and store windows were broken, and police used fire hoses on the crowd and beat individuals with billy clubs. Eventually, the riot petered out, but only temporarily (Carter 2004).

Despite the significant damage done to the Stonewall Inn, it reopened the following night, serving only soft drinks. Meanwhile, word about the riot spread quickly. By midnight, thousands of people gathered on the streets near the bar, many of them thrilled by the previous night's resistance against the police. Chants rang out in the hot and humid night, including "gay power" and "Christopher Street belongs to the queens!" Between the throng and the large police presence, tensions were high. Eventually, another melee began, with bottles thrown and trash cans set on fire. By 2:00 a.m., police were still having difficulty gaining control of the situation since rioters, especially the street youths, used the tangle of streets to play cat and mouse with them. Calm was not restored for at least another hour (Carter 2004).

While the following three nights were calm on Christopher Street, rioting resumed on Wednesday night, at least partially instigated by offensive newspaper coverage of the previous nights' riots. By then, an assortment of leftist groups had come to the Village to protest for their own purposes. The rioting began around 10:00 p.m. as it had on previous nights, resulting in many injuries, but it ended after about an hour (Carter 2004).

Many, but not all, sexual and gender minority people were inspired by these events. Lige Clarke and Jack Nichols (1969), authors of the column "The Homosexual Citizen" in the New York–based newspaper *Screw*, wrote:

> We were thrilled by the violent uprising in Sheridan Square in which homosexuals put police on notice that they'd no longer accept abuse. . . . Today . . . a new generation is angered by raids and harassment of gay bars, and last week's riots in Greenwich Village have set standards for the rest of the nation's homosexuals to follow. (p. 16)

Likewise, Ada Bello and Carole Friedman (1969) wrote in the Philadelphia-based *Homophile Action League Newsletter*, "June 28, 1969 will be viewed as a turning point in the fight for equality for homosexuals" (p. 1). However, an article in the *Advocate* that was published three months later stated, "Homosexuals simply cannot afford rioting and violence. . . . Every educated reasonable member of the gay community must aid in redirecting the anger and frustrations of the more violent and emotional members" (Jackson 1969, p. 33).

Liberation

Many sexual and gender minority people sought to harness the energy generated by the riots. At a meeting organized by the Mattachine Society of New York, an action committee decided to adopt the name Gay Liberation Front (GLF), and on July 27th it sponsored a demonstration and march to the Stonewall Inn (Carter 2004), where committee member Marty Robinson declared, "Gay power is here!" (Black 1969, p. 1). Four days later, gay

120 SEXUAL AND GENDER MINORITY HISTORY

and lesbian activists voted to establish GLF as an independent organization (Carter 2004).

GLF was exciting but highly fractious, disdaining orderly meetings and even organizational structure. Its youthful members were ambitious and idealistic. While homophile organizations sought the integration of sexual minorities into society, GLF believed sexual minorities' uniqueness held the potential for transforming society in profound ways. It established a newspaper, *Come Out*, and held wildly successful dances. In stark contrast to the oppressive bars run by organized crime, GLF dances were welcoming and supportive; they were "gay dances by gay people for gay people with the money that was handed in at the door going to gay issues and gay causes" (Carter 2004, p. 224). GLF activists were exhilarated with the experience of being openly gay on the streets of New York 24 hours a day. Many of them believed GLF should ally itself with other liberation causes, including the anticapitalist workers' rights movement, third world liberation movements, and black liberation movement. However, a proposal to donate to the Black Panthers despite their disparagement of sexual minorities caused the departure of several members who started a competing organization, Gay Activists Alliance (GAA; Carter 2004). Nevertheless, independent GLF chapters sprang up in major cities and on college campuses across the country.

GAA eschewed the liberationist goals of GLF and focused more narrowly on securing equal rights for sexual minorities. In stark contrast to GLF, it had a constitution, and its meetings were orderly and goal oriented. However, there were few women members. The organization became known for its confrontational tactics, conducting "zaps" on public figures to get their attention on sexual orientation issues. For example, GAA members infiltrated the audience of a live television interview with New York's mayor, which they proceeded to disrupt. Zaps were conducted against other politicians who were silent on sexual orientation issues, press organizations that disseminated antigay information, and television studios that produced shows that denigrated sexual minorities (Carter 2004).

In New York, neither GLF nor GAA addressed issues of importance to gender minorities, sexual and gender minority youth, or people of color. Consequently, several other organizations emerged to address them. Lee Brewster and Bunny Eisenhower founded Queens Liberation Front to advocate for the rights of drag queens and transvestites ("Queens Liberation Front—What Is It?" 1972). Beginning in 1971, it began publishing the magazine *Drag Queens* (later called *Drag*), which was distributed nationally until the 1980s. Marsha P. Johnson and Sylvia Rivera founded Street Transvestite Action Revolutionaries (STAR) to serve the needs of gender minority youth, especially those living on the streets. Both Johnson and Rivera were themselves gender minorities with a history of survival sex and life on the streets, and both were participants in the Stonewall Riots. Johnson and Rivera operated STAR House, the first American shelter for gender minority youth, until 1971 (Rubin 2020). In 1970, sexual and gender minority people of color split off from GLF in New York and Chicago to form Third World Gay Revolution (Garrido 2021; Stewart-Winter 2016). However, the Philadelphia chapter of GLF, with its Japanese American leader Kiyoshi Kuromiya, pursued a more strongly multiracial agenda (Stein 2004).

Within several months of GLF's founding, frustration mounted among women members with its lack of attention to sexism and other issues of concern to lesbians. However, the National Organization for Women (NOW), and the women's movement in general, did not welcome them either. Betty Friedan, NOW's president, had even referred to lesbians as the "lavender menace" because she believed their presence in the movement would make it less acceptable to mainstream Americans. In response, several lesbian members of GLF conducted a zap on NOW's Second Congress to Unite Women, held in May 1970 in New York. Calling themselves the Lavender Menace, they took over the opening session and distributed their manifesto, "The Woman-Identified Woman," which defined lesbians as "the rage of all women condensed to the point of explosion" (Radicalesbians 1970). In other words, all women could choose to be lesbians to free themselves from patriarchy and misogyny (Faderman 1991). By the following month, when the manifesto was published in *Come Out*, the group renamed itself Radicalesbians.

Meanwhile, Craig Rodwell had conceived of a way to revitalize the Annual Reminder by turning it into a commemoration of the Stonewall Riots. At the November 1969 meeting of ECHO, he and Ellen Broidy, from the New York University Lesbian and Gay Student Union, proposed the last Saturday in June as Christopher Street Liberation Day, to be celebrated each year with a large demonstration in New York. They also encouraged demonstrations in other cities (Carter 2004). The proposal was approved, but the first commemoration would be on Sunday, June 28, 1970 (not Saturday), when 10,000 sexual and gender minority demonstrators marched from Greenwich Village to Central Park, where they "cuddled, kissed, laughed, and

122 SEXUAL AND GENDER MINORITY HISTORY

listened to themselves being described by announcers on . . . their trans s-tor radios" (Tobin 1970, p. 12). On the same day in Los Angeles, a parade with open cars, floats, and more than 1,000 marchers took over Hollywood Boulevard, in what was called Christopher Street West ("1200 Parade in Hollywood; Crowds Line Boulevard" 1970). However, the first "gay pride" event occurred in Chicago, with 200 activists marching down Michigan Avenue to the Civic Center on Saturday, June 27th, culminating what they called "Gay Pride Week" (Stanley 1970).

Lesbian Feminism

Many lesbians became disenchanted with the male-dominated gay liberation movement and found they had more in common with the struggles of other women. "Lesbian feminists" conceptualized lesbian identity as a political choice that any woman could make, and as separatists, they considered themselves to be the purest example of women freeing themselves from misogyny and male supremacy. Lesbian feminist groups seeded the broader lesbian movement in many ways even though they themselves tended to be short lived due to infighting and lack of financial resources. In 1972, 12 women established the Furies, a lesbian feminist collective in Washington, DC. In addition to living communally, they offered training in home and auto repair and published an influential, nationally distributed newspaper. Although the Furies lasted only about a year, some of its members went on to establish Olivia Records, which moved to Los Angeles in 1973 and became the vanguard of the women's music movement. As such, it contributed significantly to the development of solidarity among lesbians throughout the country. The Gay Women's Service Center, also in Los Angeles, became one of the first organizations to provide lesbian-specific services such as support groups, referrals, and temporary housing, although, like the Furies, it lasted only about a year. After Daughters of Bilitis allowed chapters to operate independently, the Los Angeles chapter opened another center for lesbians that provided space for educational, support, and therapeutic activities. It too lasted about a year, but its newspaper, *The Lesbian Tide*, continued publishing and distributing nationally until the end of the decade (Retter 1999).

The women's music movement, led by Olivia Records and featuring music that was by, about, and for women, was especially important in the construction of a sense of community among lesbians. The company became highly successful, with its recording artists who did not hide their lesbian identities, including Cris Williams, Meg Christian, and Teresa Trull. Lesbians attended women's music festivals in droves where they heard their favorite singers and reveled in the woman-only environment. Lesbians also established literary collectives such as Naiad Press and opened women's bookstores.

These ventures drew lesbians of varying social classes, but they were mainly white (Retter 1999). African American lesbians criticized lesbian feminists for their racial myopia, and especially for their separatism. In 1973, they established the National Black Feminist Organization along with non-lesbian black women. In the following year, the Boston chapter became independent as the Combahee River Collective; its influential 1977 *Combahee River Collective Statement* was the well from which the concept of intersectional oppression developed. Barbara Smith and Audre Lorde, both Combahee River Collective members, established Kitchen Table: Women of Color Press at the end of the decade.

Gay Men

Gay men migrated increasingly to major cities, most significantly San Francisco where, with unbridled optimism and excitement, they hoped to free themselves from heterosexual pretenses and family expectations. As early as 1969, Carl Wittman described San Francisco as "a refugee camp for homosexuals. We have fled here from every part of the nation" (Wittman 1969, p. 157). By 1977, nearly 20% of the city's population was estimated to be gay (Loughery 1998), concentrated especially in the rapidly gentrifying Castro district. Gay neighborhoods like the Castro were an entirely new phenomenon, where "gay men could spend days, or an entire week, going to their offices, to the cleaner, the bank, and the health club . . ., political meetings, and . . . church without coming into contact with anyone who was not gay" (FitzGerald 1986, p. 54). Thus, the Castro represented gay men's more affluent, commercialized, and hedonistic version of lesbian separatist communities. In this environment, where nearly everyone was a potential sexual partner, gay men experimented with new forms of relationships and sexual expression.

Men danced with each other in bars and clubs where disco music blared, and they cruised each other in the streets. In addition to their own homes, they had sex, sometimes anonymously, in private spaces like bathhouses—San Francisco had more than a dozen of them—and public spaces like Buena

124 SEXUAL AND GENDER MINORITY HISTORY

Vista Park. Many men built strong friendship networks and established long-lasting love relationships through their sexual encounters, in a reversal of traditional patterns of relationship building. And for the first time, they gained a foothold in local politics. Harvey Milk moved to San Francisco in 1972 and opened a camera shop on Castro Steet. In 1973, he ran for a seat on the city's board of supervisors but didn't win. After losing again two years later, he finally won in 1977. By this time, he had developed a strong political base among the city's gay population and was the best-known openly gay man in public office.

Gender Minorities

Some development in the conceptualization of gender minority identities occurred in the years before and after the Stonewall Riots. The term *transgenderism* first appeared in the second edition of psychiatrist John Oliven's (1965) book *Sexual Hygiene and Pathology* as a correction to *transsexualism*, since the author believed gender was more important than biological sex for understanding transsexuals. During the 1970s, Virginia Prince used the term *transgenderist* to refer to gender-variant people who did not consider themselves transsexuals, particularly those who were male bodied. However, it would take until the 1990s for *transgender* to become an umbrella term for most, if not all, gender-variant people. Consequently, networks and services grew mainly among gender minority subgroups during the 1970s. For example, in 1975 mental health educator Ari Kane started the Fantasia Fair, a conference held in Provincetown, Massachusetts, for male-bodied cross-dressers that provided workshops and social events (Stryker 2008); the fair continues to operate today for a broader transgender population.

Despite their central role in the Stonewall Riots, gender-diverse people were rejected by lesbians and gay men during the 1970s. Urban gay men adopted the decidedly masculine "Castro clone" style of short hair, mustaches, flannel shirts, and jeans, in a conscious departure from the androgynous style of previous decades. They joined gyms and developed their bodies to transform themselves into manly fantasies previously embodied by heterosexual "trade." Diversity in gender expression was scorned (Loughery 1998). Among lesbian feminists, rejection of diverse gender expression was even more explicit since they believed gender roles were created by male supremacist society. Consequently, they disapproved of butch and femme roles among lesbians and drag among men. And although they promoted the view that lesbianism could be adopted by any woman as a political choice, they held essentialist beliefs about womanhood. Consequently, they condemned transsexual women as imposters (Stryker 2008).

Advances Against Discrimination

Advocacy by sexual minorities resulted in progress against all three institutional sources of discrimination against them: religious institutions, state/legal institutions, and mental health institutions. The Metropolitan Community Church grew rapidly during the 1970s, during which time a small number of Christian denominations publicly stated their opposition to discrimination against homosexuals. In 1972, the United Church of Christ ordained an openly gay minister, as did the Episcopal Church a few years later. In 1972, the first gay and lesbian synagogue, Los Angeles–based Congregation Beth Chayim Chadashim, was officially recognized by Reform Judaism. By the end of the decade, there were seven gay and lesbian synagogues, and Reform Judaism called for an end to discrimination against lesbians and gay men. A number of states repealed their sodomy laws, and a handful of municipalities passed sexual orientation nondiscrimination ordinances.

The number of sexual orientation–based advocacy organizations multiplied. On the national level, there were the law firms Lambda Legal (established 1971) and National Center for Lesbian Rights (1977) and the lobbying organizations National Gay Task Force (1973) and Gay Rights National Lobby (1976). Specific to African Americans, the National Coalition of Black Gays was established in 1978. Numerous statewide and local organizations were founded, including the Gay Coalition of Denver (1972) and the Dallas Gay Political Caucus (1975). Gay and lesbian university students established support and advocacy groups, and academic scholars founded the Gay Academic Union (GAU) in 1973, with chapters on campuses throughout the country. In 1974, lesbian members of the GAU in New York started the Lesbian Herstory Archives.

After several years of advocacy by lesbians and gay men, the American Psychiatric Association (APA) declassified homosexuality as a mental disorder in 1973. Building on scientific evidence that failed to support the theory of inherent maladjustment among homosexuals and personal narratives about the futility and harmfulness of sexual orientation change efforts, GLF and GAA activists conducted zaps on psychiatric meetings in San Francisco and Los Angeles in 1970. They gained the attention of a few sympathetic psychiatrists, which led to a panel discussion about homosexuality that included out sexual minority men and women at the next annual meeting. Its success led to a panel session at the 1972 annual meeting in which one of the presenters, John Fryer, was a gay psychiatrist. Because coming out would have ended his career, Fryer appeared in disguise, and his name was listed in the program as "Dr. H. Anonymous." Barbara Gittings, Frank Kameny, and an additional two psychiatrists also appeared on the panel, but Fryer's presentation was especially impactful. Meanwhile, an increasing number of psychiatrists were beginning to question the profession's orthodoxy about homosexuality (Bayer 1981). The 1973 annual meeting featured a symposium with four psychiatrists and one gay activist, all of whom presented papers criticizing the classification of homosexuality as a mental illness primarily on scientific grounds; two other psychiatrists on the panel argued strongly for the classification (Stoller et al. 1973). A few months later, the APA Board of Trustees announced the removal of homosexuality as a diagnostic category and the profession's opposition to discrimination against homosexuals (Bayer 1981).

Summary

The twin streams of resistance against oppression by sexual and gender minorities came together in the conflagration at the Stonewall Inn. Those who were on the margins of New York's downtown gay community, especially the "queens" and "transvestites," street youths, and butch lesbians, were like gunpowder that exploded suddenly in the early morning hours of June 28, 1969. Their brazen resistance against the police ignited simmering frustration and anger among many middle-class sexual minorities, especially younger ones, which turned the initial melee into a multinight large-scale uprising. Young, middle-class activists harnessed the tremendous energy released by the conflagration to transform the accommodationist homophile movement. Brash organizations with the word *gay* in their names demanded societal changes and promoted self-pride and being openly gay. These occurrences captured the imaginations of sexual and gender minorities across the country as they gradually learned about them in the months that followed. At first, the new movement fit firmly within the context of other liberationist movements of the 1960s and early 1970s, which targeted capitalism, colonialism, racism, and sexism, but it later focused more narrowly on equal rights for sexual minorities.

However, these new organizations were largely white, middle class, and male, and they failed to address the concerns of lesbians, gender minorities, or those who were nonwhite. Other organizations sprang up to represent and advocate for these constituencies. While it might appear that the sexual and gender minority movement quickly fragmented after the Stonewall Riots, in reality a unified movement had not yet existed. Instead, multiple sexual and gender minority communities were developing around diverse experiences of identity, marginalization, and discrimination. Gay men generally did not understand how sexism and misogyny impacted them, choosing instead to focus their advocacy efforts more narrowly on sexual orientation issues. Sexual liberation was a central issue for gay men, but not for lesbians, many of whom identified more strongly with the broader women's movement. Gay men's and lesbians' communities grew increasingly specialized and apart from each other, at least in the major cities. In both cases, the whiteness of these communities, and the organizations that represented them, resulted in a failure to recognize the relevance of racism and its impacts on sexual and gender minorities. Gender-based identity became increasingly separate from sexual orientation–based identity, with both gay men and lesbians largely rejecting gender minority people and variant gender expression among themselves. Nevertheless, the largely white and middle-class movement made significant advances against sexual orientation–based discrimination through its advocacy, and in California it gained a foothold in the political process.

Chapter 11
Turbulence and Visibility in the 1970s

The 1970s were economically and socially turbulent. The country experienced high inflation and high unemployment for most of the decade, and in 1979 it fell into a deep recession. By 1970, about four million African Americans had migrated from the rural South to cities in the North and West. But by that time, the industrial jobs that attracted them were quickly evaporating. During the 1970s, whites migrated at an accelerating rate to suburban and exurban regions, resulting in many cities becoming increasingly black and poor (Berry and Dahmann 1977). For example, Detroit became majority African American as its white population decreased by more than half. One reason for "white flight" in some cities was the implementation of desegregation busing of school children to achieve equal opportunity in education across race. In most of these situations, children were bused within the district from mostly black schools to mostly white schools, and vice versa. Desegregation busing led to protests by white parents and even violence, most notably in Boston. White flight was also encouraged by blockbusting, in which real estate agents profited from white homeowners' fears of rising crime and decreasing home values when African Americans moved into their neighborhood. Redlining, mortgage discrimination, and restrictive zoning also contributed to the urban concentration of poor African Americans (Frey 1979; Logan et al. 2017).

With the loss of older industries and affluent homeowners, many cities faced increasingly bad economic conditions. New York City was especially hard hit. By 1975, its unemployment rate reached 12%, and nearly one-fifth of its population was poor. The city teetered on the edge of bankruptcy and imposed severe budget cuts that led to police and firefighter layoffs and public service reductions. The city's subways fell into disrepair and became canvasses for street gang graffiti. On the night of July 13, 1977, lightning from thunderstorms just north of the city initiated a cascade of electrical transmission problems, leading to a total blackout lasting more than 24 hours. Widespread looting, arson, and vandalism occurred, particularly in the poorest neighborhoods of Brooklyn and the Bronx. The South Bronx

Sexual and Gender Minority History. James I. Martin, Oxford University Press. © Oxford University Press (2025).
DOI: 10.1093/9780197765500.003.0011

130 SEXUAL AND GENDER MINORITY HISTORY

was engulfed in a downward spiral of white flight, disinvestment, poverty, violent crime, and arson. By the end of the decade, with so many buildings burned out or abandoned, the South Bronx looked like it had been bombed.

Meanwhile, a great wave of immigration to the United States began in the 1970s, especially from Asia and Latin America, which continued for several decades. The Hart-Celler Act of 1965 opened the doors by doing away with national origin quotas that favored immigrants from Europe and by prioritizing immediate relatives of naturalized citizens (Coleman 2024). Also, hundreds of thousands of refugees came to American shores, especially from Southeast Asia and the Caribbean. Beginning in 1978, a tidal wave of refugees fled postwar Vietnam, so many of them in ramshackle wooden boats that they were known as "boat people." As a humanitarian crisis emerged, the United States became a primary resettlement destination in a program that continued through the 1990s (Campi 2005). And in the Mariel boatlift of 1980, more than 100,000 refugees came to Florida from Cuba and (to a lesser extent) Haiti on hundreds of boats, largely sponsored by Cuban Americans to evacuate family members to American shores. There are divergent narratives about the boatlift, with some (e.g., Triay 2019) highlighting refugees who reconnected with family and successfully integrated into American society. Others (e.g., Arenas 1993) emphasize the use of the boatlift by the Cuban government to expel the most undesired members of its society, especially homosexuals, political prisoners, and the mentally ill.

Among white Americans, attitudes toward immigration began to sour during these years, at first with respect to unauthorized immigrants. These sentiments, which were especially strong in California, Texas, and other southwestern states, gained expression in new policies that prohibited unauthorized immigrants from receiving Social Security benefits or federally funded public assistance (Fox 2016). Reports about homosexuals, political prisoners, and the mentally ill in the Mariel boatlift, many of whom were black, figured prominently in the construction of a narrative about the country being invaded by "criminal aliens" (Stephens 2021, p. 4).

The 1970s were also turbulent politically. By the end of the seven-year ratification period for the Equal Rights Amendment in 1979, 35 state legislatures had voted to ratify, just short of the required number. But in response to a wave of antifeminist activism based on hostility to nontraditional gender roles, some of those legislatures rescinded their earlier vote. Meanwhile, efforts to recriminalize abortion began soon after the Supreme Court handed down its *Roe v. Wade* decision. In 1973, several versions of the

Human Life Amendment to the US Constitution that defined human life as beginning at conception and prohibited all abortions were proposed in the House of Representatives, but they did not advance. However, the Hyde Amendment, which prohibited the use of federal funds for abortions, was approved by Congress in 1976. This law primarily impacted poor women, who were disproportionately nonwhite or immigrants.

Following the resignation of Richard Nixon in 1974, the presidency see-sawed between single-term Republicans and Democrats. Gerald Ford, the vice president at the time of the resignation, served as president for the remaining years of Nixon's second term. Only a few weeks into the presidency, Ford issued a full pardon to Nixon for any crimes he "committed or may have committed or taken part in" during his years in office. Much of the public considered the pardon to be a stain on Ford's presidency; together with the poor economy, it contributed to his defeat in the 1976 election by Jimmy Carter, a southern Democrat. However, Carter was an outsider to Washington politics and did not have good relations with members of his own party in Congress. The economy suffered through continued stagflation throughout his years in office, and there were additional shocks to the country's energy supply. In 1979, a revolution in Iran replaced a Western-friendly imperial state with an Islamic republic that viewed the United States as its arch enemy. Revolutionary students invaded the American embassy in Tehran and took more than 50 hostages, which they held for over a year. The inability to obtain their release contributed to Carter losing the 1980 election in a landslide to conservative Republican Ronald Reagan, who promised a national renewal based on limited government. Not coincidentally, the hostages were released as soon as Reagan was inaugurated, purportedly the result of a clandestine deal between the Iranian government and the Reagan presidential campaign (Baker 2023).

Ronald Reagan remained in office through most of the 1980s, as he won re-election resoundingly in 1984. The Reagan presidency ushered in neoliberal economic policies that reduced taxes, especially for wealthier individuals, and reduced federal spending on social programs. Reductions in welfare spending were predicated on differentiating between the "deserving" and "nondeserving" poor in ways that were implicitly racist, policies that were meant to appeal to conservative southerners and northern working-class whites who resented paying taxes to support poor African Americans (Spitzer 2024). Conversely, defense spending was substantially increased, and the Cold War with the Soviet Union escalated sharply.

Save Our Children

Lesbian communities developed significantly during the 1970s. Women's bookstores opened in many cities, first in Oakland, California (A Woman's Place), and Minneapolis (Amazon Bookstore), and then Los Angeles (Sisterhood Bookstore) and New York (Labyris Books). By mid-decade, there were women's bookstores in Atlanta, Ann Arbor, Boston, and Tucson. Following a number of earlier women's music festivals, the Michigan Womyn's Music Festival began in 1976. This several-day celebration of lesbian culture and community would last nearly 40 years, drawing more than 9,000 women at its height (Morris 1999). At the same time, newly visible, predominantly white gay men's communities proliferated well beyond New York, Chicago, Los Angeles, and San Francisco.

A growing number of municipalities passed sexual orientation nondiscrimination ordinances, with the college towns of East Lansing and Ann Arbor, Michigan, leading the way in 1972. In Washington, DC, a 1973 human rights ordinance banned discrimination on the basis of sexual orientation in addition to race and personal appearance. By the end of the decade, Pennsylvania and California laws provided protection against sexual orientation discrimination in state employment. Nineteen states from coast to coast repealed their sodomy laws. However, a conservative backlash to the increasing visibility of sexual minorities was brewing.

In Miami, the Dade County Coalition for the Humanistic Rights of Gays formed in 1976 to exert influence on the county's politics. Its first major action was to screen candidates for public office and offer endorsements for those with favorable positions on privacy rights, the Equal Rights Amendment, and ending discrimination against sexual minorities. When most of its endorsed candidates won election, the coalition urged the Dade County Commission to amend its human rights ordinance to prohibit discrimination on the basis of "sexual or affectional preference." The commission subsequently proposed a new ordinance, but vociferous opposition arose at a public hearing, especially from local religious leaders (Loughery 1998; Winick 2002).

Among those who spoke against the proposal was singer and author Anita Bryant. By then, Bryant had attained celebrity status as a singer, with a recording career that evolved from old standards and pop to patriotic songs and Christian hymns. She also published several books that featured advice for women from a conservative Christian perspective. Beginning in 1968, as the brand ambassador for the Florida Citrus Commission, she frequently appeared on television commercials for Florida orange juice. After hearing about the Dade County Commission's proposal, Bryant formed an organization to rally support against it, first among members of her church and then more broadly (E. Johnson 2019).

Despite the opposition, the commission voted in January 1977 to approve the ordinance. Shortly afterward, more than 30 religious and civic leaders who opposed it met at Bryant's home. They decided to build on the organization she had already established; calling their group Save Our Children, they planned a petition drive that would force a public referendum on the issue. Bryant was chosen as the group's president (Fejes 2008). Florida's social conservatives were primed for a battle over gay rights. Many of the key leaders of Save Our Children were involved in an antibusing crusade, as conflicts over desegregation busing had been riling through South Florida. In addition, conservatives had been engaged for several years in a fight to reject state ratification of the Equal Rights Amendment, often using rhetoric that played on the public's fears of racial desegregation and "gay marriage" (Frank 2013). It didn't take long for the group's petition to be signed by six times the number of voters needed to force a referendum. The state legislature decided not to ratify the Equal Rights Amendment and passed laws prohibiting "gay marriage" and "gay adoption" just two months before Election Day (Frank 2013).

A lack of diversity among the leaders of the Dade County Coalition for the Humanistic Rights of Gays, all affluent white gay men, led to a number of strategic errors. First, given their demographics, they had trouble convincing the general public they needed protection from discrimination. Assuming their cause would find little support among Cuban American voters, the coalition failed to reach out to this significant segment of the county's population. It also failed to reach out to African American voters, taking their support for granted. Much of the financial backing for its campaign came from out-of-state donors. By contrast, Save Our Children ran a well-organized grassroots campaign. In June 1977, when the votes were counted, the human rights ordinance was repealed by more than two to one (Loughery 1998).

Especially due to Anita Bryant's celebrity and effectiveness as a spokesperson, Save Our Children and its fight against gay rights gained national attention. Elated by the victory in Dade County, Bryant took the campaign to New Orleans, Washington, Houston, Tucson, Indianapolis, and Des Moines.

134 SEXUAL AND GENDER MINORITY HISTORY

Following Dade County's precedent, sexual orientation nondiscrimination ordinances were repealed in St. Paul, Wichita, and Eugene. On the other hand, the campaign motivated many gay men and lesbians to come out of the closet and become politically active. For example, prior to Bryant's appearance in Houston, there was little movement for sexual minority rights in Texas. But on the night of her appearance, as many as 10,000 men and women participated in a street protest, energizing the movement not only in Houston but also in Dallas. Throughout the country, gay men and lesbians boycotted orange juice because of its association with Bryant. Jean O'Leary and Bruce Voeller (1977), co-executive directors of the National Gay Task Force, publicly thanked the Bryant campaign for raising the public's awareness about prejudice and discrimination against sexual minorities. However, the fight was just beginning.

John Briggs, a California state legislator, sponsored a ballot initiative in 1978 with the stated aim to protect "impressionable youth" (p. 29) in the state's public schools by making it illegal for anyone who "engages in public homosexual activity and/or public homosexual conduct" (p. 29) to work as a teacher, teacher's aide, administrator, or counselor. Such people could not be hired, and if they were already employed by a district, they would have to be fired (Eu, 1978). Because California repealed its sodomy law a few years earlier, the initiative would have had the effect of partially restoring it. There was a clear connection between the "Briggs Initiative" and the Save Our Children campaign. Briggs traveled to Miami to celebrate the Dade County referendum result with Anita Bryant (Loughery 1998), and he named his own organization California Defend Our Children. But while the Florida referendum curtailed efforts to prevent discrimination against sexual minorities, the Briggs Initiative was intended to restrict their rights (Tracey 2022). Anita Bryant campaigned in favor of the initiative, as did San Francisco Supervisor Dan White. Early polling suggested it would win easily.

In San Francisco, Harvey Milk had been elected to the board of supervisors at the end of 1977. As the most prominent gay politician in the country, he took a leadership role in the fight against the Briggs Initiative. In his stirring speech at the massively attended 1978 Gay Freedom Day parade in San Francisco, he exhorted the crowd:

> My name is Harvey Milk—and I want to recruit you. I want to recruit you
> for the fight to preserve your democracy from the John Briggs and the Anita
> Bryants who are trying to constitutionalize bigotry. . . . Gay people, we will

not win our rights by staying quietly in our closets … we are coming out! We are coming out to fight the lies, the myths, the distortions! We are coming out to tell the truth about gays! (Milk 1978)

In Los Angeles, lesbians and gay men were already working together to influence the local government. By 1978, the Municipal Elections Committee of Los Angeles (MECLA), with its mixed-gender leadership and cadre of wealthy donors, was perhaps the country's most influential sexual minority political organization. To fight the initiative, MECLA members formed the New Alliance for Gay Equality, which combined high-powered fundraising with grassroots activism. Joining the fight were the Coalition for Human Rights, Southern California Women for Understanding, the Union for Lesbians and Gay Men, and the Action Coalition to Fight the Briggs Initiative (Faderman and Timmons 2006). Even the newly formed Log Cabin Club of Los Angeles joined, with its membership of Republican white gay men (Howard 2020). Affluent and working-class whites, gay men and lesbians— even those who had been separatists—and racial and ethnic minorities fought together (Faderman and Timmons 2006).

The movement to defeat the initiative obtained endorsements from California governor Jerry Brown and former president Gerald Ford. Harvey Milk lobbied President Carter for months to speak out against the initiative, which he finally did at the end of a speech in Sacramento just days before the election (Peters and Woolley n.d.). Perhaps the most important endorsement came from Ronald Reagan. David Mixner, a cofounder of MECLA, persuaded Reagan that the initiative represented a government attack on privacy and would leave teachers (regardless of their sexual orientation) vulnerable to mischief and blackmail by disgruntled students (Gabriel 2024).

When the votes were counted in November, the Briggs Initiative was soundly defeated, 58% to 42%. Adding to the night's good news for sexual minorities, an effort to repeal Seattle's sexual orientation nondiscrimination ordinance failed by an even larger margin (Fejes 2008).

Harvey Milk and the White Night Riot

Harvey Milk's success in being elected to the San Francisco Board of Supervisors, after two unsuccessful attempts, followed the city's adoption of electoral districts for board positions (previously elected on a citywide basis). Milk's district included the Castro, with its high concentration of sexual minority voters. His campaign focused on tax reform and housing and quality-of-life issues, in addition to protecting sexual minorities from discrimination. He was a strong proponent of forging coalitions among diverse constituencies. Shortly after joining the board, Milk sponsored a wide-ranging sexual orientation nondiscrimination ordinance that was subsequently approved. His high-profile, statewide campaign to defeat the Briggs Initiative added substantially to his political influence and renown well beyond San Francisco (Loughery 1998).

After less than 11 months in office, however, Harvey Milk was murdered by fellow supervisor Dan White. A former policeman, White had been elected from a conservative, largely Catholic district. At 31, he was the youngest member of the board, and due in part to his inexperience in politics, he was often outmaneuvered by Milk and the other more progressive members. In early November, shortly after the failure of the Briggs Initiative, and under the weight of financial problems and difficulties on the board, White submitted his resignation to the mayor, George Moscone. Days later, he asked the mayor to rescind his resignation, but the board had already voted to accept it. After a replacement was named for his position, White went to city hall and gunned down the mayor and then Harvey Milk (Faderman 2018).

Dianne Feinstein, who was president of the board of supervisors, heard gunfire from her office, whereupon she rushed to Milk's office and found him dead. After being notified that Moscone also had been killed, she announced the deaths in a now-iconic press conference and named Dan White as a suspect. The grief among gay and lesbian San Franciscans was immediate and intense. Thousands joined a candlelight procession to city hall, where Feinstein spoke and Joan Baez sang "Amazing Grace" (Faderman 2018).

Dan White was tried in court six months later. The prosecution was inept and outmaneuvered by the defense, which obtained an entirely heterosexual, all-white jury. During the 11-day trial, the defense team played strongly for the jury's sympathy, arguing that White was a fine young man suffering from severe depression. In what has been called the "Twinkie defense," they claimed that due to White's depression he was unable to eat normally, subsisting only on Cokes and Twinkies, with disastrous effects on his ability to think clearly. After deliberating for a day and a half, the jury returned a verdict of guilty for involuntary manslaughter, not premeditated murder. The sentence was just seven years and eight months in prison (Faderman 2018).

Upon announcement of the verdict, rage hit the streets of San Francisco in the White Night Riot. Unlike the peaceful procession six months earlier, thousands marched to city hall where, for several hours, they shattered windows with parking meters, iron grillwork torn from buildings, tree limbs, and newspaper vending boxes, and they firebombed police cars (Faderman 2018). Later, police in riot gear came to Castro Street where they chased gay men who threw bottles at them, clubbing those they could catch. Entering a popular gay bar, they smashed windows and beat customers ("Gays Riot: Why? Why Not?" 1979). The riot left nearly 130 injured, almost half of them police, and $1 million in property damage (Faderman 2018).

Conservative Christians in Politics

Meanwhile, building on the Save Our Children campaign and Briggs Initiative, conservative Christian organizations for whom vilification of sexual minorities was an animating feature began to proliferate. The first, Focus on the Family, started as a weekly radio program in 1977 by psychologist James Dobson, whose bestselling book *Dare to Discipline* advocated for strict parenting and the use of corporal punishment to discipline children. More generally, Dobson offered advice to couples and parents from an antifeminist Christian perspective that prescribed adherence to rigid gender roles. Focus on the Family grew into a highly successful fundamentalist ministry and multimedia empire. Although it did not engage directly in political activities, it encouraged conservative Christians to exert their collective power. In 1979, televangelist Jerry Falwell founded the Moral Majority, the first conservative Christian organization to enter directly into the political realm. During the 1960s, Falwell had used biblical arguments to oppose African American civil rights (Balmer 2021), and in the 1970s he participated in both the Save Our Children and Briggs Initiative campaigns. In establishing the Moral Majority, Falwell allied with conservative Catholics and nonreligious right-wing partisans in a fight against homosexuality, feminism, and abortion (Williams 2010).

Presbyterian minister Louis Sheldon, who was listed as executive director of California Defend Our Children on the organization's letterhead,

138 SEXUAL AND GENDER MINORITY HISTORY

formed the Traditional Values Coalition in 1980 as a lobbying organization for conservative Christian policies. Sheldon routinely employed inflammatory language when campaigning against lesbians and gay men, declaring "open warfare" on their supposed agenda (Lichtblau 1989). And in 1981, James Dobson formed the Family Research Council, a policy think tank that became one of the most vociferous opponents of lesbian and gay rights with claims that same-sex sexual behavior is inherently harmful and gay men are sexual predators. The organization routinely drew from pseudoscientific or otherwise discredited research in its policy statements and recommendations (Barrett-Fox 2014). Concerned Women for America and the American Family Association, both established during this period, also campaigned strongly against lesbian and gay rights.

Building Sexual Minority Communities

In spite of the forces arrayed against them, sexual minority communities continued to grow and diversify. Community centers and social service organizations were established, although in many cases their services were initially oriented toward the needs of white gay men. The Los Angeles Gay Liberation Front (GLF) opened Liberation House for homeless youth in 1971, and while GLF disbanded shortly after that, several of its leaders established the groundbreaking Gay Community Services Center in 1972. In the next few years, Chicago's Gay Horizons (1973) and Howard Brown Memorial Clinic (1974) opened, as did the Gay Community Center of Philadelphia (1975) and Houston's Montrose Counseling Center (1978).

There was considerable growth of newspapers that disseminated news and other material and advertised services and businesses within these communities. In 1971, San Francisco's *Bay Area Reporter* was established, as was *Fag Rag*, the radical gay men's Boston paper, and both *Lavender Woman* (Chicago) and *Lesbian Tide* (Los Angeles). Joining them within a few years were *Gay Community News* (Boston), *Gay Life* (Chicago), *Out Front Colorado* (Denver), *Philadelphia Gay News*, and *The Montrose Star* (Houston). In 1974, investment banker David Goodstein bought Los Angeles–based *The Advocate* and transformed it into a glossy national magazine that targeted an affluent, white, gay market. And in 1976, New York–based

Christopher Street began coverage of culture and politics for a national, mainly male, readership.

New York's Oscar Wilde Memorial Bookshop was the only gay bookstore in the country until 1974, when Lambda Rising opened in Washington. Within the next few years, Giovanni's Room (1976) opened in Philadelphia, as did A Different Light (1978) in Los Angeles. By the mid-1980s, A Different Light had opened branches in New York and San Francisco. These stores carried books and materials of interest to both gay men and lesbians. As previously mentioned, there were also lesbian-owned feminist bookstores in many cities.

To help gay men find places to meet other gay men, Los Angeles gay bar owner Bob Damron began publishing a national guide all the way back in 1964. Updated, expanded editions were released each year; listings included bars, clubs, bathhouses, and cruising areas. The Damron guide was oriented toward white gay men, and there were no comparable guides for lesbians or nonwhite gay men. However, Gayellow Pages began publishing somewhat more inclusive regional directories of gay- and lesbian-owned or -welcoming businesses in 1973.

Pride events continued to grow, diversify, and proliferate. San Francisco held its first Christopher Street West parade in 1972 and later renamed it the Gay Freedom Day parade. The rainbow flag, a symbol of sexual and gender minority pride, first flew at the Gay Freedom Day parade in 1978. Seattle celebrated its first Gay Pride Week in 1974, corresponding with the opening of its new gay community center. By mid-decade, there were pride parades in Atlanta, Boston, Denver, Philadelphia, and Washington. By the 1980s, nearly every large American city had a pride parade or celebration.

During the 1970s, gay and lesbian communities were largely adult communities, with an absence of social structures or supports for youth. Lesbians and, especially, gay men had long been accused by conservative critics of being child molesters, so they were generally wary of even social contact with underage young men and women. It was risky for fledgling sexual minority organizations to provide services to them. However, a few support services began to appear. Sexual minority students at George Washington High School in the Bronx, New York, established the first known support group for lesbian and gay youth in 1972; the racially and ethnically diverse group included lesbian and gay students and their friends (Cohan 2008).

In Boston, Project Lambda was established in 1974, with federal funding to prevent sexual minority youth from engaging in street crime. Its young adult advocates provided mentorship and support for the youth with whom they were paired (Lachman 1974). Unfortunately, the funding ran out a year later, and the program folded. In 1977, the Committee for Gay Youth was established to take its place, and a support group for sexual minority youth ran under its auspices (The Boston Alliance of LGBTQ+ Youth n.d.). In 1978, two social work graduate students facilitated a support group for lesbian and gay high school students in Ann Arbor, Michigan. The group was formed by two high school students who repeatedly called the University of Michigan's Gay Hotline, asking where they could find others like themselves. With the permission of both students, the hotline worker put them in touch with each other. The students subsequently found others to join a group, which they wrote about in their school's underground newspaper. Also in 1978, the landmark booklet *Growing Up Gay*, with most articles written by lesbian- or gay-identified high school students, was published in Ann Arbor by Youth Liberation Press.

Although disapproval or rejection by parents was commonly experienced by sexual minorities, an opposing movement of love and support originated when Jeanne Manford joined her son, Stonewall veteran and Gay Activists Alliance cofounder Morty Manford, in New York's 1972 Christopher Street Liberation Day March, carrying a sign that said, "Parents of Gays Unite in Support for Our Children." Noticing the crowd's excitement about his mother's participation in the march, Morty encouraged his parents to form a support group for parents like themselves. The next year, after advertising the group in the *Village Voice*, Jeanne and husband Jules led its first meeting with 20 other parents and named the group Parents of Gays. The Manfords gradually realized that acceptance of one's gay children was important but insufficient; parents also needed to fight for their children's rights. The group quickly gained national publicity, and Jeanne was interviewed frequently on radio and television, sometimes joined by her husband or son. Parents in cities all over the country contacted the Manfords for advice about their own children and how to start a Parents of Gays group where they lived. Local groups proliferated, but there was no national organization that connected them until 1982, when the Federation of Parents and Friends of Lesbians and Gays (PFLAG) was incorporated in California, with PFLAG-Los Angeles founder Adele Starr as its first president (PFLAG 2024; Schulz 2023).

Sexual Minorities of Color

In most large cities, advances in sexual minority advocacy and community building occurred primarily according to the interests and needs of white gay men and lesbians, seen especially in the absence of attention to issues of race and class by white-dominated advocacy organizations (Bell 2020). In addition, nonwhite sexual minorities commonly experienced racial and ethnic discrimination in white gay and lesbian communities. For example, they encountered discriminatory treatment when trying to enter gay or lesbian bars and clubs and racist attitudes among white gay men and lesbians. However, coming out within tight-knit African American, Latine, or Asian American communities was perilous. Thus, gay men and lesbians of color often found themselves without a place they could truly call home (Faderman and Timmons 2006).

Bars catering to nonwhite sexual minorities were important sites for support and community building. For example, in Los Angeles, Jewel Thais-Williams's dance bar Jewel's Catch One became a linchpin of the African American gay community after it opened in 1973 (Faderman and Timmons 2006). Later, Circus Disco played a similar role for Latino gay men (Reyes 2016), as did Mugi's for Asian American gay men (Wise 2023). Local advocacy organizations gradually developed, including the Association of Black Gays (established 1975), Asian/Pacific Lesbians and Gays (1980), and Gay and Lesbian Latinos Unidos (1981).

A national movement to address the interests and needs of African American sexual minorities began in 1979 with the founding of the National Coalition of Black Gays, with chapters in Baltimore, Washington, and Detroit. Within a few years, the organization's name was changed to the National Coalition of Black Lesbians and Gays (NCBLG), and as many as 14 additional chapters opened. Unlike white-dominated sexual minority advocacy organizations, which tended to focus narrowly on what they considered sexual orientation issues, the NCBLG also sought to address racism and other forms of prejudice and discrimination (National Coalition of Black Gays n.d.; Pritchard 2015). In 1979, it organized the National Third World Lesbian and Gay Conference, in Washington. The conference brought together diverse sexual minority activists of color to examine racism, sexism, heterosexism, and homophobia (Pritchard 2015). Audre Lorde gave a keynote address titled "When Will the Ignorance End?"

For not one of us will be free until we are all free, and until all members of our communities are free. So we are here to help shape a world where all people can flourish, beyond sexism, beyond racism, beyond ageism, beyond classism, and beyond homophobia. (Lorde 1979)

Gender Minorities

Sexual minorities disassociated themselves from gender minorities in their community development and social and political advocacy efforts during the 1970s. Among gender minorities, these years were notable for advancements in minimum standards for gender-confirming medical care. The Erickson Educational Foundation, mentioned previously, sponsored a biennial International Symposium on Gender Identity between 1969 and 1977 that brought together medical and mental health professionals to share information about the study and treatment of transsexuals. After the foundation closed in 1977, the Harry Benjamin International Gender Dysphoria Association (HBIGDA) assumed leadership on transgender healthcare (Devore and Matte 2007). In 1979, HBIGDA produced the first version of its *Standards of Care* for the medical treatment of transsexuals, which provided gatekeeping protocols for hormone treatment and gender-confirming surgery. At the same time, the American Psychiatric Association created the diagnostic categories transsexualism (for adults and adolescents) and gender identity disorder of childhood. Gender dysphoria, discomfort with one's assigned sex and associated sex roles, was required for a patient to receive either diagnosis.

According to the *Standards of Care*, hormonal treatment could be given only to adult patients who were confirmed by a mental health professional to experience considerable gender dysphoria. After one year of hormonal treatment and "real-life experience" (living as the desired gender), patients could be considered for surgical treatment and legal change of sex and name ("Standards of Care: The Hormonal and Surgical Sex Reassignment of Gender Dysphoric Persons" 1985). These guidelines were intended to provide access to gender-confirming medical treatment, and as such they were welcomed by some transgender people. However, they also pathologized transgender experience and put mental health professionals in the role of gatekeepers. In addition, insurance companies generally refused to

National March on Washington

Just before he was murdered, Harvey Milk was beginning to organize a national march on Washington in order to build a more integrated, national movement for lesbian and gay rights. Inspired by Milk's martyrdom, more than 300 lesbian and gay activists from across the country met in Philadelphia in February 1979, and they decided to hold the march later that year to coincide with the 10-year anniversary of the Stonewall Riots. Steve Ault, a former GLF-New York member, and Joyce Hunter, a social work student in New York, volunteered to be co-coordinators of the march. With a lead time of only eight months, and without the backing of a national sexual minority rights organization, they worked quickly to build support and plan the logistics for a geographically, racially, and gender-diverse event on October 14th (Ghaziani 2005). The National Coalition of Black Gays scheduled their Third World conference on the same weekend as the march, which benefited both events. To culminate the conference, a few hours before the start of the national march, they held a separate march through African American and Chinese neighborhoods of Washington, a courageous and highly meaningful event for many of the participants (Beemyn 2014).

The 1979 National March on Washington for Lesbian and Gay Rights kicked off on a chilly Sunday afternoon with Salsa Soul Sisters, a New York–based African American and Latina group, leading as many as 100,000 participants from all across the country. They marched up Pennsylvania Avenue toward the White House and then the Washington Monument, demanding legislation to protect lesbian and gay rights and an end to laws and policies that discriminate against sexual minorities. At the end of the march, they gathered around the Washington Monument, where they were entertained by gay bands and inspired by speakers including Adele Starr (PFLAG), Reverend Troy Perry (Metropolitan Community Church), Harry Britt (San Francisco Board of Supervisors), Eleanor Smeal (National Organization for Women), New York congressman Ted Weiss, and Audre Lorde. That day, a national movement for sexual minority rights seemed within reach, no longer just a visionary dream.

Summary

Within the context of the country's economic, social, and political turbulence, sexual minorities substantially increased their visibility in American life during the 1970s and built communities where they could live more openly and freely than ever before. At the same time, a movement emerged on the political right to turn back the clock and erase their visibility. Although sometimes successful, these efforts inspired sexual minorities in many cities to come out of the closet, organize, and fight for their rights. However, sexual minorities remained largely fragmented with respect to race, gender, and social class, and even by the end of the decade, there was only the beginning of a sense of national movement among them. Political and social support organizations tended to be local or, at best, statewide. In many cases, they were dominated by white gay men who focused on issues that were most familiar to them and important to their demographic, issues that were defined narrowly as "gay issues." By contrast, issues of concern to lesbians and gay men of color were inherently intersectional, that is, sexual orientation in combination with sexism, racism, and economic injustice. The social and political goals pursued by gay men and lesbians tended to ignore gender minorities altogether. These were serious shortcomings that would take considerably more time to overcome.

Nevertheless, the foundation for a broader, more inclusive movement was built during the 1970s. Coming out and living openly became important for political as well as personal reasons, although doing so remained risky in most parts of the country. Thus, many sexual minorities migrated to major cities where they could pursue life more openly. A growing lesbian and gay press helped to reduce the isolation of those who were not yet out, and it stimulated a greater sense of community among others. Among lesbians, the women's music movement served these purposes even more powerfully. Increasingly, those who were not originally thought of as members of these communities fought for inclusion. Those who were too young to access the commercial venues in which sexual minority life thrived began to find ways to connect with each other and build support. Parents countered the expectation of many lesbians and gay men that coming out meant leaving their families behind. Sexual minorities of color began building social and political structures of their own in the face of racism and lack of understanding among white lesbian and gay communities. Gender minorities were largely excluded from these communities, and they remained fragmented across diverse identities. Among those who sought medical services to aid in transitioning, there was progress in the establishment of standards for these services. Unfortunately, the standards were a devil's bargain, as the promise of access to services depended on acceptance of a pathological identity.

Chapter 12
The Deluge and Beyond

As sexual minority communities proliferated and gained strength in the 1970s, a previously unknown pathogen was circulating among their members; eventually it would be named human immunodeficiency virus (HIV). On June 5, 1981, the Centers for Disease Control and Prevention (CDC) newsletter *Morbidity and Mortality Weekly Report* announced that a rare and virulent form of pneumonia had been discovered among five gay men in Los Angeles, and one month later the *New York Times* reported that 41 previously healthy gay men in New York and California had developed a rare form of cancer. The San Francisco gay newspaper *Bay Area Reporter* soon ran articles about the "gay pneumonia" and the "gay cancer." These illnesses were devastating, as those who contracted them usually died horribly within a year. At first, no one knew what caused the pneumonia, cancer, and other unusual illnesses that were striking down gay men. By the end of 1981, it was determined that they were the result of an immune system collapse; since this syndrome was seen primarily among gay men, researchers and the press called it gay-related immune deficiency (GRID). Doing so reinforced the association of the emerging epidemic with same-sex sexuality and all of the stigma that went with it.

In the years before the cause of GRID was found to be a virus, some theories about its cause implicated gay men's sexuality even though not everyone stricken by the disease was gay, particularly hemophiliacs and intravenous drug users. Most commonly implicated were frequent casual or anonymous sex and the use of inhalants to enhance sexual experiences (e.g., Altman 1982). Although the CDC replaced the name GRID with acquired immune deficiency syndrome (AIDS) in mid-1982, the epidemic would continue to be associated with gay men, with devastating consequences.

The CDC, which normally functions like a detective agency to determine the cause of health emergencies and provide guidance to members of the public on how to safeguard their health, was underfunded by Congress and hamstrung by the Reagan administration, which did not consider the developing epidemic as important as reducing the size of the federal government

Sexual and Gender Minority History. James I. Martin, Oxford University Press. © Oxford University Press (2025). DOI: 10.1093/9780197765500.003.0012

148 SEXUAL AND GENDER MINORITY HISTORY

(Francis 2012). Even though AIDS was nearly always fatal (Kolata 1987), the National Institutes of Health, which funds research on health problems, failed to respond with any sense of emergency (Kramer 1983), and Congress appropriated no new funds to deal with the epidemic (Shilts 1987). Decisive, early action could have slowed the epidemic's growth, but through inaction the federal government allowed it to spread exponentially (Francis 2012). At the end of 1981, there were 152 identified cases (Shilts 1987), but the incubation period for AIDS was very long; a back-calculation estimate performed decades later (Bosh et al. 2021) showed that 20,000 people in the United States were likely infected by then. More than 75% of those with AIDS were gay and bisexual men, a population toward whom the Reagan administration and much of American society had extremely negative attitudes. Reagan himself had courted conservative Christians in his first presidential campaign, and during the second Reagan administration the White House communications director was Pat Buchanan, a hard right political commentator who had accused gay men of bringing the disaster on themselves by "declaring war on nature" (Shilts 1987, p. 311). President Reagan did not speak publicly about AIDS until late 1985.

The federal government's refusal to assume leadership, even as the epidemic was spiraling out of control, was catastrophic. It was impossible to know who was infected since there was no blood test for AIDS until 1985 (Pear 1985). The first antiretroviral medication to treat AIDS became available in 1987, by which time more than 10,000 Americans had died, with perhaps 1 million more HIV-infected (Taylor 1989). All previous treatments for AIDS were considered experimental, so insurers commonly denied payment for them; some patients bankrupted themselves to pay on their own. Those who became too ill to work were typically unable to receive disability payments because AIDS was not a qualifying condition. Consequently, many gay men lost their homes, and it was not uncommon for friends and family members to refuse to help them due to fear of contagion (Kramer 1983). Even though gay men were bearing the brunt of the epidemic, the first national AIDS prevention campaign, America Responds to AIDS, launched by the CDC in 1987, failed even to mention them, let alone provide them with any guidance (Ratzan et al. 1994).

Most news media outlets paid little attention to AIDS during the epidemic's first few years. For example, the *New York Times* ran only five articles about it during 1982, two of them about nongay patients with the disease, and it would take two years for an article about AIDS to appear on the paper's first page. San Francisco was unique in having regular newspaper coverage of the unfolding epidemic, with journalist Randy Shilts writing about it for the *San Francisco Chronicle.* San Francisco's NBC affiliate station carried regular coverage as well. By contrast, there was barely a mention of it on New York's television stations or on national news programs, largely due to an unwillingness to give attention to gay men or same-sex sexuality. Television talk shows and the tabloid press generally focused on the risk to nongay Americans and stoked the public's hysteria, while conservative Christian media outlets played up the supposed degeneracy of gay men and the threat they posed to American families (Tomes 2022). A national poll conducted by the *Los Angeles Times* in 1985 found that 51% of Americans believed it should be "a crime for an AIDS patient to have sex with another person," and the same percentage approved of quarantining those with AIDS. More than 40% were in favor of shutting down all gay bars, and 15% approved of tattooing people with AIDS so they could be easily identified (Balzar 1985).

Even though New York City was the epicenter of the AIDS epidemic, its municipal government also failed to provide leadership. Like President Reagan, Mayor Ed Koch refused to speak publicly about AIDS It took until 1985 for the city to start most of its efforts to address the epidemic, by which time more than 6,600 of its residents had been diagnosed with AIDS and about 3,800 had died (New York City AIDS Memorial 2011–2024). Unlike San Francisco, sexual minorities exerted little political power in New York, and Mayor Koch, who was secretly gay, avoided giving too much attention to sexual minority issues to protect his secret (Flegenheimer and Goldensohn 2022).

A Fight for Survival

Especially in New York, the catastrophe of AIDS made it clear to many gay men that the larger society considered them expendable, and if they wanted to survive, they would need to save themselves. Author and social critic Larry Kramer founded Gay Men's Health Crisis (GMHC) in early 1982 with five other gay men. Although it was conceived as a vehicle to raise funds for AIDS research, it quickly became a service organization; a hotline and a buddy program in which volunteers provided day-to-day assistance to people with AIDS were the initial services (Shilts 1987). Around the same time, activist Cleve Jones and three other gay men in San Francisco established

150   SEXUAL AND GENDER MINORITY HISTORY

the Kaposi's Sarcoma Research and Education Foundation. Like GMHC, the foundation operated a hotline. But because San Francisco's Department of Public Health had begun creating a city-wide strategy for dealing with the epidemic by then, the foundation was not alone in its efforts. In 1983, it began providing counseling services and emergency food and housing for people with AIDS, and in 1984 it reorganized as the AIDS Foundation of San Francisco (Arno 1986). The principles of safer sex were originally developed by the National Coalition of Gay STD Services in 1979 to reduce gay men's risk of contracting sexually transmitted diseases. By 1982 the principles had become "Guidelines and Recommendations for Healthful Gay Sexual Activity" with respect to AIDS and sexually transmitted diseases, which were distributed throughout San Francisco's gay community and, eventually, to gay communities throughout the country (Blair 2017).

As the AIDS epidemic spread rapidly across the country, gay communities in many cities established supportive services, often in the absence of assistance from municipal governments. The Los Angeles Gay Community Services Center held an emergency meeting about the epidemic in late 1982, which led three gay men and a straight woman—all friends—to establish a hotline. Soon after, they held a fundraiser that would yield seed money for AIDS Project Los Angeles (APLA). Among AIDS service organizations, APLA was especially notable for the strong involvement of lesbians in its leadership. APLA held its first AIDS Walk in 1985, a fundraising event that would be copied by many other cities. The organization's fundraising prowess was enhanced by its ability to draw on Hollywood's celebrity power (Faderman and Timmons 2006). In Chicago, two gay physicians set up an AIDS unit at Illinois Masonic Hospital that would become a model for AIDS hospital units elsewhere (Chicago LGBT Hall of Fame 2007). In 1985, Chicago House was established to provide emergency housing and hospice services for people with AIDS, as was the fundraising and grantmaking organization AIDS Foundation of Chicago (Chicago LGBT Hall of Fame 2009). Gay men affected by the epidemic established service and fundraising organizations in Atlanta, Dallas, and Houston.

These developments notwithstanding, rage simmered beneath the surface of gay communities. In a 1983 article published by the *New York Native*, Larry Kramer spewed vitriol about the lack of responsiveness by federal and municipal governments and the denial of the growing disaster by many gay men; the article was reprinted in gay newspapers in several other cities. Four years later in New York, Kramer formed the AIDS Coalition to Unleash

Power (ACT UP) to force change through direct political action. ACT UP's slogan "Silence = Death" meant that gay people must fight for their lives or die. The group's first action was a demonstration against overcharging by pharmaceutical corporations for AIDS medications. Demonstrators lay down on Broadway at the intersection of Wall Street and blocked traffic during rush hour, chanting, "We are angry, we want action!" Two years later, ACT UP members chained themselves to the VIP balcony of the New York Stock Exchange, dropped fake money onto the trading floor, and delayed the opening bell. ACT UP members from multiple cities protested at the headquarters of the US Food and Drug Administration (FDA) to demand faster development and approval of medications to treat AIDS. Staging a die-in, they chanted, "Hey, hey, FDA, how many people have you killed today?" Increasingly theatrical, ACT UP demonstrations effectively used the media to gain attention; these tactics led to faster access to new AIDS medications and lower costs for them (ACT UP-NY 1987–2024; Specter 2021).

The AIDS epidemic also brought an upsurge in antigay activism, as some conservatives used it in efforts to reverse progress on sexual minority rights. William Dannemeyer, who represented a California district in the House of Representatives from 1979 to 1993, advocated quarantining people with AIDS and barring them from jobs in healthcare (Roberts 2019). At the 1985 Conservative Political Action Conference, Paul Cameron, a psychologist who was expelled from the American Psychological Association for ethical violations, promoted "extermination of homosexuals" (Southern Poverty Law Center 2005). In 1986, a deceptively worded California ballot initiative asked voters to approve adding AIDS to the state's official list of communicable diseases, based on the fallacious idea that AIDS was spread through casual contact. Approval of the initiative would have required isolation and quarantine procedures for all people who were HIV positive, which meant mandatory testing, loss of employment, and potentially quarantine camps. The initiative was defeated by a large margin, inspiring aggressive AIDS activism in the state, with new organizations like Los Angeles's Stop AIDS Quarantine Committee (Faderman and Timmons 2006) and San Francisco's Citizens for Medical Justice; ACT UP chapters sprang up in both cities.

As the epidemic progressed, death notices in local gay newspapers expanded to multiple pages; in San Francisco's *Bay Area Reporter*, as many as 31 obituaries appeared in one week. In the mainstream press, obituaries for gay men who died of AIDS often obscured the cause of death. They died "after a long illness," from "heart failure," or from "cancer." For newspapers

152   SEXUAL AND GENDER MINORITY HISTORY

like the *New York Times*, and for many families of the deceased, AIDS was too stigmatized by its association with same-sex sexuality to acknowledge the actual cause of death. It was common for obituaries not to acknowledge the deceased was gay; life partners were euphemized as "friends" or "longtime companions" (Rosenzweig 2018). To memorialize and acknowledge the lives of people who died from AIDS, Cleve Jones and several friends established the NAMES Project AIDS Memorial Quilt in 1987. Anyone could contribute a panel to the quilt, and contributions from cities around the country soon poured into the San Francisco workshop where volunteers assembled them. After only four months, the quilt was displayed on the National Mall, coinciding with the second March on Washington for Lesbian and Gay Rights; its 1,920 panels covered an area larger than a football field. One year later, more than 8,000 quilt panels were displayed in front of the White House (National AIDS Memorial n.d.).

Not Only White Gay Men

The history of the AIDS epidemic most often told has been about white gay men, and much of the activism and development of care systems described above was led by them. However, men and women of color were affected by AIDS from the earliest days of the epidemic. The CDC did not begin to track AIDS by race until 1983, but nonwhites are estimated by a back-calculation method to have accounted for 44% of all new HIV infections in 1981 (Bosh et al. 2021). Gay men of color received few of the benefits of the advocacy and care described above since they were often unwelcome in white gay communities, and those efforts were largely not directed toward them or designed with them in mind. Also, in contrast to the pattern among whites, in which self-identified gay men represented the great majority of cases, many HIV infections among African American and Latine individuals derived from same-sex sexual activity between men who did not identify as gay or from intravenous drug use. In addition, AIDS tended to be viewed as a "white gay men's" disease within African American and Latine communities, which led to rejection of affected members of those communities (Friedman et al. 1987). Men of color who were gay or had sex with other men also were more likely to be poor than white gay men, with less access to good medical care and more exposure to crime and other social ills besetting racial and ethnic minority communities.

Black gay men founded several AIDS organizations in 1985. In Chicago, social worker Richard Lee Gray cofounded the Kupona Network to provide AIDS education and prevention services for black people living with AIDS. In Los Angeles, Archbishop Carl Bean of the Unity Fellowship Church founded the Minority AIDS Project to address AIDS in black and Latine communities, with informational materials in both English and Spanish. In San Francisco, the organization Black and White Men Together formed an AIDS Task Force to provide AIDS education and support within the city's black community. In Philadelphia, Blacks Educating Blacks About Sexual Health Issues was founded not by a gay man, but by an African American woman, Rashidah Hassan, who believed in the importance of outreach to black gay men within their home communities (Royles 2020).

Over the next several years, other organizations arose in several cities to focus on AIDS prevention and care in racial and ethnic minority communities. For example, Gay Men of African Descent was founded in New York to address the health of black gay men from a holistic perspective. Because a large proportion of HIV infections among African American and Latine communities were occurring for reasons other than same-sex sexual behavior, some organizations did not focus solely on men who had sex with men. Chicago's Puerto Rican Cultural Center initiated the program Vida/SIDA to provide prevention services in the city's Latine communities In Los Angeles, a committee of Gay and Lesbian Latinos Unidos eventually became an independent AIDS service organization named Bienestar. Even though AIDS incidence was relatively low among Asian American communities, gay Asian Americans faced a lack of appropriate services from white gay communities and little support from their home communities. In Los Angeles, they founded the Asian Pacific AIDS Intervention Team (Wat 2021), and in San Francisco, the Asian Pacific AIDS Coalition provided coordination and advocacy among five Bay Area organizations. In Minneapolis, Sharon M. Day, a two-spirit Ojibwe woman, founded the Minnesota American Indian AIDS Task Force.

Beginning in the mid-1980s, the World Health Organization began conceptualizing the social determinants of health, which help to explain why those who are marginalized in society experience poorer health (Braverman and Gottlieb 2014). Gender minorities, composing some of the most marginalized populations in American society, were hit hard by the AIDS epidemic. But since the CDC did not collect surveillance data about them, their situation remained largely invisible to others. Due to widespread

154   SEXUAL AND GENDER MINORITY HISTORY

discrimination in education and employment, many engaged in sex work for survival and injected illicit drugs to manage their desperate circumstances. In addition, appropriate healthcare services for transgender people hardly existed during the 1980s and 1990s. Among gender minorities, the epidemic devastated black transgender women in particular, as they inhabited perhaps the most marginalized social position of all (Gossett and Hayward 2020).

Expanding Public Awareness

When AIDS began to strike celebrities and more people who were not gay, society's interest in the epidemic increased. In 1985, Rock Hudson's publicist acknowledged that the famous actor, who was secretly gay, had AIDS. Soon after this announcement was made, the Los Angeles–based National AIDS Research Foundation merged with the New York–based AIDS Medical Foundation to form the American Foundation for AIDS Research (AmfAR), with superstar Elizabeth Taylor as its national chair. Within one year, AmfAR distributed more than $1.5 million in research grants (AmfAR 2024). Coinciding with Hudson's death, Congress allocated approximately $190 million for AIDS research, far more than the Reagan administration had requested but far less than what was needed. Ryan White, an Indiana boy, contracted AIDS from a blood transfusion when he was 13 years old. The discrimination he encountered in school because of his illness became national news, and people throughout the country empathized with the plight of the young "innocent victim" of AIDS. With White's death in 1990, Congress finally passed comprehensive AIDS care legislation and named it the Ryan White CARE Act. In 1991, basketball star Magic Johnson announced that he had contracted HIV as a result of sexual experiences with women. Subsequently, as a spokesman for the promotion of AIDS awareness and safer sex, Johnson had an especially important impact on African American men (Kalichman and Hunter 1992).

AIDS and the activism that arose in response to it caused sexual minorities to come out of the closet in increasing numbers. The arts world, in which gay men were overrepresented, was decimated by AIDS; many leading actors, dancers, singers, musicians, painters, and photographers died. Actors Equity, the stage actors' union, was supporting 600 members living with AIDS by 1990 (Mitchell 1990). A wave of creative works focusing on AIDS and same-sex sexuality emerged in the late 1980s and 1990s. Among them, Keith Haring's graffiti-based artwork may be the best known, but artist and author David Wojnarowicz, authors Andrew Holleran and Paul Monette, and composer John Corigliano were other important contributors, as were documentary filmmaker Marlon Riggs and author Essex Hemphill, both African American. Larry Kramer's play *The Normal Heart* and Tony Kushner's two-part *Angels in America* were highly successful, with film adaptations years later. Hollywood failed to address AIDS until 1993, when the popular film *Philadelphia*, with nongay stars Denzel Washington and Tom Hanks, was released. These works raised the public's awareness about AIDS and brought same-sex sexuality into the public discourse to a far greater extent than it had ever been before. And with the wave of coming out during these years, a greater proportion of the general public became aware of having sexual minority family members, friends, or acquaintances.

Concurrent with sexual minorities' increased visibility was a sharp increase in violent attacks on them, especially gay men. Although lesbians also experienced attacks, the greater visibility of gay men in public spaces and their association with AIDS led them to be the more frequent victims of "gay bashing," which left them severely injured if not dead. Organizations like New York City's Gay and Lesbian Anti-Violence Project and San Francisco's Community United Against Violence worked to document violent incidents and advocate for strategies to protect their communities (Greer 1986).

Beyond the AIDS Epidemic: Sexual Minorities

Concurrent with the AIDS epidemic, sexual minorities in many states continued to find themselves on the wrong side of the law. In 1982, an Atlanta gay man named Michael Hardwick was arrested in his own bedroom by a police officer serving an invalid warrant who subsequently witnessed him engaging in sex with another man. Hardwick was charged under Georgia's sodomy law, and although the charge was later dismissed, the American Civil Liberties Union filed a complaint against the state law that eventually made its way to the US Supreme Court. In a decision handed down in 1986, the court upheld Georgia's sodomy law, claiming that gay people did not have a right to privacy with respect to their sexual behavior (Barrett 2024). About half of the states still had a sodomy law at that time, and it would take another 17 years for the court to reverse its 1986 decision and strike down these laws.

156 SEXUAL AND GENDER MINORITY HISTORY

Effective treatment of AIDS with a combination of antiviral medications became available in 1996, by which time half a million Americans were stricken and more than 300,000 had died. These medications changed AIDS from a fatal disease to a manageable, chronic condition. However, the new treatment was accessed at a much higher rate by people with AIDS who were white (mainly gay men) than those who were racial minorities, likely due to stigma about AIDS and differential access to quality healthcare services in racial and ethnic minority communities. Accordingly, the main benefits of these medications, enhanced health and lower mortality, were experienced to a much greater degree in white (gay) communities (Rubin et al. 2009). That said, these communities had been devastated, with virtually an entire generation of gay men dead. Little attention was given to the impact of these losses on those who survived the epidemic until 1995, when psychologist Walt Odets published *In the Shadow of the Epidemic*. Many of these men had lost their entire support system and learned to associate intimate contact with illness and death. Meanwhile, the larger society continued to blame them for the epidemic, and traditional approaches to AIDS prevention devalued their sexuality. The next generation of gay men, who understandably wanted to get on with their lives, had little appreciation for the trauma their elders endured.

In the midst of the devastation it caused, the AIDS epidemic led to lesbians working together with gay men to a much greater extent. The San Diego Blood Sisters were lesbians who organized blood donation drives to counter a shortage in the blood supply during the early years of the epidemic. First held in 1983, their blood drives were conceived as a way to help gay men stricken with AIDS, many of whom needed transfusions to stay alive. The drives continued in Southern California for nearly a decade, and they were replicated by lesbians in many other cities (Hutchison 2015). Lesbian social worker Caitlin Ryan was the founding director of Atlanta's first AIDS service organization in 1982, and in the following year she helped to establish the National Association of People with AIDS (Ryan 2001). Lesbian psychotherapist Candy Marcum cofounded the first organization to provide AIDS services in Dallas (Wilder 2020). Many lesbians provided direct care to people with AIDS when others refused (Laird 2022), and lesbians protested alongside gay men as members of ACT UP (Roth 1998).

Increasingly, lesbians assumed leadership roles in local sexual minority organizations. One reason was the decimation of gay men by AIDS. However, the experience many lesbians had gained in the women's movement, and their feminist perspective, made them especially valuable as leaders (Faderman and Timmons 2006). Lesbians began to take on the leadership of national organizations as well. Jean O'Leary, who had been codirector of the National Gay Task Force in the late 1970s, became director of National Gay Rights Advocates, a public interest law firm. Lesbians assumed sole leadership of the Task Force beginning in 1982, with the appointment of Ginny Apuzzo. A few years later, the organization was renamed the National Gay and Lesbian Task Force, and Urvashi Vaid became the first immigrant and nonwhite lesbian director in 1989.

Beginning in the late 1980s, increasing numbers of lesbians were choosing to have children through donor insemination. Before then, lesbians were more likely to have had children before they came out, within the context of marriage to a man. Upon coming out, it was not uncommon for their husbands to divorce them and take custody of their children. Through donor insemination, lesbians were free to raise a family on their own as openly lesbian mothers (Faderman 1991). Doing so raised the visibility of sexual minorities in settings where they had previously been invisible, such as pediatrician practices, childcare settings, and schools. Eventually, gay men began to contribute to the "gayby boom," especially through foster parenting and adoption. These developments contributed to a growing desire among sexual minorities for legal sanction of their relationships.

Beginning in the 1980s, lesbians got elected to local and state government. When West Hollywood became an independent city in 1984, three of its five elected city council members were sexual minorities, among whom a lesbian, Valerie Terrigno, served as mayor. In Santa Monica, California, Judy Abdo served as mayor for three years in the early 1990s. And in 1994, Sheila Kuehl was elected to the California State Assembly for the first of three terms. This trend would expand over the next couple of decades. In 2010, Annise Parker was elected mayor of Houston, the first out lesbian to lead a major American city. Nine years later, Lori Lightfoot, an African American lesbian, was elected mayor of Chicago. An increasing number of gay men would also pursue elected office. Gerry Studds was in the closet when he was elected to the House of Representatives from Massachusetts in 1973, but after being outed in a 1983 scandal, he was re-elected six times. Massachusetts congressman Barney Frank was also closeted upon election in 1981, but after coming out in 1987 he was re-elected 13 times. In 2012, Californian Mark Takano became the first openly gay Asian American member of Congress, and the first openly gay congressmen of African and Afro-Latino descent, Mondaire

158   SEXUAL AND GENDER MINORITY HISTORY

Jones and Ritchie Torres, were elected in 2021 from New York. By 2023, three states would elect governors whose sexual minority identity was not a secret, 49 state legislatures would have at least one out sexual minority member, and nearly a dozen states would elect out sexual minorities to Congress.

By the 1990s, the liberationist goals of sexual minority activists of the early 1970s were largely abandoned, and the movement dominated by white gay men and lesbians was pursuing a narrower goal of equality within the existing social, economic, and political system. In her 1994 book, *Virtual Equality*, Urvashi Vaid argued that among many organizations working on behalf of sexual and gender minorities, the need to rely on funds from wealthy donors had skewed their objectives toward the interests of afflu- ent, white, gay men and lesbians. Same-sex marriage became one of the movement's primary objectives in the 1990s. Although this was certainly an important objective for many gay men and lesbians, it was less of a priority for sexual minorities of color, among whom racism, poverty, and violence were more pressing problems, and it was irrelevant to gender minorities, who were just beginning to demand their place in a broader movement for sexual and gender minority rights.

Beyond the AIDS Epidemic: Gender Minorities

In the early 1990s, transwoman Holly Boswell and butch lesbian Leslie Fein- berg were the first to promote *transgender* as an umbrella term for all gender minorities. Feinberg also encouraged people to reject the medical model of transsexualism and to adopt a more democratic understanding of gen- der variance in which all experiences of gender are valued equally (Stryker 2008). *Transgender* gradually gained popularity as a self-identifier. With a greater sense of shared community, gender minorities began to fight for inclusion in and respect from sexual minority communities and organiza- tions. Although some organizations started to broaden their focus to include gender minorities, it would take at least another decade for many of them to include *transgender* in their names. For example, New York City's Lesbian and Gay Community Center, which was established in 1983, changed its name in 2001 to the Lesbian, Gay, Bisexual, and Transgender Community Center, and the National Gay and Lesbian Task Force became the National LGBTQ Task Force in 2014 (the "Q" representing "queer").

Well into the 2000s, some organizations continued to place less value on the experiences and needs of gender minorities. For example, New York

State's leading lobbying organization for sexual minority issues, Empire State Pride Agenda, advocated strongly for a sexual orientation–only nondiscrimination bill in 2002, based on the belief that the state legislature would not pass a bill that included gender identity. While a sexual orientation nondiscrimination law was passed that year, after numerous unsuccessful attempts since 1971, it would take another six years for gender identity protections to be added to the state's human rights law.

By the 1990s, nearly half of the states allowed transgender people to change the sex listed on their birth certificate and the name on their driver's license, but it would take longer for protections from discrimination to be won. The International Conference on Transgender Law and Employment Policy, organized in 1992 by Phyllis Frye, a transgender lawyer and activist in Houston, accelerated advocacy for gender minority rights. Three years later, transgender activist Riki Wilchins founded the Gender Political Advocacy Coalition (GenderPAC), the first national gender minority advocacy organization. Research published by GenderPAC demonstrated that transgender people experienced a high rate of violence. The problem of deadly violence against gender minorities was introduced to the general public in 1999 by the award-winning film *Boys Don't Cry*, which dramatized the rape and murder of a young transman named Brandon Teena (Stryker 2008). In the same year, transgender activist Gwendolyn Ann Smith established November 20th as Transgender Day of Remembrance to memorialize transgender victims of deadly violence, which became an annual event. Most of these victims were, and continue to be, transwomen of color.

Reimagining Sexual and Gender Identities

Outrage over violence perpetrated against sexual minority men and women led to several members of ACT UP New York to form a new organization in 1990, Queer Nation. Their reclamation of *queer* from its decades-long use as a derogatory slur expressed defiance in the face of discrimination and violence. With its emblematic chant, "We're here! We're queer! Get used to it!" and militant, direct-action tactics, Queer Nation challenged the perceived passivity of sexual minorities as well as the assimilationist politics that had become dominant among them. Seemingly overnight, chapters opened in many cities. While most of them disbanded after several years, the organization's reclamation of *queer* had lasting impact. Concurrently, feminist scholar Teresa de Lauretis coined the term *queer theory*, although she did

160 SEXUAL AND GENDER MINORITY HISTORY

not apply it to sexual minorities. However, queer theory soon developed as a challenge to binary concepts of sexual orientation and gender as well as the supposed fundamental difference between them (Warner 1991). Consequently, some sexual minorities adopted *queer* as an umbrella term just as *transgender* was adopted by gender minorities. Over time, *queer* also became an identity for those who opposed categorization with respect to their sexual orientation and gender.

Summary

Upon accepting the Republican nomination for president in 1980, Ronald Reagan promised to welcome everyone "into a great national crusade to make America great again" (Editors of National Review 2004, p. 22). Early in his first administration, AIDS began striking down previously healthy gay men; it would soon devastate their communities and, increasingly, communities marginalized by their gender identity, race, ethnicity, and economic status. Because the epidemic struck sexual minority men first, it would always be stigmatized by its association with same-sex sexuality. The inaction of the Reagan administration toward the epidemic during its first few years showed that "everyone" did not include sexual minorities, even those who were white, male, and affluent. The Reagan administration was not alone in its failure to slow the epidemic's growth. New York City's mayor, at the epicenter of the epidemic, also failed to act. In the 1980s, same-sex sexuality was disapproved of by a majority of the public, and most state and local governments were uninterested or unwilling to do anything that might be seen as supportive of sexual minorities.

The AIDS epidemic impacted sexual and gender minorities in multiple ways. Virtually an entire generation of gay men died, including pioneers and leaders of the movement for sexual minority rights, community leaders, authors, artists, performers, lovers, family members, and friends. In the absence of government action, sexual minorities learned to take care of themselves. They devised the strategy of safer sex to reduce the risk of transmitting HIV; started community organizations with hotlines to provide information and referrals, and buddy programs to provide day-to-day support for people with AIDS; raised money for AIDS research; advocated for government action and better treatment options; and memorialized their dead. The epidemic also resulted in a lessening of the divisions between lesbians and gay men that had developed since Stonewall, and lesbians began to take leadership positions that previously were not open to them. Because many of these developments occurred within the context of white sexual minority communities, parallel developments transpired among African American, Latine, Asian American, and Native American communities The AIDS epidemic also led sexual minorities to come out of the closet in much greater numbers, which contributed to an increase in acceptance of them by the general public. The extreme marginalization of gender minorities, especially black transwomen, resulted in a disproportionate rate of AIDS illness and death among them. But by the second decade of the epidemic, a greater sense of commonality among gender minorities through the shared self-identifier *transgender* and increased visibility allowed them to press more strongly for social justice and equal rights under the law.

By the end of the 20th century, sexual minorities had long since abandoned the liberationist goals that emerged following the Stonewall Riots. Pursuing the narrower goal of equality within the existing social, political, and economic system, they were getting elected to public office in increasing numbers and advocating for nondiscrimination laws, protection from violence, and legal recognition for their relationships. At the same time, some sexual minorities were beginning to adopt queer identities that were revolutionary in their challenge to the system of fixed, binary sexual orientation that developed over the previous decades as well as the idea that sexual orientation and gender were unrelated aspects of identity.

Chapter 13
Summary and Conclusions

This counter-narrative documents the presence of sexual and gender diversity in the United States from its very beginning until the end of the 20th century and the German origins of American sexual and gender minority identities. It also describes efforts to suppress and remove sexual and gender diversity from both German and American consciousness, which helps to explain its virtual absence from the public history of both countries. Europeans imposed on North America a xenophobic moral code dating from the Middle Ages that prioritized control and restriction of sexuality. Especially through the influence of revolutionary France, much of Europe modified its views of private sexual behavior by the 19th century, but an independent United States did not. Sodomy laws carried harsh penalties, and laws against cross-dressing made same-sex sexual behavior and variant gender expression illegal.

However, Americans found ways to escape rigid gender roles and expectations for their sexuality, especially in the frontier West. Women dressed as men, became soldiers, did "men's work," and led independent lives. Men found companionship and perhaps love in all-male cowboy communities and mining, logging, and railroad camps. In the East, women's colleges opened the doors to economic independence among middle-class white women, and with it the possibility for two women to live together in a committed relationship. Although higher education and economic independence were not available to working-class and nonwhite women, there is evidence of long-lasting and passionate relationships among them as well.

At the dawn of the 20th century, before the concept of homosexuality was popularized in the United States, immigrant and working-class men who flamboyantly violated sexual and gender role expectations in New York City thought of themselves as women in male bodies and enjoyed the favors of conventionally masculine men. Middle-class men found ways to signal their sexual interest in other men more privately, without the expression of variant gender. Both of these identity constructions approximated those established earlier in Germany. By the beginning of the 1920s, many American men

Sexual and Gender Minority History. James I. Martin, Oxford University Press. © Oxford University Press (2025).
DOI: 10.1093/9780197765500.003.0013

164 SEXUAL AND GENDER MINORITY HISTORY

with same-sex desires had learned there were others like them through serving in the Army during the First World War, and women found expanded opportunities for independence in noncombat roles and on the home front. Prohibition and women's suffrage brought significant social changes during the 1920s. The Pansy Craze swept the nation in these years before the public associated variant gender expression with deviant sexuality. The beginnings of American sexual and gender minority communities appeared amid the Harlem Renaissance and the Greenwich Village bohemians in New York, in the female impersonator clubs of San Francisco, and among the silent film–era moviemakers of Hollywood, while Berlin grew to be a world capital of sexual and gender minority life. A short-lived attempt to advocate for the rights of sexual minority men occurred in Chicago, influenced by the decades-long German movement.

The Great Depression brought economic pain and social retrenchment to both countries. In the United States, opportunities for independence among women evaporated, and those who were sexual minorities became increasingly isolated. With the repeal of Prohibition, states and municipalities sought to reverse the social experimentation that flourished during the previous decade. In New York, the state alcohol control board and the city's police force worked to remove sexual and gender minorities from the public's view. In the late 1930s, a national panic about deviant sexuality was whipped up by an unscrupulous press, law enforcement agencies, and the ascendant profession of psychiatry. Sexual psychopath laws were used by police in tandem with psychiatrists, most notably in Los Angeles, to ruin the lives of sexual minority men. In Germany, the National Socialist government destroyed the country's sexual and gender minority community as part of its murderous effort to build a racially pure society.

As with the First World War but on a much larger scale, the Second World War provided numerous opportunities for American sexual and gender minorities to find others like themselves and develop a shared identity. The military accepted sexual minorities into their ranks because they needed the man- and womanpower, but it was not a welcoming institution. Witch hunts and blue discharges destroyed the lives of many sexual and gender minority men and women. Nevertheless, veterans, along with the many women and men who migrated for jobs in expanding industries, formed the beginnings of sexual and gender minority communities in New York, Los Angeles, Chicago, Washington, and San Francisco.

SUMMARY AND CONCLUSIONS   165

During the 1950s, the American public became more aware of same-sex sexuality, while government agencies defined sexual minorities as grave threats to the nation's security. A massive purge from civil service employment spread to the private sector, and police sweeps and lurid press coverage pushed them deep into the shadows of American life. However, a sense of shared identity strengthened within those shadows, particularly among middle-class sexual minority men and women. The first wave of resistance, the homophile movement, began in Los Angeles and San Francisco. Ideas generated by Mattachine, Daughters of Bilitis, and ONE Inc. percolated across the country, and the gender minority identities of transvestite and transsexual, which had originated in Germany, began to emerge.

Severe repression of sexual and gender minorities continued through the 1960s. However, resistance to police harassment and violence occurred in several cities. In most of these cases, working-class, nonwhite, and gender minority people rebelled openly, and middle-class, white, and sexual minority people supported them through orderly, direct action. A new generation of activists pushed homophile organizations to engage in public demonstrations against discrimination, especially in Washington and New York, and activists across the country made the first attempts to coordinate their efforts. In California, gender minorities identifying as transvestites and transsexuals established their first organizations.

By the end of the 1960s, sexual minorities in California had established their right to assemble and be served in bars, especially in San Francisco, where an organization of bar owners became an important pillar of the community. But in New York, home of the country's largest sexual and gender minority community, the environment continued to be extremely repressive. A routine police raid on the Stonewall Inn on a hot and humid night in June set off a riot by gender-diverse street youth that spread to middle-class sexual minorities. In the wake of three nights of rioting, youthful activists established the gay liberation movement, which soon eclipsed the older homophile movement in the imaginations of sexual and gender minorities. However, the ambitious aims and anarchism of gay liberation led to a competing, more narrowly focused movement of activist middle-class, white gay men. Lesbians formed their own liberationist organizations that aligned with the larger women's movement.

Gay men's communities in the largest American cities grew exponentially during the 1970s, while many lesbians rejected gay men's hedonism and pursued a separatist society that was free from patriarchal oppression. Sexual minority and gender minority identities grew increasingly separate from each other, as lesbians and gay men developed rigid expectations for gender role behavior among themselves and marginalized those who did not conform. Conservative Christians strongly disapproved of the increasing visibility of sexual minorities, and they initiated a national campaign to reverse it.

The AIDS epidemic began in the early 1980s, and it was stigmatized from the very beginning by its association with same-sex sexuality. Virtually an entire generation of gay men died while the federal government and most municipal governments did little to prevent it. Despite the devastation it caused, the epidemic resulted in lesbians and gay men beginning to work together on shared goals. Intense activism by gay men and lesbians, and an upsurge in coming out among them, resulted in greatly increased visibility and, gradually, better acceptance among the general public. In the 1990s, American gender minorities began to establish a sense of shared community under the umbrella identity of *transgender*, and they began their own push for rights and social justice. By the end of the 20th century, sexual minorities were starting to acknowledge their kinship with gender minorities, but many of the organizations that represented them pursued goals of particular interest to their most affluent members.

This counter-narrative began in Germany, where the first constructions of sexual and gender minority identities developed and the first movement for sexual and gender minority rights occurred. That movement was brutally crushed by the National Socialist government, and the country was subsequently destroyed by war, divided, and occupied. Postwar West Germany retained the Nazi-era sodomy law and continued prosecutions based on it. But two decades later, after years of advocacy for reform, same-sex sexual behavior among adults finally was legalized. In 1971, activist filmmaker Rosa von Praunheim instigated a new gay liberation movement with his film *It Is Not the Homosexual Who Is Perverse, But the Society in Which He Lives*. In 1979, Christopher Street (Liberation) Day marches were held for the first time in Berlin and Bremen, and by the end of the 20th century they were held in all major cities. In 2002, the German government annulled Nazi-era convictions under Paragraph 175, and 15 years later it pardoned men who were convicted after 1945 and offered reparations to those who were still living. In 2009, the European Union, of which Germany is a founding member, adopted the Charter of Fundamental Rights that prohibits discrimination on the basis of sex and sexual orientation. But as in the United States, it took longer for gender minority rights to advance. Beginning in 1980 gender minorities could change their legal gender, although it would take several decades more for the onerous conditions for doing so to be swept away.

Lessons About Social Justice, Resilience, and Diversity

This counter-narrative shows that periods of progress for sexual and gender minorities have been followed repeatedly by periods of repression and backsliding, and even—in the case of Germany—catastrophe. Recent efforts in the United States to ban books and restrict the visibility and rights of sexual and gender minorities suggest this pattern is unlikely to end. Although the cyclical recurrence of backsliding might be disheartening, it does provide an important lesson. That is, social justice for sexual and gender minorities should not be seen as an endpoint that will be reached one day when everyone will live happily ever after. Instead, it is an ideal that requires perpetual work and vigilance since efforts to reverse it will keep coming. This counter-narrative also shows that sexual and gender minorities are enormously resilient. Even though recurrent efforts to render them invisible and powerless have caused great suffering, they found ways to adapt to and ultimately surmount these efforts. Under the most repressive conditions, they found each other, developed identities and communities, and advocated for their rights and freedoms.

Because sexual and gender diversity is not limited to specific demographics, those who identify as sexual and gender minorities are extremely diverse. This counter-narrative describes how social positioning in American society is largely reproduced among sexual and gender minorities, with those who are white, male, middle class and affluent, and cisgender experiencing more opportunities for self-expression and self-determination than those who are nonwhite, female, working class and poor, and noncisgender. Nevertheless, many of the shoulders on which today's sexual and gender minorities stand are those of people who were doubly and triply marginalized. From the drag balls, rent parties, and buffet flats of Jazz Age Harlem; the pansy clubs of Bronzeville; and the butch and femme lesbian bars and female impersonator and drag performers of San Francisco to the interracial founders of ONE Inc. and Daughters of Bilitis, transgender women of Compton's Cafeteria, and multiethnic street youth of the Stonewall Inn, the history of sexual and gender minorities in the United States is a rainbow history. This is not meant to diminish the important contributions of those who were less marginalized, including organization founders and leaders from Henry Gerber to Harry Hay, Frank Kameny to Troy Perry, and Craig Rodwell to Harvey Milk. Marlene Dietrich and other boundary-pushing Hollywood stars, Bob Mizer and his beefcake photography, and Ann Bannon and her pulp novels all played important parts in the development of shared identities and the construction of sexual and gender minority communities.

Standpoint theory asserts that the experiences and perspectives of people on the margins of society are particularly important for understanding social reality, and for advancing social justice. This assertion is as applicable when considering sexual and gender minorities alone as it is for society in general. While Daughters of Bilitis was an organization of primarily middle-class, white lesbians, the original idea for it came from working-class, nonwhite lesbians. While the gay and lesbian liberation movement was propelled largely by middle-class, white gay men and lesbians, it came into being because working-class and poor, multiethnic, and gender-diverse youth started a riot. By the end of the 20th century, mainstream sexual minority organizations had begun to acknowledge the needs and experiences of gender minorities and nonwhite sexual minorities, but they continued to be dominated by the interests of middle-class, white, cisgender gay men and lesbians. This counter-narrative indicates that each sexual and gender minority subcommunity has needed its own process of self-discovery, identity development, and community building. But it also shows how sexual and gender minorities have benefited from the interaction among these subcommunities from Los Angeles to New York, and from Miami to Washington, at nearly every inflection point from the Jazz Age to the AIDS epidemic.

Self-Definition and Control of the Narrative

Erasure of sexual and gender minorities from the narrative of American history reflects, and acts to maintain, their disempowerment. Since there are no enduring stories about them, it is easy for those with greater power to define who they are. This counter-narrative shows that the state defined them as criminals, religious institutions defined them as evil, and the medical/psychiatric establishment defined them as mentally ill. It also describes how sexual and gender minorities suffered individually from the destructive impact of being defined in these ways, and how they began to define themselves more authentically as they came together and formed communities. Out of the self-knowledge formed in these communities, they were able to assert with increasing confidence and force that they were not criminal, evil, or sick, and they demanded their place in state, religious, and health-based institutions. It is telling that with an upsurge in coming out among sexual minorities during the AIDS epidemic, acceptance of them by the general public gradually increased. In other words, as the erasure of sexual minorities from the general public's consciousness decreased, they were more likely to be viewed authentically.

But since sexual and gender minorities are so diverse, there are many forms of authenticity. For example, this counter-narrative shows that sexual and gender variance are closely related, and sexual minorities generally did not define themselves separately from gender minorities until the second half of the 20th century. This divergence was led primarily by middle-class, white gay men and lesbians who hoped to retain the privileges that social status and white racial identification brought them. That is, sexuality privately expressed, out of the awareness of the public, does little to threaten the façade of "normality." Variant gender expression, which is public by definition, is a direct attack on that façade. Similar ideas contributed to the abandonment of the liberationist goals of the early 1970s in favor of the narrower goal of equality. By the end of the 20th century, sexual minorities had made considerable progress toward this goal, but their erasure from the dominant narrative of American history remained largely intact. Much like other minority populations, sexual and gender minorities would continue to struggle for decades to come for inclusion in the American story.

References

"1200 Parade in Hollywood: Crowds Line Boulevard." 1970. *The Advocate*, July 22, p. 6. Reprinted in *The Stonewall Riots: A Documentary History*, edited by Marc Stein, 2019, pp. 279–280. New York: New York University Press.

Achenbach, Joel. 2018. "'A Party That Had Lost Its Mind': In 1968, Democrats Held One of History's Most Disastrous Conventions." *Washington Post*, August 27. https://www.washingtonpost.com/news/retropolis/wp/2018/08/24/a-party-that-had-lost-its-mind-in-1968-democrats-held-one-of-historys-most-disastrous-conventions/

ACT UP-NY. 1987–2024. "ACT UP Accomplishments 1987–2012." https://actupny.com/actions/

Adely, Hannan. 2020. "NJ Schools Get Early Start on LGBTQ History Lessons, Soon to Be Required by Law." Northjersey.com, January 7. https://www.northjersey.com/story/news/education/2020/01/07/nj-schools-to-teach-lgbtq-history-months-before-new-state-law-requiring-such-lessons/2712628001/

Aldrich, Robert. 2012. *Gay Lives*. New York: Thames & Hudson.

Altman, Lawrence K. 1982. "New Homosexual Disorder Worries Officials." *New York Times*, May 11, pp. C1, 6. https://www.nytimes.com/1982/05/11/science/new-homosexual-disorder-worries-health-officials.html?searchResultPosition=1

American Civil Liberties Union. 2024. "Mapping Attacks on LGBTQ Rights in U.S. State Legislatures in 2024." https://www.aclu.org/legislative-attacks-on-lgbtq-rights-2024

American Library Association. 2024. "Banned and Challenged Books." https://www.ala.org/bbooks

AmfAR. 2024. "A Brief History of AmfAR." https://www.amfar.org/about-amfar/a-brief-history-of-amfar/

Amspacher, Shelby. 2020. "Stagecoach Mary Fields." National Postal Museum blog, April 1, Smithsonian Institution. https://postalmuseum.si.edu/stagecoach-mary-fields

"A New African American Identity: The Harlem Renaissance." n.d. National Museum of African American History and Culture, Smithsonian Institution. https://nmaahc.si.edu/explore/stories/new-african-american-identity-harlem-renaissance

"Antisemitism in the 1920s and 1930s." 2024. Abraham Lincoln Brigade Archives. https://alba-valb.org/resource/anti-semitism-in-the-1920s-and-1930s/

Arenas, Reinaldo. 1993. *Before Night Falls* (trans. Dolores M. Koch). New York: Penguin Books.

Arno, Peter. S. 1986. "The Nonprofit Sector's Response to the AIDS Epidemic: Community-Based Services in San Francisco." *American Journal of Public Health* 76 (11): pp. 1325–1330. https://doi.org/10.2105/AJPH.76.11.1325

Avildsen, John G. (dir.) 1970. *Joe*. Cannon Films.

172 REFERENCES

Baker, Peter. 2023. "43-Year Secret of Sabotage: Mission to Subvert Carter Is Revealed." *New York Times*, March 19, p. A1. https://www.nytimes.com/2023/03/18/us/politics/jimmy-carter-october-surprise-iran-hostages.html?searchResultPosition=1

Baldwin, James. 1965. "The White Man's Guilt." *Ebony* 20 (10): pp. 47–48.

Balkin, Steven. 2017. "What the Children Said." In *Detroit 1967: Origins, Impacts, Legacies*, edited by Joel Stone, pp. 213–217. Detroit: Wayne State University Press.

Balmer, Randall. 2021. *Bad Faith: Race and the Rise of the Religious Right*. Grand Rapids, MI: William B. Eerdmans Publishing Co.

Balzar, John. 1985. "The Times Poll: Tough New Government Action on AIDS Backed." *Los Angeles Times*, December 19. https://www.latimes.com/archives/la-xpm-1985-12-19-mn-30337-story.html

Barnett, Tracy. 2024. "Bowers v. Hardwick." *New Georgia Encyclopedia*, June 24. https://www.georgiaencyclopedia.org/articles/government-politics/bowers-v-hardwick/

Barrett-Fox, Rebecca. 2014. "Family Research Council." In *The Social History of the American Family: An Encyclopedia*, edited by Lawrence H. Ganong and Marilyn J. Coleman, pp. 509–510. Thousand Oaks, CA: Sage Publications. https://doi.org/10.4135/9781452286143.n217

Bayer, Robert. 1981. *Homosexuality and American Psychiatry: The Politics of Diagnosis*. New York: Bantam Books.

Beachy, Robert. 2014. *Gay Berlin: Birthplace of a Modern Identity*. New York: Alfred A. Knopf.

Beemyn, Brett G. 2006. "The Americas: From Colonial Times to the 20th Century." In *Gay Life and Culture: A World History*, edited by Robert Aldrich, pp. 146–165. New York: Universe Publishing.

Beemyn, Genny. 2014. *A Queer Capital: A History of Gay Life in Washington D.C.* New York: Routledge.

Bell, Jonathan. 2020. "Introduction: Privilege, Power, and Activism in Gay Rights Politics Since the 1970s." In *Beyond the Politics of the Closet: Gay Rights and the American State Since the 1970s*, edited by Jonathan Bell, pp. 1–15. Philadelphia: University of Pennsylvania Press.

Bellafaire, Judith A. 2005. "The Women's Army Corps: A Commemoration of World War II Service." CMH Publication 72–15. https://history.army.mil/brochures/wac/wac.html

Bello, Ada, and Carole Friedman. 1969. "Give Me Liberty Or . . ." Homophile Action Newsletter, August, pp. 1–2. Reprinted in *The Stonewall Riots: A Documentary History*, edited by Marc Stein, 2019, pp. 177–179. New York: New York University Press.

Benemann, William E. 2006. *Male-Male Intimacy in Early America: Beyond Romantic Friendships*. New York: Harrington Park Press.

Berry, Brian J. L., and Donald C. Dahmann. 1977. "Population Redistribution in the United States in the 1970s." *Population and Development Review* 3 (4): pp. 443–471. https://doi.org/10.2307/1971685

Bérubé, Allan. 2010. *Coming Out Under Fire: The History of Gay Men and Women in World War II*. 20th anniversary ed. Chapel Hill: University of North Carolina Press.

Biles, William R. 1981. "Mayor Edward J. Kelly of Chicago: Big City Boss in Depression and War." Doctoral dissertation, University of Illinois at Chicago.

Bishop, Thomas. 2022. "Digging Up the History of the Nuclear Fallout Shelter." *Smithsonian Magazine* (History), April 25. https://www.smithsonianmag.com/history/digging-up-the-history-of-the-nuclear-fallout-shelter-180979956/

Black, Jonathan. 1969. "Gay Power Hits Back." *Village Voice* 14 (42). https://www.villagevoice.com/in-the-wake-of-stonewall-gay-power-hits-back/

Blair, Thomas R. 2017. "Safe Sex in the 1970s: Community Practitioners on the Eve of AIDS." *American Journal of Public Health* 107 (6): pp. 872–879. https://doi.org/10.2105/AJPH.2017.303704

Blevins, John. 2011. "When Sodomy Leads to Martyrdom: Sex, Religion, and Politics in Historical and Contemporary Contexts in Uganda and East Africa ' *Theology and Sexuality* 17 (1): pp. 51–74. https://doi.org/10.1558/tse.v17i1.51

"Blue and 'Other than Honorable' Discharges." n.d. National Park Service, Golden Gate National Recreation Area. https://www.nps.gov/articles/000/blue-and-other-than-honorable-discharges.htm#:~:text=During%20WWII%2C%20to%20cut%20costs,African%20Americans%2C%20and%20LGBTQ%20servicemen.

Boon, L. J. 1989. "Those Damned Sodomites: Public Images of Sodomy in the Eighteenth Century Netherlands." *Journal of Homosexuality* 16 (1–2): pp. 237–248. https://doi.org/10.1300/j082v16n01_13

"Boots on the Ground." n.d. National Museum of African American History and Culture, Smithsonian Institution. https://nmaahc.si.edu/explore/stories/boots-ground

Bosh, Karin A., H. Irene Hall, Laura Eastham, Demetre C. Daskalakis, and Jonathan H. Mermin. 2021. "Estimated Annual Number of HIV Infections—1981–2019." *Morbidity and Mortality Weekly Report* 70 (June 4): pp. 801–806.

Boswell, John. 1980. *Christianity, Social Tolerance, and Homosexuality: Gay People in Western Europe from the Beginning of the Christian Era to the Fourteenth Century.* Chicago: University of Chicago Press.

Boswell, John. 1994. *Same-Sex Unions in Premodern Europe.* New York: Villard Books.

Boyd, Dick. 2010. "Before the Castro: North Beach, A Gay Mecca." Found SF: San Francisco Digital Archive. https://www.foundsf.org/index.php?title=Before_the_Castro:_North_Beach,_a_Gay_Mecca

Boyd, Nan A. 2003. *Wide Open Town: A History of Queer San Francisco to 1965.* Berkeley: University of California Press.

Bradner, Liesl. 2019. "How Alcohol Still Seeped into Los Angeles During Prohibition." Public Media Group of Southern California, October 30. https://www.kcet.org/shows/lost-la/how-alcohol-still-seeped-into-los-angeles-during-prohibition

Brand, Adolf. 1925/1991. "What We Want." In *Homosexuality and Male Bonding in Pre-Nazi Germany*, edited by Harry Oosterhuis and Hubert Kennedy (trans. Hubert Kennedy), pp. 155–166. New York: Routledge.

Brand, Adolf. 1931/1991. "Political Criminals: A Word About the Röhm Case." In *Homosexuality and Male Bonding in Pre-Nazi Germany*, edited by Harry Oosterhuis and Hubert Kennedy (trans. Hubert Kennedy), pp. 235–239. New York: Routledge.

Braverman, Paula, and Laura Gottlieb. 2014. "The Social Determinants of Health: It's Time to Consider the Causes of the Causes." *Public Health Reports* 129 (Suppl 2): pp. 19–31.

Brecht, Bertolt, and Kurt Weill. 1928. *Threepenny Opera.*

174 REFERENCES

Brecht, Bertolt, and Kurt Weill. 1930. *The Rise and Fall of the City of Mahagonny*.

Bronski, Michael. 2011. *A Queer History of the United States*. Boston: Beacon Press.

Bronski, Michael, Kit Heyam, and Valerie Traub (Eds.). 2023. *The LGBTQ+ History Book*. New York: DK Publishing.

Brown, Daniel J. 2021. *Facing the Mountain: A True Story of Japanese American Heroes in World War II*. New York: Viking.

Burnie, Melanie. 2019. "World War II Veteran Calls Honorable Discharge from Army to Correct an 'Injustice' Nearly 75 Years Later 'a Miracle'." *Philadelphia Inquirer*, June 5. https://www.inquirer.com/news/philadelphia/nelson-henry-veteran-army-blue-discharge-philadelphia-20190604.html#:~:text=World%20War%20II%20vete ran%20Nelson,the%20color%20of%20his%20skin

Burns, Stewart. 1997. *Daybreak of Freedom: The Montgomery Bus Boycott*. Durham: University of North Carolina Press.

Campi, Alicia. 2005. "From Refugees to Americans: Thirty Years of Vietnamese Immigration to the United States" [Policy Brief]. Immigration Policy Center, American Immigration Law Foundation. https://www.americanimmigrationcouncil.org/research/refugees-americans-thirty-years-vietnamese-immigration-united-states

Capers, Bennett. 2008. "Cross Dressing and the Criminal." *Yale Journal of Law & the Humanities* 20 (1): pp. 1–30. https://doi.org/10.1300/J082v16n01_13

Carden, Michael. 2014. *Sodomy: A History of a Christian Biblical Myth*. New York: Routledge.

Carter, David. 2004. *Stonewall: The Riots That Sparked the Gay Revolution*. New York: St. Martin's Griffin.

Chafe, William H. 1981. *Civilities and Civil Rights: Greensboro, North Carolina, and the Black Struggle for Freedom*. New York: Oxford University Press.

Charles, Douglas M. 2015. *Hoover's War on Gays: Exposing the FBI's 'Sex Deviates' Program*. Lawrence: University Press of Kansas.

Chauncey, George. 1994. *Gay New York: Gender, Urban Culture, and the Making of the Gay Male World, 1890–1940*. New York: Basic Books.

Chicago LGBT Hall of Fame. 2007. "David Blatt and David Moore." https://chicagolgbthalloffame.org/blatt-david/

Chicago LGBT Hall of Fame. 2009. "AIDS Foundation of Chicago." https://chicagolgbthalloffame.org/aids-foundation-of-chicago/

Chou, Wah-Shan. 2000. *Tongzhi: Politics of Same-Sex Eroticism in Chinese Societies*. Binghamton, NY: Haworth Press.

Clarke, Lige, and Jack Nichols. 1969. "Pampered Perverts." *Screw*, July 25. Reprinted in *The Stonewall Riots: A Documentary History*, edited by Marc Stein, 2019, pp. 166–169. New York: New York University Press.

Cohan, Stephan L. 2008. *The Gay Liberation Youth Movement in New York*. New York: Taylor & Francis.

Coleman, Sarah R. 2024. "Immigration After 1965." Organization of American Historians. https://www.oah.org/tah/immigration-history/immigration-post-1965/

Collins, Patricia H. 1997. "Comment on Hekman's 'Truth and Method: Feminist Standpoint Theory Revisited': Where's the Power?" *Signs* 22 (2): pp. 375–381. https://doi.org/10.1086/495162

"Congressional Gold Medal to the Tuskegee Airmen." 2006. Public Law 109-213, *Congressional Record* 152. https://www.govinfo.gov/content/pkg/PLAW-109publ213/html/PLAW-109publ213.htm

Consulting GPA. 2023. "Los Angeles Citywide Historic Context Statement: Lesbian, Gay, Bisexual, and Transgender (LGBT) Context Statement." Survey LA: Los Angeles Historic Resources Survey. Prepared for City of Los Angeles Department of City Planning, Office of Historic Resources, September 2014, Revised February 2023. https://planning.lacity.org/odocument/23b499c0-1f2e-49cc-842e-8744c439acf6/LosAngeles_LGBT_HistoricContext.pdf

Cook, Christopher C. H. 2021. "The Causes of Human Sexual Orientation." *Theology & Sexuality* 27 (1): pp. 1–19. https://doi.org/10.1080/13558358.2020.1813541

Crafts, Nicholas, and Peter Fearon. 2013. "Depression and Recovery in the 1930s: An Overview." In *The Great Depression of the 1930s: Lessons for Today*, edited by Nicholas Crafts and Peter Fearon, pp. 1–44. New York: Oxford University Press.

Crenshaw, Kimberlé. 1989. "Demarginalizing the Intersection of Race and Sex: A Black Feminist Critique of Antidiscrimination Doctrine, Feminist Theory and Antiracist Politics." *University of Chicago Legal Forum* 140: pp. 139–167.

Crompton, Louis. 1981. "The Myth of Lesbian Impunity Capital Laws from 1270 to 1791." *Journal of Homosexuality* 6 (1–2): pp. 11–25. https://doi.org/10.1300/J082v06n01_03

Daniels, Roger. 2011. *Asian America: Chinese and Japanese in the United States Since 1850*. Seattle: University of Washington Press.

Del Castillo, Richard Griswold. 2000. "The Los Angeles 'Zoot Suit Riots' Revisited: Mexican and Latin American Perspectives." *Mexican Studies/Estudios Mexicanos* 16 (2): pp. 367–392.

De La Croix, St. Sukie. 2012. *Chicago Whispers: A History of LGBT Chicago Before Stonewall*. Madison: University of Wisconsin Press.

D'Emilio, John. 1983. *Sexual Politics, Sexual Communities: The Making of a Homosexual Minority in the United States, 1940–1970*. Chicago: University of Chicago Press.

D'Emilio, John. 2023. "Troubles I've Seen: Rustin and the Price of Being Gay." In *Bayard Rustin: A Legacy of Protest and Politics*, edited by Michael G. Long, pp. 131–143. New York: New York University Press.

Devore, Aaron, and Nicholas Matte. 2007. "Building a Better World for Transpeople: Reed Erickson and the Erickson Educational Foundation." *International Journal of Transgenderism* 10 (1): pp. 47–68.

Dose, Ralf. 2014. *Magnus Hirschfeld: The Origins of the Gay Liberation Movement* (trans. Edward H. Willis). New York: Monthly Review Press.

Downey, H. R. 2017. "Removing Homosexuality from Sodom: Contextualizing Genesis 19 with Other Biblical Rape Narratives." MHum thesis, Wright State University.

Drescher, Jack. 2013. "Controversies in Gender Diagnoses." *LGBT Health* 1 (1): pp. 10–14. https://doi.org/10.1089/lgbt.2013.1500

Duberman, Martin. 1993. *Stonewall*. New York: Dutton.

Editors of National Review. 2004. *Tear Down This Wall: The Reagan Revolution—A National Review History*. New York: Continuum International Publishing Group.

Edmonds, Michael (Ed.). 2014. *Risking Everything: A Freedom Summer Reader*. Madison: Wisconsin Historical Society Press.

176   REFERENCES

Ehrhardt, Anke A. 2007. "John Money, PhD." *Journal of Sex Research* 44 (3): pp. 223–224. https://doi.org/10.1080/00224490701580741

Eig, Jonathan. 2023. "Rustin and King: Stony the Road They Trod." In *Bayard Rustin: A Legacy of Protest and Politics*, edited by Michael G. Long, pp. 75–86. New York: New York University Press.

Elk Grove Historical Society. n.d. "Stagecoach Driver Charley Parkhurst." https://elkgrovehistoricalsociety.com/history-stagecoach-driver-charley-parkhurst/

"Entrapment Attacked." 1966. *The Ladder* 10 (9): pp. 12–13. https://documents.alexanderstreet.com/d/1003347905

Epstein, Catherine. 2015. *Nazi Germany: Confronting the Myths*. Chichester, UK: John Wiley & Sons.

Estrada, Josue. 2006. "Brown Beret Chapters 1969–1972." Mapping American Social Movements Project, Civil Rights and Labor History Consortium, University of Washington. https://depts.washington.edu/moves/brown_beret_map.shtml

Eu, March Fong. 1978. "California Voters Pamphlet: General Election November 7, 1978." Secretary of State, State of California. https://web.archive.org/web/20060818145437/http://library.uchastings.edu/ballot_pdf/1978g.pdf

Faderman, Lillian. 1991. *Odd Girls and Twilight Lovers: A History of Lesbian Life in 20th Century America*. New York: Columbia University Press.

Faderman, Lillian. 1999. *To Believe in Women: What Lesbians Have Done for America—A History*. Boston: Houghton Mifflin Co.

Faderman, Lillian. 2018. *Harvey Milk: His Lives and Death*. New Haven, CT: Yale University Press.

Faderman, Lillian, and Stuart Timmons. 2006. *Gay L.A.: A History of Sexual Outlaws, Power Politics, and Lipstick Lesbians*. New York: Basic Books.

Fausto-Sterling, Anne. 2000. *Sexing the Body: Gender Politics and the Construction of Sexuality*. New York: Basic Books.

Fejes, Fred. 2008. *Gay Rights and Moral Panic: The Origins of America's Debate on Homosexuality*. New York: Palgrave Macmillan.

FitzGerald, Frances. 1986. *Cities on a Hill: A Journey Through Contemporary American Cultures*. New York: Simon & Schuster.

Flegenheimer, Matt, and Rosa Goldensohn. 2022. "The Secrets Ed Koch Carried." *New York Times*, May 7. https://www.nytimes.com/2022/05/07/nyregion/ed-koch-gay-secrets.html?searchResultPosition=1

Folsom, Ed, and Kenneth M. Price. n.d. "Walt Whitman." In *The Walt Whitman Archive*, edited by Matt Cohen, Ed Folsom, and Kenneth M. Price. https://whitmanarchive.org/whitmans-life/biography

Forrest, Katherine V. 2005. *Lesbian Pulp Fiction: The Sexually Intrepid World of Lesbian Paperback Novels, 1950–1965*. San Francisco: Cleis Press.

Fox, Cybelle. 2016. "Unauthorized Welfare: The Origins of Immigrant Status Restrictions in American Social Policy." *Journal of American History* 102 (4): pp. 1051–1074. https://doi.org/10.1093/jahist/jav758

Francis, Donald P. 2012. "Deadly AIDS Policy Failure by the Highest Levels of the US Government: A Personal Look Back 30 Years Later for Lessons to Respond Better to Future Epidemics." *Journal of Public Health Policy* 33 (3): pp. 290–300.

Frank, Gillian. 2013. "The Civil Rights of Parents: Race and Conservative Politics in Anita Bryant's Campaign Against Gay Rights in 1970s Florida." *Journal of the History of Sexuality* 22 (1): pp. 126–160. https://doi.org/10.7560/JHS22106

Frey, William H. 1979. "Central City White Flight: Racial and Nonracial Causes." *American Sociological Review* 44 (3): pp. 425–448. https://doi.org/10.2307/2094885

Friedländer, Benedict. 1907/1991. "Memoir for the Friends and Contributors of the Scientific Humanitarian Committee in the Name of the Secession of the Scientific Humanitarian Committee." In *Homosexuality and Male Bonding in Pre-Nazi Germany*, edited by Harry Oosterhuis and Hubert Kennedy (trans. Hubert Kennedy), pp. 71–84. New York: Routledge.

Friedman, Samuel R., Jo L. Sotheran, Abu Abdel-Quader, Beny J. Primm, Don C. Des Jarlais, Paula Kleinman, Conrad Mauge, Douglas C. Goldsmith, Wafaa El-Sadr, and Robert Maslansky. 1987. "The AIDS Epidemic among Blacks and Hispanics." *Milbank Quarterly* 65 (Suppl 2, Part 2): pp. 455–499.

Gabriel, Trip. 2024. "David Mixner, Fierce Fighter for Gay Rights, Is Dead at 77." *New York Times*, March 12. https://www.nytimes.com/2024/03/12/us/politics/david-mixner-dead.html?searchResultPosition=1

Gallo, Marcia M. 2007. *Different Daughters: A History of the Daughters of Bilitis and the Rise of the Lesbian Rights Movement*. Emeryville, CA: Seal Press.

Garrido, German. 2021. "The World in Question: A Cosmopolitical Approach to Gay/Homosexual Liberation Movements in/and the 'Third World' (from Argentina to the United States)." *GLQ: A Journal of Lesbian and Gay Studies* 27 (3): pp. 379–406.

"Gays Riot: Why? Why Not?" 1979. *Bay Area Reporter* 9 (11), May 24: pp. 1–2. https://archive.org/details/BAR_19790524/mode/2up

Gerassi, John. 1966. *The Boys of Boise: Furor, Vice and Folly in an American City*. New York: Macmillan.

Gerber, Henry. 1962. "The Society for Human Rights-1925." *ONE Magazine* 10 (9): pp. 5–11.

Gertten, Magnus (dir.). 2023. *Nelly & Nadine*. Wolfe Video.

Ghaziani, Amin. 2005. "Breakthrough: The 1979 National March." *Gay and Lesbian Review Worldwide* 12 (2): pp. 31–32.

Gierach, Ryan. 2003. *West Hollywood*. Charleston, SC: Arcadia Publishing.

Gill, Thomas P. 1950. "The State Board of Equalization and Liquor Control." *California Law Review* 38 (5): pp. 875–896.

Gnuse, Robert K. 2015. "Seven Gay Texts: Biblical Passages Used to Condemn Homosexuality." *Biblical Theology Bulletin: Journal of Bible and Culture* 45 (2): pp. 68–87. https://doi.org/10.1177/0146107915577097

Gossett, Che, and Eva Hayward. 2020. "Trans in a Time of HIV/AIDS." *Transgender Studies Quarterly* 7 (4): pp. 527–553.

REFERENCES

Gowing, Laura. 2018. "LGBT Histories and the Politics of Identity." In *History, Memory, and Public Life: The Past in the Present*, edited by Anna Maerker, Simon Sleight, and Adam Sutcliffe, pp. 294–316. London: Routledge.

Greenwood, Len. 2017. "Trail of Tears from Mississippi Walked by Our Ancestors." Choctaw Nation of Oklahoma School of Choctaw Language. https://choctawschool. com/home-side-menu/history/trail-of-tears-from-mississippi-walked-by-our-ancestors.aspx

Greer, William R. 1986. "Violence Against Homosexuals Rising, Groups Seeking Wider Protection Say." *New York Times*, November 23, p. A36. https://www.nytimes. com/1986/11/23/us/violence-against-homosexuals-rising-groups-seeking-wider-protection-say.html?searchResultPosition=1

Grünzweig, Walter. 1995. "Whitman in the German-Speaking Countries." In *Walt Whitman and the World*, edited by Ed Folsom and Gay W. Allen, pp. 160–230. Iowa City: University of Iowa Press.

Hansen, Karen V. 1995. "'No Kisses Is Like Youres': An Erotic Friendship Between Two African-American Women During the Mid-Nineteenth Century." *Gender & History* 7 (2): pp. 153–182. https://doi.org/10.1111/j.1468-0424.1995.tb00019.x

Harding, Sandra. 1997. "Comment on Hekman's 'Truth and Method: Feminist Standpoint Theory Revisited': Whose Standpoint Needs the Regimes of Truth and Reality?" *Signs* 22 (2): pp. 382–391. https://doi.org/10.1086/495163

Hartsock, Nancy C. M. 1983. *Money, Sex, and Power: Toward a Feminist Historical Materialism*. New York: Longman.

Harvey, A. D. 1978. "Prosecutions for Sodomy in England at the Beginning of the Nineteenth Century." *Historical Journal* 21 (4): pp. 939–948. https://doi.org/10.1017/S0018246X00000753

Heger, Heinz. 1972. *The Men with the Pink Triangle*. Hamburg, Germany: Merlin-Verlag.

Hessisches Ministerium für Soziales und Integration. n.d. *Shameless: Lesbian Women and Gay Men in Hesse from 1945 to 1985* (trans. N. Y. Molitor). Exhibition documentation about the research project Revisiting the Lives of the Victims of Former Section 175 of the German Criminal Code in Hesse.

Hofman, Elwin. 2020. "The End of Sodomy: Law, Prosecution Patterns, and the Evanescent Will to Knowledge in Belgium, France, and the Netherlands, 1770–1830." *Journal of Social History* 54 (2): pp. 480–502. https://doi.org/10.1093/jsh/shz068

Holtfrerich, Carl L. 1986. *The German Inflation 1914–1923: Causes and Effects in International Perspective* (trans. Theo Balderston). New York: Walter De Gruyter.

Hooker, Evelyn. 1957. "The Adjustment of the Male Overt Homosexual." *Journal of Projective Techniques* 21 (1): pp. 18–31. https://doi.org/10.1080/08853126.1957.10380742

Hoover, J. Edgar. 1937. "War on the Sex Criminal!" *New York Herald Tribune*, September 26, pp. SM2, 23.

Howard, Clayton. 2020. "Gay and Conservative: An Early History of the Log Cabin Republicans." In *Beyond the Politics of the Closet: Gay Rights and the American State since the 1970s*, edited by Jonathan Bell, pp. 141–164. Philadelphia: University of Pennsylvania Press.

REFERENCES   179

Hurewitz, Daniel. 1997. *Stepping Out: Nine Walks Through New York City's Gay and Lesbian Past*. New York: Henry Holt and Co.

Hurewitz, Daniel. 2007. *Bohemian Los Angeles and the Making of Modern Politics*. Berkeley: University of California Press.

Hutchison, Beth. 2015. "Lesbian Blood Drives as Community-Building Activism in the 1980s." *Journal of Lesbian Studies* 19 (1): pp. 117–128. https://doi.org/10.1080/10894160.2015.963079

Hyde, Janet S., Rebecca S. Bigler, Daphna Joel, Charlotte C. Tate, and Sari M. van Anders. 2019. "The Future of Sex and Gender in Psychology: Five Challenges to the Gender Binary." *American Psychologist* 74 (2): pp. 171–193. https://doi.org/10.1037/amp0000307

Jackson, Don. 1969. "Reflections on the N.Y. Riots." *Los Angeles Advocate* 11 (October): p. 33. Reprinted in *The Stonewall Riots: A Documentary History*, edited by Marc Stein, 2019, pp. 182–184. New York: New York University Press.

Jacobs, Sue-Ellen, Wesley Thomas, and Sabine Lang. 1997. "Introduction." In *Two-Spirit People: Native American Gender Identity, Sexuality, and Spirituality*, edited by Sue-Ellen Jacobs, Wesley Thomas, and Sabine Lang, pp. 1–19. Urbana: University of Illinois Press.

Jeffries, Hasan Kwame. 2018. "April 2018: The Assassination of Dr. Martin Luther King, Jr." *Origins: Current Events in Historical Perspective* 11 (7): pp. 1–6.

Jelavich, Peter. 1993. *Berlin Cabaret*. Cambridge, MA: Harvard University Press.

Jenkins, Keith. 2003. *Rethinking History*. 2nd ed. New York: Routledge.

John F. Kennedy Presidential Library and Museum. n.d. "The Modern Civil Rights Movement and the Kennedy Administration." https://www.jfklibrary.org/learn/about-jfk/jfk-in-history/civil-rights-movement

Johnson, David K. 2004. *The Lavender Scare: The Cold War Persecution of Gays and Lesbians in the Federal Government*. Chicago: University of Chicago Press.

Johnson, David K. 2019. *Buying Gay: How Physique Entrepreneurs Sparked a Movement*. New York: Columbia University Press.

Johnson, Emily S. 2019. *This Is Our Message: Women's Leadership in the New Christian Right*. New York: Oxford University Press.

Johnson, Serena. 2020. "Sodomy Laws in France: How the 1791 French Penal Code Decriminalized Sodomy Without the Will of the People." Young Historians Conference, April 27, Portland State University. https://archives.pdx.edu/ds/psu/32888

Johnson, Thomas A. 1966. "3 Deviates Invite Exclusion by Bars." *New York Times*, April 22, p. 43. https://www.nytimes.com/1966/04/22/archives/3-deviates-invite-exclusion-by-bars-but-they-visit-four-before.html?searchResultPosition=1

Johnson, Troy. 2019. "We Hold the Rock: The Alcatraz Indian Occupation." National Park Service. https://www.nps.gov/alca/learn/historyculture/we-hold-the-rock.htm

Kalichman, Seth C., and Tricia L. Hunter. 1992. "The Disclosure of Celebrity HIV Infection: Its Effects on Public Attitudes." *American Journal of Public Health* 82 (10): pp. 1374–1376. https://doi.org/10.2105/AJPH.82.10.1374

180 REFERENCES

Kim, Woojin. 2022. "Television and American Consumerism." *Journal of Public Economics* 208 (April): pp. 1–17. https://doi.org/10.1016/j.jpubeco.2022.104609

Kolata, Gina. 1987. "15% of People with AIDS Survive 5 Years." *New York Times*, November 19. https://archive.nytimes.com/www.nytimes.com/library/national/science/aids/111987sci-aids-2.html

Kolb, Eberhard. 2005. *The Weimar Republic* (trans. P. S. Falla and R. J. Park). 2nd ed. New York: Routledge.

Kramer, Larry. 1983. "1,112 and Counting." *New York Native*, March 14–27, pp. 1, 18–19, 21–23.

Lachman, Linda. 1974. "Meetinghouse Receives $52,371." *Gay Community News* 2 (26), December 21: pp. 1–2. https://repository.library.northeastern.edu/files/neu:m046gk586

Laird, Cynthia. 2022. "SF Was at Epicenter of Lesbians Helping Gay Men During AIDS Crisis." *Bay Area Reporter*, November 16. https://www.ebar.com/story.php?ch=news&sc=news&id=320607

Lang, Fritz (dir.). 1927. *Metropolis*. Universum Film.

Lang, Fritz (dir.). 1931. *M*. Nero-Film AG.

Lang, Sabine. 2016. "Native American Men-Women, Lesbians, Two-Spirits: Contemporary and Historical Perspectives." *Journal of Lesbian Studies* 20 (3–4): pp. 299–323. https://doi.org/10.1080/10894160.2016.1148966

Lareau, Alan. 2005. "Lavender Songs: Undermining Gender in Weimar Cabaret and Beyond." *Popular Music and Society* 28 (1): pp. 15–33. https://doi.org/10.1080/0300776042000300954

Lave, Tamara R. 2009. "Only Yesterday: The Rise and Fall of Twentieth Century Sexual Psychopath Laws." *Louisiana Law Review* 69 (3): pp. 549–591.

Layton, Geoff. 2015. *Democracy and Dictatorships in Germany 1919–1963*. 2nd ed. London: Hodder Education.

Leck, Ralph M. 2016. *Vita Sexualis: Karl Ulrichs and the Origins of Sexual Science*. Urbana: University of Illinois Press.

Legg, W. Dorr. 1994. *Homophile Studies in Theory and Practice*. San Francisco: ONE Institute Press and GLB Publishers.

Leidinger, Christiane. 2004. "'Anna Rüling': A Problematic Foremother of Lesbian Herstory." *Journal of the History of Sexuality* 13 (4): pp. 477–499. https://doi.org/10.1353/sex.2005.0030

Leng, Kirsten. 2013. "Sex, Science, and Fin-de-Siècle Feminism: Johanna Elberskirchen Interprets the Laws of Life." *Journal of Women's History* 25 (3): pp. 38–61. https://doi.org/10.1353/jowh.2013.0034

Leng, Kirsten. 2014. "Permutations of the Third Sex: Sexology, Subjectivity, and Antimaternalist Feminism at the Turn of the Twentieth Century." *Signs: Journal of Women and Culture in Society* 40 (1): pp. 227–254. https://doi.org/10.1086/676899

Lewis, John. 1998. *Walking with the Wind: A Memoir of the Movement*. New York: Simon and Schuster.

Lewy, Guenter. 2016. *Harmful and Undesirable: Book Censorship in Nazi Germany*. New York: Oxford University Press.

Lichtblau, Eric. 1989. "A Savvy 'Free Agent for God': The Rev. Louis Sheldon Is Part Fiery Preacher, Part Cool-Headed Lobbyist. Opponents Question His Support but Don't

Deny His Political Clout." *Los Angeles Times*, November 26. https://www.latimes.com/archives/la-xpm-1989-11-26-mn-348-story.html

Lo, Malinda. 2021. "The Women of Color Behind the Daughters of Bilitis." Blog, June 15. https://www.malindalo.com/blog/2021/6/15/daughters-of-bilitis

Loftin, Craig M. 2007. "Unacceptable Mannerisms: Gender Anxieties, Homosexual Activism, and Swish in the United States." *Journal of Social History* 40 (3): pp. 577–596. https://doi.org/10.1353/jsh.2007.0053

Logan, John R., Weiwei Zhang, and Deirdre Oakley. 2017. "Court Orders, White Flight, and School Desegregation, 1970–2010." *Social Forces* 95 (3): pp. 1049–1075. https://doi.org/10.1093/sf/sow104

Lorde, Audre. 1979. "When Will the Ignorance End? Keynote Speech at National Conference of 3rd World Lesbians and Gay Men." *Off Our Backs* 9 (10): pp. 8–9.

Lorde, Audre. 1984. *Sister Outsider*. Berkeley, CA: Crossing Press.

Loughery, John. 1998. *The Other Side of Silence: Men's Lives and Gay Identities: A Twentieth Century History*. New York: Henry Holt and Co.

Maeda, Daryl Joji. 2016. "The Asian American Movement." *Oxford Research Encyclopedias, American History*. https://doi.org/10.1093/acrefore/9780199329175.013.21

Magee, Sharon S. 2003. "American Indians and the War Effort." In *Arizona Goes to War: The Home Front and the Front Lines During World War II*, edited by Brad Melton and Dean Smith, pp. 71–87. Tucson: University of Arizona Press.

Marhoefer, Laurie. 2015. *Sex and the Weimar Republic: German Homosexual Emancipation and the Rise of the Nazis*. Toronto: University of Toronto Press.

Marhoefer, Laurie. 2016. "Lesbianism, Transvestism, and the Nazi State: A Microhistory of a Gestapo Investigation, 1939–1943." *American Historical Review* 121 (4): pp. 1167–1195. https://doi.org/10.1093/ahr/121.4.1167

Marotta, Toby. 2004. "Rodwell, Craig." In *Encyclopedia of Lesbian, Gay, Bisexual, and Transgender History in America* (Vol. 3), edited by Marc Stein, pp. 44–46. New York: Charles Scribner's Sons.

Martin, Kali. 2020. "It's Your War Too: Women in World War II." National World War II Museum, March 13. https://www.nationalww2museum.org/war/articles/its-your-war-too-women-world-war-ii

Martin, Katrina. 2016. "New Acquisitions Roundup—Celebrating the 60th Anniversary of The Ladder: A Lesbian Review." The Devil's Tale: Dispatches from the David M. Rubenstein Rare Book & Manuscript Library, Duke University, November 14. https://blogs.library.duke.edu/rubenstein/2016/11/14/new-acquisitions-roundup-celebrating-60th-anniversary-ladder-lesbian-review/

Matysik, Tracie. 2004. "In the Name of the Law: The 'Female Homosexual' and the Criminal Code in Fin de Siècle Germany." *Journal of the History of Sexuality* 13 (1): pp. 26–48. https://doi.org/10.1353/sex.2004.0051

McFadden, Robert D. 2018. "Dick Leitsch, Whose 'Sip In' Was a Gay Rights Milestone, Dies at 83." *New York Times*, June 23, p. A19. https://www.nytimes.com/2018/06/22/obituaries/dick-leitsch-dead.html?searchResultPosition=1

McGirr, Lisa. 2016. *The War on Alcohol: Prohibition and the Rise of the American State*. New York: W. W. Norton.

McWilliams, Carey. 1949. *California: The Great Exception*. Berkeley: University of California Press.

182 REFERENCES

Members of the Gay and Lesbian Historical Society of Northern California. 1998. "M⁻F Transgender Activism in the Tenderloin and Beyond, 1966–1975." *GLQ: A Journal of Lesbian and Gay Issues* 4 (2): pp. 349–372. https://dor.org/10.1215/10642684-4-2-349

Milk, Harvey. 1978. "That's What America Is." Speech delivered at the San Francisco Gay Freedom Day Parade, June 28. https://www.oneinstitute.org/wp-content/uploads/2015/05/1978_harvey_milk_gay_freedom_day_speech.pdf

Mississippi Band of Choctaw Indians. 2016. "History." https://www.choctaw.org/aboutmbci/history/index.html

Mitchell, Sean. 1990. "AIDS and the Arts: Behind the Scenes of a Tragedy." *Los Angeles Times*, December 26. https://www.latimes.com/archives/la-xpm-1990-12-26-ca-1044-story.html

Money, John. 1955. "Hermaphroditism, Gender and Precocity in Hyperadrenocorticism: Psychologic Findings." *Bulletin of Johns Hopkins Hospital* 96: pp. 253–264.

Money, John. 1985. "The Conceptual Neutering of Gender and the Criminalization of Sex." *Archives of Sexual Behavior* 14 (3): pp. 279–290. https://doi.org/10.1007/BF01542110

Morgan, Iwan. 2018. "Introduction: Hollywood and the Great Depression." In *Hollywood and the Great Depression: American Film, Politics, and Society in the 1930s*, edited by Iwan Morgan and Philip J. Davies, pp. 1–26. Edinburgh, UK: Edinburgh University Press.

Morris, Bonnie J. 1999. *Eden Built by Eves: The Culture of Women's Music Festivals*. Los Angeles: Alyson Books.

Morsch, Günter, and Astrid Ley (Eds.). 2011. *Sachsenhausen Concentration Camp 1936–1945: Events and Developments*. Berlin: Metropol Verlag.

Mumford, Kevin. 2016. *Not Straight, Not White: Black Gay Men from the March on Washington to the AIDS Crisis*. Chapel Hill: University of North Carolina Press.

Muñoz, Jr., Carlos. 2018. "The Chicano Movement: Mexican American History and the Struggle for Equality." *Perspectives on Global Development and Technology* 17 (1–2): pp. 31–52. https://doi.org/10.1163/15691497-12341465

Munslow, Alun. 2006. *Deconstructing History*. 2nd ed. New York: Routledge.

National AIDS Memorial. n.d. "The History of the Quilt." https://www.aidsmemorial.org/quilt-history

National Coalition of Black Gays. n.d. Brochure downloaded from University of Florida Digital Collections. https://original-ufdc.uflib.ufl.edu/AA00001470/00001/1j

National Organization for Women. 1970. "NOW (National Organization for Women) Bill of Rights." In *Sisterhood Is Powerful: An Anthology of Writings from the Women's Liberation Movement*, edited by Robin Morgan, p. 576. New York: Vintage Books.

National Park Service. 2021. "The Little Rock Nine: Little Rock High School National Historic Site." https://www.nps.gov/people/the-little-rock-nine.htm

Newton, Alistair. 2012. "Children of a Lesser Holocaust." *Gay & Lesbian Review Worldwide* 19 (1): pp. 18–20.

New York City AIDS Memorial. 2011–2024. "HIV/AIDS Timeline." https://www.nycaidsmemorial.org/timeline

Office of the Historian. n.d. "American Isolationism in the 1930s." US Department of State. https://history.state.gov/milestones/1937-1945/american-isolationism

O'Leary, Jean, and Bruce Voeller. 1977. "Anita Bryant's Crusade." *New York Times*, June 7, p. 35. https://www.nytimes.com/1977/06/07/archives/anita-bryants-crusade.html?searchResultPosition=1

Oosterhuis, Harry. 2012. "Sexual Modernity in the Works of Richard von Krafft-Ebing and Albert Moll." *Medical History* 56 (2): pp. 133–155. https://doi.org/10.1017/mdh.2011.30

"Operation Alert, Los Angeles, 1957." 2013. Cold War: LA. http://www.coldwarla.com/operation-alert.html

Orwell, George. 1949. *1984*. New York: Harcourt, Brace and Co.

Painter, George. 1991–2005. "The Sensibilities of Our Forefathers: The History of Sodomy Laws in the United States." Sodomy Laws. http://www.glapn.org/sodomylaws/sensibilities/introduction.htm

Pear, Robert. 1985. "AIDS Blood Test to Be Available in 2 to 6 Weeks." *New York Times*, March 3. https://archive.nytimes.com/www.nytimes.com/library/national/science/aids/030385sci-aids.html

Peck, James. 1962. *Freedom Ride*. New York: Simon and Schuster.

Perry, David G., Rachel E. Pauletti, and Patrick J. Cooper. 2019. "Gender Identity in Childhood: A Review of the Literature." *International Journal of Behavioral Development* 43 (4): pp. 289–304. https://doi.org/10.1177/0165025418811129

Peters, Gerhard, and John T. Woolley. n.d. "Sacramento California Remarks at a 'Get Out the Vote Rally.'" American Presidency Project. https://www.presidency.ucsb.edu/node/243861

Petrick, Rachel A. 2019. "Blue-Ticket Discharge: A Color That Has Stained the Lives of WWII-Era Veterans for Over 75 Years." Mason Veterans and Servicemembers Legal Clinic blog, May 17, Antonin Scalia Law School, George Mason University. https://mvets.law.gmu.edu/2019/05/17/the-blue-ticket-discharge-a-color-that-has-stained-the-lives-of-wwii-era-veterans-for-over-75-years/#_edn8

Pettis, Ruth M. 2005. "Roellig, Ruth Margarete (1878–1969)." GLBTQ Archives. http://www.glbtqarchive.com/literature/roellig_rm_L.pdf

PFLAG. 2024. "Our Story." https://pflag.org/our-story/

Plant, Richard. 1986. *The Pink Triangle*. New York: Henry Holt and Co.

"Portraits in Oversight: Joe McCarthy's Oversight Abuses." 2024. Carl Levin Center for Oversight and Democracy, Wayne State University Law School. https://www.levin-center.org/joe-mccarthys-oversight-abuses/

President's Commission on the Status of Women. 1963. *American Women: Report of the President's Commission on the Status of Women*. Washington, DC: US Government Printing Office. https://www.dol.gov/sites/dolgov/files/WB/media/American-Women-Report.pdf

Pretsell, Douglas O. 2020. *The Correspondence of Karl Heinrich Ulrichs, 1846–1894*. Cham, Switzerland: Palgrave Macmillan.

Pritchard, Eric D. 2015. "As Proud of Our Gayness, as We Are of Our Blackness: Racing Sexual Rhetorics in the National Coalition of Black Lesbians and Gays." In *Sexual*

184 REFERENCES

Rhetorics: Methods, Identities, Publics, edited by Jonathan Rhodes and Jacqueline Alexander, pp. 159–171. New York: Routledge.

Pruitt, Sarah. 2019. "How 'Duck-and-Cover' Drills Channeled America's Cold War Anxiety." History, A&E Television Networks, March 26. https://www.history.com/news/duck-cover-drills-cold-war-arms-race

Puff, Helmut. 2000. "Female Sodomy: The Trial of Katerina Hetzeldorfer (1477)." *Journal of Medieval and Early Modern Studies* 30 (1): pp. 41–61. https://doi.org/10.1215/10829636-30-1-41

"Queens Liberation Front—What Is It?" 1972. *Drag* 2 (6): pp. 13–14. Reprinted in *The Stonewall Riots: A Documentary History*, edited by Marc Stein, 2019, pp. 212–213. New York: New York University Press.

Radicalesbians. 1970. "The Woman-Identified Woman." *Come Out*, June, pp. 12–13. Reprinted in *The Stonewall Riots: A Documentary History*, edited by Marc Stein, 2019, pp. 200–203. New York: New York University Press.

Ratzan, Scott C., Gregory Payne, and Holly A. Massett. 1994. "Effective Health Message Design: The America Responds to AIDS Campaign." *American Behavioral Scientist* 38 (2): pp. 197–380. https://doi.org/10.1177/0002764294038002010

Rauchway, Eric. 2008. *The Great Depression and the New Deal: A Very Short Introduction*. New York: Oxford University Press.

Ray, Ebenezer. 1938. "Fifteen Arrested by Police as 'Fairies' Turn 'Em On." *New York Age*, March 5.

Reiffegg. 1902/1991. "The Significance of Youth-Love for Our Time." In *Homosexuality and Male Bonding in Pre-Nazi Germany*, edited by Harry Oosterhuis and Hubert Kennedy (trans. Hubert Kennedy), pp. 167–177. New York: Routledge.

Retter, Yolanda G. 1999. "On the Side of Angels: Lesbian Activism in Los Angeles, 1970–1990." Doctoral dissertation, University of New Mexico.

Reyes, Emily A. 2016. "Deal with Developers Will Recognize Circus Disco's Place in Hollywood Gay History." *Los Angeles Times*, January 22. https://www.latimes.com/local/california/la-me-circus-disco-20160122-story.html

Ring, Trudy. 2017. "Women Who Paved the Way: Cabaret Singer Claire Waldoff." The Advocate, March 22. https://www.advocate.com/women/2017/3/22/women-who-paved-way-cabaret-singer-claire-waldoff

Roberts, Sam. 2019. "William Dannemeyer, 89, California Archconservative, Dies." *New York Times*, July 16. https://www.nytimes.com/2019/07/16/us/william-dannemeyer-dead.html?searchResultPosition=1

Robertson, Stephen, Shane White, Stephen Garton, and Graham White. 2012. "Disorderly Houses: Residency, Privacy, and the Surveillance of Sexuality in 1920s Harlem." *Journal of the History of Sexuality* 21 (3): pp. 443–466. https://doi.org/10.7560/JHS21303

Roelens, Jonas. 2015. "From Slurs to Silence? Sodomy and Medicants in the Writings of Catholic Laymen in Early Modern Ghent." *Sixteenth Century Journal* 46 (3): pp. 629–649. https://doi.org/10.1086/scj4603005

REFERENCES 185

Rojas, Rick, and Khorri Atkinson. 2017. "Five Days of Unrest That Shaped, and Haunted, Newark." *New York Times*, July 11. https://www.nytimes.com/2017/07/11/nyregion/newark-riots-50-years.html?searchResultPosition=1

Romm, James. 2021. *Sacred Band: Three Hundred Theban Lovers Fighting to Save Greek Freedom*. New York: Scribner.

Roots of Equality. 2011. *Lavender Los Angeles*. Charleston, SC: Arcadia Publications.

Rosario, Vernon. 2022. "Sex and Gender in Native America." *Gay & Lesbian Review Worldwide* 29 (4): pp. 15–17.

Rosenzweig, Leah. 2018. "Cause of Death." *Slate*, November 30. https://slate.com/human-interest/2018/11/aids-new-york-times-obituary-history.html

Roth, Benita. 1998. "Feminist Boundaries in the Feminist-Friendly Organization: The Women's Caucus of ACT UP/LA." *Gender and Society* 12 (2): pp. 129–145. https://doi.org/10.1177/089124398012002002

Royles, Dan. 2020. *To Make the Wounded Whole: The African American Struggle Against HIV/AIDS*. Chapel Hill: University of North Carolina Press.

Rubin, Marcie S., Cynthia G. Colen, and Bruce G. Link. 2009. "Examination of Inequalities in HIV/AIDS Mortality in the United States from a Fundamental Cause Perspective." *American Journal of Public Health* 100 (6): pp. 1053–1059. https://doi.org/10.2105/AJPH.2009.170241

Rubin, Lena. 2020 "Revolutionaries on East Second Street: STAR House" Off the Grid: Village Preservation blog, October 29. https://www.villagepreservation.org/2020/10/29/revolutionaries-on-east-second-street-the-star-house/

Ruffalo, Mark L. 2018. "The Psychoanalytic Tradition in American Psychiatry: The Basics." *Psychiatric Times*, January 24. https://www.psychiatrictimes.com/view/psychoanalytic-tradition-american-psychiatry-basics

Rupp, Leila J. 2006. "Loving Women in the Modern World." In *Gay Life and Culture: A World History*, edited by Robert Aldrich, pp. 223–248. New York: Universe Publishing.

Ryan, Caitlin. 2001. "My Roots as an Activist." *Journal of Lesbian Studies* 5 (3): pp. 141–149. https://doi.org/10.1300/J155v05n03_17

Samuel, Lawrence R. 2013. *Shrink: A Cultural History of Psychoanalysis in America*. Lincoln: University of Nebraska Press.

Saunt, Claudio. 2019. "Financing Dispossession: Stocks, Bonds, and the Deportation of Native Peoples in the Antebellum United States." *Journal of American History* 106 (2): pp. 315–337. https://doi.org/10.1093/jahist/jaz344

Schilt, Kristen, and Laurel Westbrook. 2009. "Doing Gender, Doing Heteronormativity: 'Gender Normals,' Transgender People, and the Social Maintenance of Heterosexuality." *Gender & Society* 23 (4): pp. 440–464. https://doi.org/10.1177/0891243209340034

Schulz, Kathryn. 2023. "Family Values: How a Mother's Love for Her Gay Son Started a Revolution." *New Yorker*, April 17, pp. 42–49. https://www.newyorker.com/magazine/2023/04/17/how-one-mothers-love-for-her-gay-son-started-a-revolution

Schwules Museum Berlin and Andreas Sternweiler. 2008. *Self-Confidence and Persistence: Two Hundred Years of History*. 2nd ed. Berlin: Schwules Museum.

186 REFERENCES

Shilts, Randy. 1987. *And the Band Played On: People, Politics, and the AIDS Epidemic.* New York: St. Martin's Press.

Shively, Charles (Ed.). 1989. *Drum Beats: Walt Whitman's Civil War Boy Lovers.* San Francisco: Gay Sunshine Press.

Sibalis, Michael. 2006. "Male Homosexuality in the Age of Enlightenment and Revolution, 1680–1850." In *Gay Life and Culture: A World History*, edited by Robert Aldrich, pp. 103–123. New York: Universe Publishing.

Siegessäule. 2021. "Schöneberg Was So Lesbian in the Weimar Republic." Place2Berlin. https://www.place2be.berlin/en/discover-berlin/schöneberg-was-so-lesbian-in-the-weimar-republic/

Slide, Anthony. 1999. "The Silent Closet." *Film Quarterly* 52 (4): pp. 24–32.

Smith, Mapheus. 1947. "Population Characteristics of American Servicemen in World War II." *Scientific Monthly* 65 (3): pp. 246–252.

"Sodomy Law: Pennsylvania, December 7, 1682." n.d. OutHistory.org. https://outhistory.org/exhibits/show/the-age-of-sodomitical-sin/1680s/sodomy-law-pennsylvania-decemb

Southern Poverty Law Center. 2005. "History of the Anti-Gay Movement Since 1977." *Intelligence Report*, April 28. https://www.splcenter.org/fighting-hate/intelligence-report/2005/history-anti-gay-movement-1977

Specter, Michael. 2021. "How ACT UP Changed America." *New Yorker*, June 7. https://www.newyorker.com/magazine/2021/06/14/how-act-up-changed-america

Spitzer, Scott J. 2024. "Racial Politics and Welfare Retrenchment During the Reagan Presidency." *Congress & the Presidency* 51 (1): pp. 31–61. https://doi.org/10.1080/07343469.2023.2289874

"Standards of Care: The Hormonal and Surgical Sex Reassignment of Gender Dysphoric Persons." 1985. *Archives of Sexual Behavior* 14 (1): pp. 79–90. https://doi.org/10.1007/BF01541354

Stanley, Bob. 1970. "Gay Pride Week 1970: That Was the Week That Was." *Mattachine Midwest Newsletter*, June, p. 1. Reprinted in *The Stonewall Riots: A Documentary History*, edited by Marc Stein, 2019, pp. 280–281. New York: New York University Press.

Stein, Marc. 2004. *City of Sisterly and Brotherly Loves.* Philadelphia: Temple University Press.

Stein, Marc (Ed.). 2019. *The Stonewall Riots: A Documentary History.* New York: New York University Press.

Stephens, Alexander M. 2021. "Making Migrants 'Criminal': The Mariel Boatlift, Miami, and U.S. Immigration Policy in the 1980s." *Anthurium: A Caribbean Studies Journal* 17 (2): pp. 1–18.

Stewart-Winter, Timothy. 2016. *Queer Clout: Chicago and the Rise of Gay Politics.* Philadelphia: University of Pennsylvania Press.

Stoller, Robert, Judd Marmor, Irving Bieber, Ronald Gold, Charles W. Socarides, Richard Green, and Robert L. Spitzer. 1973. "A Symposium: Should Homosexuality Be in the APA Nomenclature?" *American Journal of Psychiatry* 130 (11): pp. 1207–1216. https://doi.org/10.1176/ajp.130.11.1207

REFERENCES 187

Storer, Colin. 2013. *A Short History of the Weimar Republic*. London: I. B. Tauris & Co.

Streitmatter, Rodger. 1998. "Vice Versa: America's First Lesbian Magazine." *American Periodicals* 8: pp. 73–95.

Stryker, Susan. 2008. *Transgender History*. Berkeley, CA: Seal Press.

Sutherland, Edwin H. 1950. "The Sexual Psychopath Laws." *Journal of Criminal Law and Criminology* 40 (5): pp. 543–554.

Takacs, Judit. 2004. "The Double Life of Kertbeny." In *Past and Present of Radical Sexual Politics*, edited by Gert Hekma, pp. 26–40. Amsterdam, Netherlands: Mosse Foundation.

Tamagne, Florence. 2006. "The Homosexual Age, 1860–1940." In *Gay Life and Culture: A World History*, edited by R. Aldrich, pp. 169–195. New York: Universe Publishing.

Taylor, Jeremy M. 1989. "Models for the HIV Infection and AIDS Epidemic in the United States." *Statistics in Medicine* 8 (1): pp. 45–58. https://doi.org/10.1002/sim.4780080107

Taylor, Mara, and Michael T. Taylor. 2017. "Sentimentalizing the Case Study: Emma Trosse's Deviant Genre." In *Not Straight from Germany: Sexual Publics and Sexual Citizenship Since Magnus Hirschfeld*, edited by Michael T. Taylor, Annette F. Timm, and Rainer Herrn, pp. 243–282. Ann Arbor: University of Michigan Press.

"The Blacklist and the Greylist." 1955. *Hollywood Review* 2 (2): pp. 9–10.

The Boston Alliance of LGBTQ+ Youth. n.d. "BAGLY History." https://www.bagly.org/where-we-came-from

The Chickasaw Nation. 2023. "Removal." https://www.chickasaw.net/our-nation/history/removal.aspx

"The Gay Civil Rights Movement Turns to Public Picketing." n.d. Rainbow History Project. https://web.archive.org/web/20110517153305/http://www.rainbowhistory.org/Pickets.htm

"The Trail of Broken Treaties, 1972." n.d. National Park Service. https://www.nps.gov/articles/000/trail-of-broken-treaties.htm

Tillet, Salamishah. 2015. "Nina Simone's Time Is Now, Again." *New York Times*, June 21, p. AR 1.

Timberg, Scott. 2017. "30 Years After His Death, James Baldwin Is Having a New Pop Culture Moment." *Los Angeles Times*, February 23. https://www.latimes.com/entertainment/movies/la-et-james-baldwin-pop-culture-20170223-story.html

Timmons, Stuart. 1990. *The Trouble with Harry Hay: Founder of the Modern Gay Movement*. Boston: Alyson Publications.

Tobin, Kay. 1965. "Picketing: The Impact & the Issues." *The Ladder* 9 (12): pp. 4–8.

Tobin, Kay. 1970. "Thousands Take Part in Gay Marches." *GAY*, July 20, p. 12. Reprinted in *The Stonewall Riots: A Documentary History*, edited by Marc Stein, 2019, pp. 277–279. New York: New York University Press.

Tomes, Nancy. 2022. "A 'Creation of the Media': AIDS, Sensationalism, and Media Portrayals of Epidemic Risk." *Feminist Media Histories* 8 (4): pp. 85–116.

Tosh, John. 2018. "Historical Scholarship and Public Memory in Britain: A Case of Oil and Water?" In *History, Memory and Public Life: The Past in the Present*, edited by Anna Maerker, Simon Sleight, and Adam Sutcliffe, pp. 29–47. New York: Routledge.

188 REFERENCES

Tracey, Liz. 2022. "Proposition 6 (the Briggs Initiative): Annotated." *JSTOR Daily*, October 28. https://daily.jstor.org/proposition-6-the-briggs-initiative-annotated/

Triay, Victor Andres. 2019. *The Mariel Boatlift: A Cuban-American Journey*. Gainesville: University of Florida Press.

Turner, Frederick J. 1893. "The Significance of the Frontier in American History." Edited and reprinted by the American Historical Association, 2023. https://www.historians. org/about-aha-and-membership/aha-history-and-archives/historical-archives/the-significance-of-the-frontier-in-american-history-(1893)

US Holocaust Memorial Museum. 2021. "Paragraph 175 and the Nazi Campaign Against Homosexuality." Holocaust Encyclopedia. https://encyclopedia.ushmm.org/content/en/article/paragraph-175-and-the-nazi-campaign-against-homosexuality

US Holocaust Memorial Museum. n.d. "How Did Public Opinion About World War II Change Between 1939 and 1941?" Americans and the Holocaust. https://exhibitions. ushmm.org/americans-and-the-holocaust/us-public-opinion-world-war-II-1939-1941

US Census Bureau. 2021. "Decennial Official Census Publications." https://www.census. gov/programs-surveys/decennial-census/decade/decennial-publications.1920.html

US National Archives and Records Administration. 2001. "FDR's 'Day of Infamy' Speech. *Prologue Magazine* 33 (4). https://www.archives.gov/publications/prologue/2001/winter/crafting-day-of-infamy-speech.html

Verge, Arthur C. 1994. "The Impact of the Second World War on Los Angeles." *Pacific Historical Review* 63 (3): pp. 289–314.

Vergun, David. 2020. "During WWII, Industries Transitioned from Peacetime to Wartime Production." US Department of Defense, March 27. https://www. defense.gov/News/Feature-Stories/story/Article/2128446/during-wwii-industries-transitioned-from-peacetime-to-wartime-production/

Voigt, Matthias Andre. 2021. "Warriors for a Nation: The American Indian Movement, Indigenous Men, and Nation Building at the Takeover of Wounded Knee in 1973." *American Indian Culture and Research Journal* 45 (2): pp. 1–38. https://doi.org/10. 17953/aicrj.45.2.voigt

Warner, Michael. 1991. "Introduction: Fear of a Queer Planet." *Social Text* 29: pp. 3–17.

Wat, Eric C. 2021. *Love Your Asian Body: AIDS Activism in Los Angeles*. Seattle: University of Washington Press.

Welch, Paul. 1964. "Homosexuality in America." *Life*, June 26, pp. 65–80.

West Hollywood Marketing Corporation. 2024. "WeHo's Infamous Past & Colorful History." https://www.visitwesthollywood.com/history-of-west-hollywood/

Whitman, Walt. 1855/2018. *Leaves of Grass*. Auckland, New Zealand: The Floating Press.

Whisnant, Clayton J. 2016. *Queer Identities and Politics in Germany: A History, 1880–1945*. New York: Harrington Park Press.

Wiene, Robert (dir.). 1920. *The Cabinet of Dr. Caligari*. Decla-Bioscop AG.

Wilder, Terri. 2020. "Candy Marcum, a Therapist and Lesbian, Has Helped Gay Men in Texas Since the Early Days of AIDS." The Body, March 31. https://www.thebody.com/article/candy-marcum-therapist-since-aids-early-days

REFERENCES 189

Williams, Daniel K. 2010. *God's Own Party: The Making of the Christian Right.* New York: Oxford University Press.

Wilson, James F. 2010. *Bulldaggers, Pansies, and Chocolate Babies: Performance, Race, and Sexuality in the Harlem Renaissance.* Ann Arbor: University of Michigan Press.

Winick, Bruce J. 2002. "The Dade County Human Rights Ordinance of 1977: Testimony Revisited in Commemoration of Its Twenty-Fifth Anniversary." *Tulane Journal of Law and Sexuality* 11: pp. 1–9.

Wise, Camille. 2023. "Before the 'Rice Bar': A History of Mugi's." Mapping the Gay Guides, July 25. https://www.mappingthegayguides.org/articles/beyond-the-rice-bar/

Wittman, Carl. 1969. "Refugees from Amerika: A Gay Manifesto." Reprinted in *The Homosexual Dialectic*, edited by Joseph A. McCaffrey, 1972, pp. 157–171. Englewood Cliffs, NJ: Prentice-Hall.

"Women in World War I." 2022. National Park Service. https://www.nps.gov/articles/women-in-world-war-i.htm

Wong, K. Scott. 2005. *Americans First: Chinese Americans and the Second World War.* Cambridge, MA: Harvard University Press.

Index

For the benefit of digital users, indexed terms that span two pages (e.g., 52–53) may, on occasion, appear on only one of those pages.

Abdo, Judy, 157–158
abortion, 114–115
acquired immune deficiency syndrome (AIDS)
  association with same-sex sexuality, 166
  and gender minorities, 158–159
  non-white population affected by, 152–154
  origins and early responses to crisis, 147–149
  political legacy of AIDS epidemic, 160–161, 168–169
  and public awareness, 148–149, 154–155
  scope and impact of crisis, 149–152
  and sexual and gender identities, 159–160
  and sexual minorities, 155–158
Action Coalition to Fight the Briggs Initiative, 135
Actors Equity, 154–155
Addams, Eve, 50–51
Addams, Jane, 38–39
Adely, Hannan, 1
adoption, 157–158
Advocate, The, 116, 119, 138–139
African Americans
  and AIDS crisis, 154, 157–158, 160–161
  black feminist standpoint theory, 4
  black gay men, 153
  "Black is Beautiful" slogan, 109
  Black Panther Party, 113
  Black Power, 110, 113
  black transgender women, 153–154
  and civil rights activism, 99–102, 111–112
  community-building among sexual minorities, 141
  and conservative Christian politics of the 1970s, 137
  and direct action in support of sexual and gender minorities, 106–107
  and drag balls, 50
  and Great Migration, 45, 47, 54–55
  and Harlem Renaissance, 47–49
  impact of Great Depression on, 57

and marginalization of sexual minorities in New York, 60
military service and sexual and gender minorities, 74
and One Inc., 91–92
reversals of social justice progress, 30
romantic friendships among women, 39–40
sexual minorities in the 1960s, 109–110
and support networks for sexual and gender minorities, 89
and transgression of gender norms, 34
and wartime environment for sexual and gender minorities, 70, 74, 78–80
and "white flight," 129
Agnew, Spiro, 114
Ai, Emperor of Han, 5–6
AIDS Coalition to Unleash Power (ACT UP), 150–151, 156, 159–160
AIDS Foundation of Chicago, 150
AIDS Foundation of San Francisco, 149–150
AIDS Medical Foundation, 154
AIDS Project Los Angeles (APLA), 150
AIDS Task Force, 153
AIDS Walk, 150
Alcatraz Island, 115–116
alcohol, 66–67. *See also* Prohibition
Alexander the Great, 5–6
Amazon Bookstore, 132
American Civil Liberties Union, 1, 92–93, 155
American Communist Party, 89–90
American Family Association, 137–138
American Foundation for AIDS Research (AmfAR), 154
American Historical Association, 35
American Law Institute, 105
American Psychiatric Association (APA), 125–126, 142–143
American Psychological Association, 151
America Responds to AIDS, 148
androgyny, 62, 124–125
Angels in America (play), 154–155

192 INDEX

Ann Arbor, Michigan, 132, 139–140
Annex Buffet, 60–61
Annual Reminder, 107–108
antifeminists, 17, 130–131, 137
antigay activism, 120, 151
antiretroviral medications, 148, 156
Antisemitism, 70
antiwar activism, 102, 114
Apuzzo, Ginny, 156–157
Aquinas, Thomas, 9
Armed Forces Disciplinary Control Board, 78–79
Armstrong, Louis, 48
Army Air Corps, 74–75
Army Review Board for Correction of Military Records, 74
Arzner, Dorothy, 51–52
Asian Americans, 115, 141, 153, 157–158, 160–161
Asian Pacific AIDS Coalition, 153
Asian Pacific AIDS Intervention Team, 153
Asian/Pacific Lesbians and Gays, 141
assassinations, 100–102
Association of Black Gays, 141
Astor Hotel Bar, 59–60
Athletic Model Guild, 79–80, 87–88, 108–109
Atlanta, Georgia, 155
Auden, H., 23–24
Ault, Steven, 143
Austria-Hungary, 21

baby boom, 83
Baez, Joan, 136
Baldwin, James, 3, 110
Ballyhoo Club, 52–53
Bamberger, Rose, 93–94
Bankhead, Tallulah, 62
Bannon, Ann (Ann Weldy), 88–89, 167–168
bars, 61, 76–77, 165. *See also* speakeasies
Battle of Chaeronea, 5–6
Bauhaus architecture, 21–22
Bavarian Criminal Code of 1813, 10–11
Bay Area Reporter, 138–139, 147, 151
"B.D. Woman Blues" (Bogan), 47
beach culture, 79–80
Beachy, Robert, 22–23
Bean, Carl, 153
Beebo Brinker (fictional character), 88–89
Beemyn, Brett G., 35
Bello, Ada, 119
Ben, Lisa (Edythe Eyde), 79, 87
Benjamin, Harry, 111

Benny the Bums bar, 77
Bentley, Gladys, 47–49, 60
berdaches, 31
Berlin, Germany, 15, 17–18, 22–25, 26–27, 28–30, 53–54, 163–164, 166–167
Berlin, Irving, 76
Berlins Lesbische Frauen, 23
Beverly Hills, California, 61–62
Bible, 9–10
Bienestar, 153
Biltmore Hotel, 63
binary gender and sex assumption, 6–7
Bird, Merton, 89, 91–92
bisexuality, 147–148
Black and White Men Together, 153
Black Cat bar in San Francisco, 78–79
Black Cat bar in Los Angeles, 104–105
black feminist standpoint theory, 4
black gay men, 153
"Black is Beautiful" slogan, 109
Black Panther Party, 113
Black Power, 110, 113
Blacks Educating Blacks About Sexual Health Issues, 153
black transgender women, 153–154, 160–161
Bleecker Street, 50–51
Blevins, John, 5–6
Block, Martin, 91–92
Bloody Sunday, 101
blue discharges, 73–75, 89, 164
boat people, 130
Bogan, Lucille, 47
bohemian culture, 51–52, 163–164
Boise, Idaho, 87
bombings, 100
bookstores, 108–109, 122–123, 132, 139
bootlegging, 51–52, 58
Boston, Massachusetts, 129, 138–139
Boston marriages, 38–40
Boswell, Holly, 158
Boswell, John, 9
Boys Don't Cry (film), 159
Brand, Adolf, 16–17, 43, 53–54
Brass Rail bar, 78–79
Brecht, Bertolt, 84
Bremen, Germany, 166–167
Brewster, Lee, 120–121
Briggs, John, 134
Briggs Initiative, 134–137
Britt, Harry, 143
Broidy, Ellen, 121–122

INDEX   193

Bronzeville neighborhood (Chicago), 52–53, 60–61, 167–168
"Brother Can You Spare a Dime" (song), 57
Brown, Addie, 39–40
Brown Berets, 115
Brown v. Board of Education, 99
Bryant, Anita, 132–134
Bryn Mawr College, 39
Buchanan, Pat, 147–148
Buena Vista Park, 123–124
buffet flats, 48–49, 54–55, 167–168
Buford, Harry (Loreta Velasquez), 33
Buggery Act, 32
Bund für Menschenrecht, 53–54
busing desegregation, 129, 133
butch lesbians, 75–76, 88–89, 94, 118, 124, 126–127, 158, 167–168

Cabinet of Dr. Caligari, The (film), 21–22
Cabin Inn, 60–61
Calamus (Whitman), 36
California
    and AIDS crisis, 147, 151, 156–158
    alcohol beverage control board, 66–67
    and anti-immigrant sentiment, 130
    and Briggs Initiative, 134–135
    community-building among sexual minorities, 140, 165
    and conservative Christian politics of the 1970s, 137–138
    gold rush, 52
    and marginalization of sexual and gender minorities 1, 61–63, 65
    and nondiscrimination ordinances, 132
    repeal of Prohibition, 58
    women's bookstores, 132
    See also Los Angeles, California; San Francisco, California
California Defend Our Children, 134, 137–138
California State Assembly, 157–158
California State Department of Education, 93
California Supreme Court, 116
Cameron, Paul, 151
Campaign for a Clean Reich, 26–27
Capers, Bennett, 33
capitalism, 3–4. *See also* economic conditions
capital punishment, 10, 32–33
Caribbean, 130
Carlyle, Thomas, 91–92
Carousel bar, 77
Carpenter, Edward, 13, 37–38, 89–90
Carter, Jimmy, 131, 135

Cashier Albert (Jennie Hodgers), 33
Castro district, 123, 135–137
Catholic Church, 9–11, 55
Catholic Germans, 46
censorship, 22, 24–25, 26–27, 60–61, 62–63
Center for Special Problems, 104–105
Centers for Disease Control and Prevention (CDC), 147–148, 152–154
Central Park, 121–122
Century of Progress International Exposition (Chicago World's Fair), 60–61
Charleston (dance), 48–49
Charter of Fundamental Rights, 166–167
Chauncey, George, vii, 40–41, 46, 49–50
Chicago, Illinois
    and AIDS crisis, 150, 153, 157–158
    and community-building efforts, 138–139
    and counterculture of the 1960s, 113
    and gender identities in the 1920s, 54–55
    and Gerber's background, 53–54
    and lesbian bars in 1930s, 65–66
    and marginalization of sexual and gender minorities, 60–61, 67
    and Prohibition, 46
    and support networks for sexual and gender minorities, 104–106
    and urban growth of the 1920s, 45
    and wartime environment for sexual and gender minorities, 71, 77, 164
Chicago House, 150
Chicano/a identity, 115
Chickasaw people, 31–32
Children of Adam (Whitman), 36
Children's Hour, The (play), 60–61
China, 69
Chinese Exclusion Act, 70
Chinese immigrants, 70
Choctaw people, 31–32
Christian, Meg, 122–123
Christian, Paula (Yvonne MacManus), 88–89
Christians and Christianity, 5–6, 9, 62–63, 132–133, 137–138, 147–148, 165–166
Christopher Street (newspaper), 138–139
Christopher Street, Greenwich Village, 118–119
Christopher Street Liberation Day, 121–122, 140, 166–167
Christopher Street West parade, 121–122, 139
Cimitière de la Caucade, 26–27
Circus Disco, 141
cisgender identity, 8
Citizens for Medical Justice, 151

194   INDEX

Civil Rights Act of 1964, 100–101, 102–103
civil rights movement, 99–103, 106–110, 113, 137
civil service, 85–86
Civil Service Commission, 106–107
Civil War (US), 33, 37
Clark, Mary Ann (Henry Clark), 33
Clarke, Lige, 119
class identities, 50
clothing styles, 33
Club Abbey, 52–53, 58
Club New Yorker, 52–53
Coalition for Human Rights, 135
Cold War, 83–84, 131
colonialism, 5–6, 31–32
Colorado, 1
Colvin, Claudette, 99
Combahee River Collective, 123
Combahee River Collective Statement, 123
Come Out, 120–121
"coming out," 14–15, 126–127, 134, 141, 144–145, 154–155, 157–158, 166, 168–169
Commission on the Status of Women, 102–103
Committee for Gay Youth, 139–140
Communist Party, 69, 84, 90–91
community-building efforts, 138–140
Community United Against Violence, 155
Compton's Cafeteria, 104–105, 167–168
Comstock Act, 92–93
concentration camps, 28–30
Concerned Women for America, 137–138
Confederate Army, 33
Congregation Beth Chayim Chadashim, 125
Congress of Racial Equality, 99–100
Connecticut, 32–33
conservatism, 62–63, 132–133, 137–138, 139–140, 147–148, 151, 165–166
Conservative Political Action Conference (CPAC), 151
Constructing the Self, Constructing America (Cushman), vii
consumerism, 83
Continental Army, 33
Conversion Our Goal, 104–105
Cooper Do-nuts, 103–104
Corbin, Joan, 91–92
Corigliano, John, 154–155
corruption, 58
Cotton Club, 48, 60
Coughlin, Charles, 70
Council on Religion and the Homosexual, 104–105

counterculture movement, 113
counter-narratives, 2, 18–19, 30, 42–43, 163, 166–167, 168–169
courts martial, 72
Cozy Corner bar, 78
Crenshaw, Kimberlé, 4
criminalization of sexual and gender minorities, 32–33, 64, 65–66, 168–169
Crompton, Louis, 10
cross-dressing, 22–23, 33, 81, 95–96. *See also* transvestism and transvestites
Crusades, 9
Crystal Beach, 79–80
Cuba and Cuban refugees, 106–107, 130
Cullen, Countee, 47
Cushman, Philip, vii
"cut sleeve," 5–6

Dade County Coalition for the Humanistic Rights of Gays, 132–133
Dade County Commission, 132–134
Dallas, Texas, 133–134
Dallas Gay Political Caucus, 125
Damron, Bob, 139
Dance of the Fairies, 50
Dannemeyer, William, 151
Dare to Discipline (Dobson), 137
Das Lila Lied, 22
Daughters of Bilitis, 93–95, 96–97, 104–107, 109–110, 122, 165, 167–168
Day, Sharon M., 153
death penalty, 10, 32–33
decriminalization of same-sex sexuality, 11–12, 13–15, 22–23, 109
definitions of sexual and gender minorities, 5–6
Democratic National Convention, 102, 109
Democratic Party, 113–114
Denver, Colorado, 138–139
Der Eigene, 16, 23, 24–25, 26–27, 53–54
Der Kreis, 92–93
desegregation, 99–100, 129
Detroit, Michigan, 45, 101, 129
"deviant" sexuality, 63–64, 87–88, 163–164
Dewey's, 103–105
Diamond Lil's, 52–53
Die Freundin, 23, 24–25, 26–27
Die Freundschaft, 23, 24–25
Die Gemeinschaft der Eigenen (club), 16
Die Insel, 23
Dietrich, Marlene, 22, 62, 167–168
Different Light, A (bookstore), 139
Dionings, 12

direct action, 106–108
disco music, 123–124
discrimination, 92–93, 125–126, 141, 153–154
Disney, Walt, 84
Dobson, James, 137–138
dominant narratives, 2 *See also* counter-narratives
Dong Xian, 5–6
Doyle, Peter, 37
draft, 70
drag
  drag balls, 24, 49–50, 52–53, 54–55, 58, 167–168
  drag performance 1, 61, 72–73, 77
  drag queens, 120–121, 126–127
Drag Queens (later *Drag*), 120–121
Drum, 108–109, 112
dubads, 31
Dust Bowl, 57

East Coast Homophile Organizations (ECHO), 105–107, 109, 121–122
Eastern European immigrants, 54–55
East Lansing, Michigan, 132
East Los Angeles, California, 115
economic conditions, 25–26, 54–55, 57, 66, 129, 131. *See also* Great Depression
Edmonds, Sarah Emma, 33
Edmund Pettus Bridge, 101
Educational Amendments of 1972, 114–115
18th Amendment, 45–46, 58
Einstein, Albert, 14–15
Eisenhower, Bunny, 120–121
Eisenhower, Dwight, 85, 99
Elberskirchen, Johanna, 17–18
Eldorado nightclub, 22–23, 26–27
Ellington, Duke, 48
Eltinge, Julian, 51–52
Emancipation, 34
Empire State Pride Agenda, 158–159
employment discrimination, 102–103
Enlightenment, 10
Episcopal Church, 125
Equal Rights Amendment, 114–115, 130–133
Erickson, Reed, 111
Erickson Educational Foundation, 111, 142
ethnic minorities, 46
European colonialism, 31–32
European Union, 166–167
Executive Order 10450, 85
Eyde, Edythe (Lisa Ben), 79, 87

fascism, 69–70
Faggots Ball, 50
Fag Rag, 138–139
fairies, 40–43, 46, 50–51, 52–53, 95–96
Falwell, Jerry, 137
Family Policy Alliance of New Jersey, 1
Family Research Council, 137–138
Fantasia Fair, 124
Fawcett Gold Medal Books, 88–89
Federal Bureau of Investigation (FBI)
  and African American sexual minorities, 110
  campaign against sexual and gender minorities in 1960s, 103
  and Daughters of Bilitis, 95
  and direct action in support of sexual and gender minorities, 106–107
  and Lavender Scare, 85–87
  and Mattachine Society, 90–91
  and One Inc., 92–93
  and pathologizing of sexual difference, 64, 66
  and rise of social justice movements, 113
Federal Civil Defense Administration, 83–84
Federation of Parents and Friends of Lesbians and Gays (PFLAG), 140, 143
Federation of Uranians, 12
Feinberg, Leslie, 158
Feinstein, Dianne, 136
Feminine Mystique, The (Friedan), 102–103
feminism
  and AIDS crisis, 156–157
  antifeminists, 17, 130–131, 137
  black feminist standpoint theory, 4
  and community-building efforts, 139
  and Elberskirchen's writings, 17–18
  feminist standpoint theory, 3–4
  first wave feminism, 39
  lesbian feminist groups, 122
  and Rüling's writings, 18
  second wave feminism, 102–103
  and Trosse's writings, 17
femme lesbians, 124, 167–168
femme men, 75–76
Fields, Mary, 34
film industry, 62–63, 65
Finocchio's, 61, 72–73
first wave feminism, 39
First World War, 45–46, 50–51, 54–55, 69–70, 163–164
fiscal policy, 25
Florida, 1
Florida Citrus Commission, 132–133
Focus on the Family, 137

196 INDEX

Ford, Gerald, 131
Foster, Marcia, 93–94
Foundation for Personality Expression, 111
Four Horsemen of the Apocalypse (film), 51–52
442nd Infantry Regiment, 74–75
Fourth Massachusetts Regiment, 33
France, 21, 69–70, 83–84
Franco, Francisco, 69–70
Frank, Barney, 157–158
Frankfurter Engel memorial, 29–30
Freedom Riders, 99–100
Freedom Summer, 100–101
French Enlightenment, 11
French Revolution, 10–11
Freundschaft und Freiheit, 53–54
Frey, Noni, 93–94
Friedan, Betty, 102–103, 121
Friedman, Carole, 119
Friedrichstrasse, Berlin, 23–24
Friendship and Freedom, 53–54
frontier environment, 35, 42–43, 163
Frye, Phyllis, 159
Fryer, John, 125–126
Furies, The, 122
"Furtive Fraternity, The," 103
F. W. Woolworth, 100

Garbo, Greta, 62
Gay Academic Union (GAU), 125
Gay Activists Alliance (GAA), 120–121,
    125–126, 140
gay adoption, 133
Gay and Lesbian Anti-Violence Project, 155
Gay and Lesbian Latinos Unidos, 141, 153
"gayby boom," 157
Gay Coalition of Denver, 125
Gay Community Center of Philadelphia, 138
Gay Community News, 138–139
Gay Community Services Center, 138
Gayellow Pages, 139
Gay Freedom Day, 134, 139
Gay Girls' Guide, A, 87
Gay Horizons, 138
Gay Hotline (University of Michigan), 139–140
"Gay Is Good" slogan, 109
Gay Liberation Front (GLF), 119–121,
    125–126, 138, 143
gay liberation movement, 122, 165–168
Gay Life, 138–139
gay men
    activism and liberation movement, 123–124

and advances against discrimination,
    125–126
and AIDS crisis, 147–152, 153, 154–158,
    160–161, 166
and community-building efforts, 138–140,
    144–145, 165–166
community development of the 1970s, 132
and conservative Christian politics of the
    1970s, 137–138
and divisions between sexual and gender
    minorities, 127, 135
and "Gay is Good" movement, 108–109
and Greenwich Village culture, 117
and intersectional identities, 30
and National March on Washington for
    Lesbian and Gay Rights, 143
and "perversion" view of sexual minorities,
    103
and political activism of the 1970s, 133–134
and rise of German National Socialism,
    26–27
and sexual minorities of color, 141
and standpoint theory, 168
and Stonewall riots, 118, 124–125, 126–127
and support networks for sexual and gender
    minorities, 105–106, 112
and value of counter-narrative, 169
in Weimer Berlin, 23–25
and White Night Riot, 135–137
Gay Men of African Descent, 153
Gay Men's Health Crisis (GMHC), 149–150
Gay New York (Chauncey), vii
Gay Pride Week, 121–122, 139
gay-related immune deficiency (GRID), 147
Gay Rights National Lobby, 125
Gay Women's Service Center, 122
Gee, Emma, 115
gender identity
    defined, 7–8
    and definitions of sexual and gender
        minorities, 6–7
    and drag balls, 50
    gender-confirming medical care, 142,
        144–145
    gender-confirming surgery, 95–96
    gender expression and behaviors, 8, 12,
        42–43
    gender minorities, 8, 124–125, 142–143,
        153–154, 158–159
    gender norms, 33–35, 116–117
    gender roles, 28, 40–41, 42–43, 45–46, 55,
        96, 137, 163

vs. sexual orientation 127

Gender Political Advocacy Coalition (GenderPAC), 159

George Washington High School, 139–140

Georgia, 32–33

Gerber, Henry, 53–54, 167–168

German Communist Party, 26

Germany, vii–viii
 and constructions of sexual and gender identities, 13, 18–19, 163–165
 and First World War, 21
 and gender identities in the 1920s, 54–55
 German Empire, 11, 21
 German Jews, 69–70
 German masculinists, 37, 41
 and historical examples of sexual and gender minorities, 6
 homosexual liberation movement, 37–38
 parliament, 25
 and rise of National Socialism, 69–70, 164
 and Second World War, 69–71
 and sodomy laws, 10–11
 and uneven progress for gender and sexual minorities, 166–167

Germany and "Golden Twenties," 25–26

Germany and hyperinflation, 25–26

Gernreich, Rudi, 89–90

Gershwin, George, 48

Ghent, Belgium, 10

Giovanni's Room, 139

Gittings, Barbara, 106–107, 125–126

Glide Memorial United Methodist Church, 104–105

Gloria's, 59

Gold Rush, 35

Goodstein, David, 138–139

Gorney, Jay, 57

Grant, Cary, 62

Grapes of Wrath, The (Steinbeck), 57

Gray, Richard Lee, 153

Great Britain, 21, 69–70, 83–84

Great Depression
 impact on African Americans, 57
 impact on Germany, 26
 and lesbians in the 1930s, 65–66
 and marginalization of sexual minorities, 60, 62–63, 66–67
 and pathologizing of sexual difference, 66
 political response to, 58
 scope of impact, 57
 and wartime environment for sexual and gender minorities, 80, 164

and Weimar Germany, 23–24

Greater Philadelphia, 103

Great Migration, 45, 47

Greece, 17, 37

Greenwich Village, 50–51, 52–53, 54–55, 108–109, 119, 121–122

Growing Up Gay, 139–140

"Guidelines and Recommendations for Healthful Gay Sexual Activity" (National Coalition of Gay STD Services), 149–150

Haines, William, 51–52, 62

Haitian refugees, 130

Hall, Radclyffe, 14, 52–53

Hamilton Lodge Ball, 50, 60

Hanks, Tom, 154–155

Hansberry, Lorraine, 109–110

Harburg, Yip, 57

Hardwick, Michael, 155

Haring, Keith, 154–155

Harlem, New York, 50, 54–55, 60, 66–67, 167–168

Harlem Renaissance, 47–49, 66–67, 163–164

Harry Benjamin International Gender Dysphoria Association (HBIGDA), 142

Harry Hansberry's Clam House, 48–49

Hart-Celler Act, 130

Hartley, Marsden, 23–24

Hartsock, Nancy, 3–4

Hassan, Rashidah, 153

Hay, Harry, 89–92, 96–97, 167–168

Hellman, Lillian, 60–61

Hemphill, Essex, 154–155

Hepburn, Kathryn, 62

heterogenit, 13–14

heterosexuality, 13–14, 17–18, 42–43

Hiroshima bombing, 83–84

Hirschfeld, Magnus, 14–16, 22–23, 26–27, 37–38, 95–96, 111

Hitler, Adolf, 26–27, 69–70

Hodgers, Jennie, 33

Holleran, Andrew, 154–155

Hollywood, California, 61–62, 67

Hollywood Boulevard, 121–122

Holy Roman Empire, 9

homoerotic physique publications, 79–80, 86, 87–88, 96–97, 108–109, 112

Homophile Action League, 109, 119

Homophile Action League Newsletter, 119

Homophile Bill of Rights, 109

homophile movement, 83
 and Daughters of Bilitis, 93–95

198 INDEX

homophile movement, (*Continued*)
    and Lavender Scare, 85–87
    legacy of, 96–97
    and Mattachine Society, 89–91
    and ONE Inc., 91–93
    and public awareness of same-sex sexuality,
        86–87, 96–97, 165
    and Red Scare, 83–85
    self-identification and network-building,
        87–89
    and trans visibility, 95–96
"Homosexual Citizen, The" (column), 119
"Homosexuality in America" (Welch), 103
homosexual liberation movement, 37–38
Hooker, Evelyn, 91
Hoover, J. Edgar, 64, 66, 86–87
hormone treatments, 95–96
Hose and Heels Club, 111
Hot Cha bar, 48–49
House Committee on Military Affairs, 74
House Un-American Activities Committee, 84
housing discrimination, 129
Houston, Texas, 133–134, 138–139, 157–158
Howard Brown Memorial Clinic, 138
Hudson, Rock, 154
Hughes, Langston, 47
Hull, Bob, 89–90
Hull House, 38–39
human immunodeficiency virus (HIV), 147,
    152. *See also* acquired immune deficiency
    syndrome (AIDS)
Human Life Amendment, 130–131
Hunter, Alberta, 47
Hunter, Joyce, 143
Hurston, Zora Neale, 47
Hwang, Nadine, 28

Ichioka, Yuji, 115
"I Have a Dream" (King), 100–101
Illinois, 1, 65. *See also* Chicago, Illinois
Illinois Masonic Hospital, 150
immigrants and immigration, 42, 46, 54–55,
    130
imprisonment of sexual and gender minorities,
    72. *See also* criminalization of sexual and
    gender minorities
Independence Hall, 106–107
Indian Removal Act, 31–32
Indians of All Tribes, 115–116
Indigenous Americans, 31–32, 43, 74–75,
    115–116, 153
industrialization, 25

inflation, 23–24, 25–26, 114, 129. *See also*
    economic conditions
Inkwell Beach, 79–80
Institute for Sexual Science, 15, 26–27
Institute for the Study of Human Resources,
    111
Intermediate Sex, The (Carpenter), 37–38
International Conference on Transgender Law
    and Employment Policy, 159
International Symposium on Gender Identity,
    142
interracial sexual minority couples, 89
intersectionality, 4–5, 30
intersex people, 6–7
Interstate Commerce Commission, 99–100
In the Shadow of the Epidemic (Odets), 156
inverts, 41–42
Iranian Revolution, 131
Irish immigrants, 46
Isherwood, Christopher, 23–24
isolationism, 69
Italian immigrants, 46
Italy, 10–11, 69–70
*It Is Not the Homosexual Who Is Perverse, But
    the Society in Which He Lives* (film),
    166–167

Jackson, Jimmie Lee, 101
Jackson State University, 114
Jahrbuch für sexuelle Zwischenstufen, 15, 37–38
Janus Society, 104–106, 108–109
Japan, 69, 83–84
Japanese Americans, 70, 74–75, 91–92,
    120–121
Jazz Age, 45, 48, 54–55, 167–168
jazz clubs, 50
Jenkins, Keith, 1–2
Jennings, Dale, 89–90, 91–92
Jewel's Catch One, 141
Jewish Americans, 70, 91–92
Jim Crow segregation, 100, 111–112
Jimmy's Backyard, 52–53
Joe (film), 114
Johnson, Earvin "Magic," 154
Johnson, Lyndon, 100–102
Johnson, Marsha P., 120–121
Johnson, Philip, 23–24
Jones, Cleve, 149–150, 151–152
Jones, Mondaire, 157–158
Jorgensen, Christine, 95–96
Julber, Eric, 92–93
Julius's bar, 108

K

K-9 Club, 60–61
Kameny, Frank, 105–108, 125–126, 167–168
Kane Ari, 124
Kansas City, 109
Kaposi's Sarcoma Research and Education
Foundation, 149–150
Kay Tobin (Kay Lahusen), 107
Kelly, Edward, 60–61
Kennedy, John F., 100–101, 102–103, 105–106
Kennedy, Robert F., 102
Kent State University, 114
Kertbeny, Károly Mária, 13–14
King, Martin Luther, Jr., 100–102, 110
Kingdom of Prussia, 11
Kinsey, Alfred, 86–87
Kitchen Table: Women of Color Press, 123
Knights of the Clocks, 89, 91–92
Koch, Ed, 149
Kohout, Josef, 29
Kovert, Frederick, 79–80
Krafft-Ebing, Richard von, 14
Kramer, Larry, 149–151, 154–155
Kuehl, Sheila, 157–158
Ku Klux Klan, 100–101
Kupona Network, 153
Kuromiya, Kiyoshi, 120–121
Kushner, Tony, 154–155
kwidó, 31

L

Labyris Books, 132
Ladder, The, 95, 96–97, 106–107, 109–110
Lafayette Park, 78
Lahusen, Kay (Kay Tobin), 106–107
Lakota Sioux people, 31
Lambda Rising bookstore, 139
Latine Americans, 141, 160–161
Latino men, 141
Lauretis, Teresa de, 159–160
Lavender Menace (activist group), 121
Lavender Scare, 85–87, 94, 105–106
Lavender Woman, 138–139
Leaves of Grass (Whitman), 36–38
Legg, W. Dorr, 89, 91–92
legislation and legal codes, 1, 32. *See also*
Briggs, John; criminalization of sexual
and gender minorities; decriminalization
of same-sex sexuality
Leitsch, Dick, 106, 108
Lesbian, Gay, Bisexual, and Transgender
Community Center, 158
Lesbian and Gay Community Center (NYC),
158

Lesbian Herstory Archives, 125
lesbians
and advances against discrimination,
125–126
and AIDS crisis, 150–153, 155, 156–158,
160–161, 166
and Boston marriages, 38–39
and community-building efforts, 138–140,
144–145
community development of the 1970s, 132
and conservative Christian politics of the
1970s, 137–138
and divisions between sexual and gender
minorities, 122–123, 127, 135, 160–161,
165–166
and Elberskirchen's writings, 17–18
and "Gay is Good" movement, 108–109
and Gay Liberation Front, 119–120, 121–122
and historical examples of sexual and gender
minorities, 5–6
and intersectional identities, 30
and Kraft-Ebing's *Psychopathia Sexualis*, 14
lesbian feminism, 122–123
lesbian liberation movement, 168
and marginalization of sexual minorities,
60–61, 65–66
and National March on Washington, 143
and political activism of the 1970s, 133–136
and "pulp" novels, 88
and rise of German National Socialism,
26–27, 28–29
and sexual minorities of color, 141
and standpoint theory, 168
and Stonewall riots, 117–118, 124–127
and value of counter-narrative, 169
and wartime environment for sexual and
gender minorities, 72, 79
and Weimar Germany, 22
in Weimer Berlin, 23–25
Lesbian Tide, The, 122, 138–139
Lesbos, 5–6
Leslie, Edgar, 52–53
Lewis, John, 99–101
lha'mana, 31
Liberation House, 138
liberationist aims, 169
Life, 103
Lightfoot, Lori, 157–158
Lindsay, John, 108
linguistics, 6–7
Lion, Margo, 22
Little Rock Central High School, 99

200 INDEX

locker clubs, 77
Log Cabin Club of Los Angeles, 135
Lorde, Audre, 4, 123, 141, 143
Los Angeles, California
  and advances against discrimination,
    125–126
  and AIDS crisis, 150–151, 153–154
  and Asian American activism, 115
  and community-building efforts, 138–140
  and founding of *The Advocate*, 116
  and gay pride parades, 121–122
  and gender identities in the 1920s, 51–52
  and Lavender Scare, 87
  and marginalization of sexual and gender
    minorities, 61–63, 67
  and origins of homophile movement, 92–93,
    165
  and pathologizing of sexual difference, 64
  and support networks for sexual and gender
    minorities, 104–105
  and urban growth of the 1920s, 45
  and wartime environment for sexual and
    gender minorities, 71, 81, 164
  women's bookstores, 132
Los Angeles County Sheriff, 61–62
Los Angeles Gay Community Services Center,
  150
Los Angeles Police Department, 61–62
Los Angeles Times, 148–149
Los Angeles Vice Squad, 104
Louÿs, Pierre, 93–94
Love of the Third Sex, The (Elberskirchen),
  17–18
Lyon, Phyllis, 93–94

M (film), 21–22
MacArthur, Douglas, 74–75
MacDougal Street, 50–51
MacManus, Yvonne (Paula Christian), 88–89
Mädchen in Uniform (play), 23
Malin, Gene, 52–53
Manford, Jeanne, 140
Manford, Jules, 140
Manford, Morty, 140
Mann, Thomas, 14–15
March on Washington for Jobs and Freedom,
  100–101, 110
March on Washington for Lesbian and Gay
  Rights, 143, 151–152
Marcum, Candy, 156
Mariel boatlift, 130
Marine Corps Women's Reserve, 72

marriage, 38–40, 83, 133, 158
Martin, Del, 93–94
Marx, Karl, 3–4
"Masculine Women Feminine Men" (Leslie),
  52–53
masculinity, 16–17, 40–41
masquerade balls, 49–50. *See also* drag
Massachusetts, 32–33. *See also* Boston,
  Massachusetts
Massachusetts Bay Colony, 32
mass media, 83
Master's Tools Will Never Dismantle the
  Master's House, The (Lorde), 4
Mattachine Society, 89–91, 94–95, 96–97,
  104–107, 108–109, 119–120, 165
Mattachine Young Adults, 106
May Act, 72–73
Mayer, Louis B., 84
McCarthy, Joseph, 84–85
Meaker, Marijane (Vin Packer), 88–89
media, 148–149
medicalization of sexuality, 16–17, 41–42, 90,
  144–145, 168–169
Men with the Pink Triangle, The (Heger), 29
Mescalero Apache people, 31
Metropolis (film), 21–22
Metropolitan Community Church, 116, 125,
  143
Mexican Americans, 74–75, 91–92, 115
Miami, Florida, 132
Michigan, 65. *See also* Detroit, Michigan
Middle Ages, 163
military service and sexual and gender
  minorities, 33, 45–46, 54–55, 71–76,
  163–164
Milk, Harvey, 106, 123–124, 134–137, 143,
  167–168
Minneapolis, Minnesota, 132, 153
Minnesota, 65. *See also* Minneapolis,
  Minnesota
Minnesota American Indian AIDS Task Force,
  153
Minority AIDS Project, 153
Mississippi, 31–32, 114
"Mississippi Goddam" (Simone), 110
Mixner, David, 135
Mizer, Bob, 79–80, 87–88, 167–168
Monaco, James, 52–53
Mona's bar, 61, 65–67, 78–79
monetary policy, 25
Monette, Paul, 154–155
Money, John, 6–8

INDEX 201

Moniac, Hildegard, 17–18
monosexual, 13–14
Montgomery Bus Boycott, 99
Montrose Counseling Center, 138
Montrose Star, The, 138–139
moral codes, 32
Moral Majority, 137
Morbidity and Mortality Weekly Report, 147
Morocco (film), 62
mortgage discrimination, 129
Moscone, George, 136
Mount Holyoke College, 39
Mount Morris Baths, 48–49
Mousset-Vos, Nelly, 23
Municipal Elections Committee of Los Angeles
    (MECLA), 135
Murnau, F. W., 51–52
Muscle Beach, 79–80
Mwanga II, King of Buganda, 5–6

nádleeh, 31
Nagasaki bombing, 83–84
Naiad Press, 122–123
Naldi, Nita, 51–52
NAMES Project AIDS Memorial Quilt,
    151–152
Napoleon I, 10–11
National AIDS Research Foundation, 154
National Association for the Advancement of
    Colored People, 99
National Association of People with AIDS, 156
National Black Feminist Organization, 123
National Center for Lesbian Rights, 125
National Chicano Youth Liberation
    Conference, 115
National Coalition of Black Gays, 125, 141, 143
National Coalition of Black Lesbians and Gays
    (NCBLG), 141
National Coalition of Gay STD Services,
    149–150
National Gay and Lesbian Task Force, 156–158
National Gay Rights Advocates, 156–157
National Gay Task Force, 125, 133–134,
    156–157
National Institutes of Health (NIH), 147–148
National LGBTQ Task Force, 158
National March on Washington for Lesbian
    and Gay Rights, 100–101, 110, 143,
    151–152
National Organization for Women (NOW),
    102–103, 121, 143

National Socialism (Germany), 26–30, 69–70,
    164, 166–167
National Third World Lesbian and Gay
    Conference, 141
National Transsexual Counseling Unit, 111
Native Americans, 115–116, 160–161
Navaho people, 31, 74–75
Nazimova, Alla, 51–52
Nazism, 26–30, 69–70, 164, 166–167
Nde'isdzan, 31
Negri, Pola, 51–52
Netherlands, 10
Nevada, 1, 52
New Alliance for Gay Equality, 135
Newark, New Jersey, 101
New Deal, 58, 66–67
Newgate Prison, 10
New Hampshire, 32–33
New Haven Colony, 32
New Jersey, 1, 32–33
New Objectivity movement, 21–22
Newton, Huey, 113
New York City
    and AIDS crisis, 148–151, 153–154, 158, 160
    and Asian American activism, 115
    and community-building efforts, 139
    and conservative backlash against social
        justice, 114
    and constructions of sexual and gender
        identities, 163–164
    and counterculture of the 1960s, 113
    and direct action in support of sexual and
        gender minorities, 108
    and Harlem Renaissance, 47
    and Lavender Scare, 87
    and marginalization of sexual and gender
        minorities, 60, 66–67, 164–165
    and Mattachine Society, 90–91
    opposition to Prohibition, 46
    and pathologization of sexual behavior,
        63–65
    and police raids, 72–73
    and pre-gay identities among men, 40–42
    and repeal of Prohibition, 59, 164
    and support networks for sexual and gender
        minorities, 87, 104–106
    and urban growth of the 1920s, 45

202 INDEX

New York City (*Continued*)
  and wartime environment for sexual and
    gender minorities, 71, 81, 164
  and "white flight," 129–130
  women's bookstores, 132
New York City Police Department, 117–119
New York Civil Liberties Union, 108
New York Herald, 64
New York Native, 150–151
New York Public Library, 109–110
New York State, 58, 59–60, 66–67, 157–159
New York Times, 114, 147, 148–149, 151–152
New York University, vii
New York University Lesbian and Gay Student
    Union, 121–122
New York World's Fair, 59
Nichols, Jack, 105–107, 119
Night of the Long Knives, 27
Niles, Blair, 52–53
1984 (Orwell), 3
19th Amendment, 41–42
95th Illinois Infantry, 33
Ninth Circuit Court of Appeals, 92–93
Nixon, Richard, 114, 131
Nobel Peace Prize, 38–39
Nob Hill bar, 78
Nojima, John, 91–92
nonviolent protest, 100
Normal Heart, The (play), 154–155
North American Conference of Homophile
    Organizations (NACHO), 109
North Beach neighborhood, 78–79
North Carolina, 32–33
North German Confederation, 11
Novarro, Ramon, 51–52
nuclear weapons, 83–84
Nugent, Richard Bruce, 47

Oakland, California, 132
Oak Room, 59–60
Odets, Walt, 156
Oglala Lakota people, 115–116
Ohio National Guardsmen, 114
oil embargo (1973), 114
Oklahoma, 31–32
Old Adobe bar, 78–79
O'Leary, Jean, 133–134, 156–157
Oliven, John, 124
Olivia Records, 122–123
158th Infantry, 74–75
ONE Inc., 91–93, 95, 96–97, 105, 165, 167–168
ONE Institute, 93

ONE Institute Quarterly of Homophile Studies,
    93
ONE Magazine, 91–93, 96–97
Operation Alert, 83–84
Oregon, 1
organized crime, 46, 58–61
Oscar Wilde Memorial Bookshop, 108–109,
    139
Out Front Colorado, 138–139

Packer, Vin (Marijane Meaker), 88–89
Page, Joy, 77
Paiute people, 31
Palmer House Hotel, 77
pansies and pansy craze, 52–53, 58, 60–61,
    95–96, 163–164, 167–168
Paragraph 175, 27–29, 166–167
parents of gender and sexual minorities, 140,
    144–145
Parker, Annise, 157–158
Parkhurst, Charley, 33–34
Parks, Rosa, 99
"passing," 33–35
pathologization of sexual behavior, 14, 63–65
patriarchy, 17–19
Pearl Harbor, 70–71
Penal Code of 1810, 10–11
Pennsylvania, 32, 132. *See also* Philadelphia,
    Pennsylvania
Pentagon, 106–107
Perry, Troy, 116, 143, 167–168
Pershing Square, 63, 79–80
Personal Rights in Defense and Education
    (PRIDE), 104–105
"perversion" view of sexual minorities, 41–42,
    64, 85, 88, 103
Philadelphia (film), 154–155
Philadelphia, Pennsylvania
  and AIDS crisis, 153
  and community-building efforts, 138–139
  and "Gay is Good" movement, 109
  and Lavender Scare, 87
  and National March on Washington, 143
  and support networks for sexual and gender
    minorities, 104–105
  and urban growth of the 1920s, 45
Philadelphia Gay News, 138–139
Philip of Macedon, 5–6
Physique Pictorial, 87–88, 96–97
Pink Triangle Park, 29–30
Pittsburgh Courier, 74
Plaza Hotel, 59–60

INDEX 203

Plymouth Colony, 32
Polak, Clark, 108–109
Poland, 69–70
police raids and harassment
    and Cooper Do-nuts riot, 103–104
    and Daughters of Bilitis, 94
    and homophile activism, 165
    and Lavender Scare, 37
    and lesbians in the 1930s, 65–66
    and the May Act, 72–73
    and New York State Liquor Authority,
        116–117
    and Stonewall riots, 116–117
    and support networks for sexual and gender
        minorities, 104–105
    in Weimar-era Berlin, 24–25
political violence, 26
popular music, 52–53
pornography, 24–25
ports of embarkation, 76–77
Pratt, John, 10
Praunheim, Rosa von, 166–167
Pregnancy Discrimination Act of 1978,
    114–115
Primrose Path bar, 77
Primus, Rebecca, 39–40
Prince, Virginia, 95–96, 111, 124
Problem in Greek Ethics, A (Symonds), 37–38
Production Code, 62–63
Prohibition
    and bootlegging, 51–52, 58
    and gender identities in the 1920s, 54–55
    and Harlem Renaissance, 48
    in Los Angeles, 51–52
    opposition to, 46
    and pansy craze, 52–53
    repealed, 58–59, 66–67, 164
    in San Francisco, 52
    social change associated with, 163–164
Project Lambda, 139–140
prostitution, 72–73
"Prove It on Me" (Rainey), 48
Prussia, 11–12, 13–14
psychedelic drugs, 113
psychiatry, 63–64
psychoanalysis, 63–64, 65–66
Psychopathia Sexualis (Krafft-Ebing), 14
public history, 2
Public Morals Squad (NYPD), 117–119
Puerto Rican Cultural Center, 153
Puerto Ricans, 113
Puff, Helmut, 10

"pulp" novels, 88–89

Queen Christina (film), 62
Queens Liberation Front, 120–121
queer identities, 41–42, 159–161
Queer Nation, 159–160

racial identity and dynamics, 27–28, 46, 50,
    80–81, 99, 110, 112, 141–142
Rainbow Room, 59–60
Rainey, Ma, 47–48
Raisin in the Sun, A (Hansberry), 109–110
Raus mit den Männern aus dem Reichstag, 22
Ravensbrück concentration camp, 28–29
Reagan, Ronald, 131, 135, 147–149, 154, 160
recessions, 129. See also economic conditions;
    Great Depression
Red Cross, 45–46
red-light districts, 72–73
redlining, 129
Red Power movement, 115–116
Red Scare, 83–85
Reform Judaism, 125
Reich Central Office for the Combat of
    Homosexuality and Abortion, 27
Reichstag, 14–15
rent parties, 48–49, 54–55, 167–168
Republican Party, 58, 114, 135
Reyes, Tony, 91–92
RheinMain University of Applied Sciences,
    vii–viii
Rhode Island, 32–33
Riggs, Marlon, 154–155
Rise and Fall of the City of Mahagonny, The
    (Brecht and Weill), 21–22
Rivera, Sylvia, 120–121
RKO Studios, 79
Robinson, Marty, 119–120
Rockefeller Center, 59–60
Rockland Palace, 50
Rodwell, Craig, 106–107, 108–110, 121,
    167–168
Roeder, Olly von, 22
Roe v. Wade, 114–115, 130–131
Röhm, Ernst, 27
romantic friendships, 38–40
Roosevelt, Franklin D., 58, 60–61, 70–71
Rosa Winkel Plaque, 29–30
Roselle Inn bar, 60–61, 65–66
Rosie the Riveter, 71
Rowland, Chuck, 89–91
Russia, 21

204 INDEX

Rustin, Bayard, 110
Ryan, Caitlin, 156
Ryan White CARE Act, 154

Sachsenhausen concentration camp, 29–30
Sacred Band of Thebes, 5–6
safer sex, 160–161
saloons, 61
Salsa Soul Sisters, 143
same-sex marriage, 38–40, 83, 133, 158
Sampson, Deborah, 33
San Diego Blood Sisters, 156
San Francisco, California
    and advances against discrimination,
        125–126
    and AIDS crisis, 148–150, 151–153, 155
    and Asian American activism, 115
    and community-building efforts, 138–139,
        163–164
    and constructions of sexual and gender
        identities, 163–164
    and counterculture of the 1960s, 113
    and diversity of sexual and gender
        minorities, 167–168
    and gay activism, 123
    and "Gay is Good" movement, 109
    and gender identities in the 1920s, 52, 54–55
    Harvey Milk and White Night Riot, 135–137
    and Lavender Scare, 87
    and lesbian bars in 1930s, 65–66
    and marginalization of sexual and gender
        minorities, 61
    and Mattachine Society, 90–91
    opposition to Prohibition, 46
    and origins of homophile movement, 165
    and origins of transgender movement, 111
    and police raids, 72–73
    and pre-gay identities among men, 42
    and support networks for sexual and gender
        minorities, 104–105
    Tavern Guild in, 116, 165
    and wartime environment for sexual and
        gender minorities, 71, 76–77, 81, 164
San Francisco Board of Supervisors, 116,
    134–136, 143
San Francisco Chronicle, 148–149
San Francisco Department of Public Health,
    149–150
San Francisco Public Health Department,
    104–105
San Francisco State University, 115
Sappho, 5–6

Save Our Children, 133–134, 137
Savoy Ballroom, 48
school segregation, 99
Schwabach, Kurt, 22
Scientific Humanitarian Committee, 14–15,
    17–18
Scott, Randolph, 62
Screen Actors Guild, 84
Screw, 119
Seale, Bobby, 113
Seattle, Washington, 115, 139
Second Congress to Unite Women, 121
Second Sex Conference, 4
second wave feminism, 102–103
Second World War
    American mobilization, 71–72
    causes of, 69–70
    and Chicago, 77
    impact on gender roles, 76–77
    and Los Angeles, 79–80
    military service and sexual and gender
        minorities, 71–76, 85–86, 96
    positive experiences of sexual and gender
        minorities, 75–76, 164
    and San Francisco, 78–79
    and Washington, D.C., 78
security clearances, 85–86
segregation, 70, 74–75, 99, 110
Selective Service and Training Act, 70
Selma-to-Montgomery March, 101
Senate Committee on Government
    Operations, 84–85
Sepia Gloria Swanson, 60–61
Sepia Mae West, 60–61
"Seven Sisters" colleges, 39
Sex Bureau (Los Angeles), 64
Sex Deviates Program (FBI), 86
sex employment discrimination, 102–103
Sexual Behavior in the Human Female
    (Kinsey), 86–87
Sexual Behavior in the Human Male (Kinsey),
    86–87
Sexual Hygiene and Pathology (Oliven), 124
sexual intermediacy, 15, 16–17, 41–42
sexual orientation, 7
sexual psychopath laws, 64–65
sex workers, 153–154
Sheldon, Louis, 137–138
Shilts, Randy, 148–149
Shonone people, 31
Showboat, The, 78
Shurtleff, Robert (Deborah Sampson), 33

Sierra gold rush, 52
silent films, 51–52
Silver Dollar bar, 78–79
Simone, Nina, 110
Sisterhood Bookstore, 132
sit-ins, 102–104
Sixteenth Street Baptist Church bombing, 100
Sixth Congress of German Jurists, 11–12
Slater, Don, 91–92
slavery and enslaved persons, 34
Slieper, Rosemary, 93–94
Small's Paradise, 48–49
Smeal, Eleanor, 143
Smith, Barbara, 123
Smith, Gwendolyn Ann, 159
Smith, John, 10
Smith, Mary Rozet, 38–39
"Smoke, Lilies, and Jade" (Nugent), 47
smuggling, 51–52
social change, 41–42
social class, 3–4
social conservatives, 66
social inequality, 25
social justice, 30, 113, 167–168
Social Service Division (of ONE, Inc.), 92–93
social work, viii
Society for Human Rights, 53–54, 89–90
sodomy laws, 9–11, 13–14, 32–33, 53–54, 81, 155, 163, 166–167
Songs of Bilitis (Sappho), 93–94
South Carolina, 32–33
Southeast Asia, 130
Southern California Women for Understanding, 135
Southern European immigrants, 54–55
Southern Poverty Law Center, 151
Soviet Union, 69–70, 83–84, 131
Spaish Civil War, 69–70
speakeasies, 46, 48–49, 51–53, 54–55, 61–62
Special Services Branch (US Army), 76
Spoliansky, Mischa, 22
Spring Fire (Packer), 88–89
Sprüngli, Theodora Ana (Anna Rüling), 18
Stafford, Harry, 37
stagflation, 131. *See also* economic conditions
Stalin, Joseph, 69
Standards of Care, 142–143
standpoint theory, vii, 3–5, 168
STAR House, 120–121
Starr, Adele, 143
Starr, Ellen Gates, 38–39
Star Route Carrier, 34

State Liquor Authority (SLA), 59, 66–67, 108, 116–117, 164
Steinbeck, John, 57
stock market crash (1929), 57
Stonewall Inn and riots
    causes and extent of, 117–119, 165
    and Gay Liberation Front, 119–121
    impact on gender minority identities, 124–125
    origins and clientele of Stonewall Inn, 117
    social and political legacy of, 126–127, 140, 143, 160–161, 167–168
Stop AIDS Quarantine Committee, 151
Strange Brother (Niles), 52–53
Street Transvestite Action Revolutionaries (STAR), 120–121
street youths, 126–127
Strength & Health, 79–80
Stryker, Susan, 33–35
Studds, Gerry, 157–158
student strikes, 102
suffrage, 45–46, 54–55
suicide, 15, 85–86
Summa Theologiae (Thomas Aquinas), 9
Sunset Boulevard, 61–62
swishes, 95–96
Switzerland, 26–27
Symonds, John Addington, 13, 37–38

tabloid press, 148–149
Tactical Patrol Force (NYPD), 118
Taft-Hartley Act, 84
tainna wa'ippe, 31
Takano, Mark, 157–158
Tavern Guild of San Francisco, 116, 165
taxation and tax policy, 131
Taylor, Elizabeth, 154
Teena, Brandon, 159
television, 83
Tellier, Andre, 52–53
Tenderloin district, San Francisco, 78–79, 104
Terrigno, Valerie, 157–158
Tewa Pueblo people, 31
Texas, 133–134. *See also* Dallas, Texas; Houston, Texas
Thais-Williams, Jewel, 141
Theban Army, 5–6
The Lavender Song, 22
third sex intermediacy, 16–17, 37–38
Third World Gay Revolution, 120–121, 143
Third World Liberation Front, 115
This Is the Army, 76

206 INDEX

Thompson, Franklin (Sarah Emma Edmonds), 33
Threepenny Opera, The (Brecht and Weill), 21–22
Thurmond, Strom, 110
Times Square, 59, 67
Timmons, John, 108
Title IX, 114–115
Tolstoy, Leo, 14–15
Tommy's Joint, 78–79
Torres, Ritchie, 157–158
Torres, Tereska, 88–89
Tosh, John, 2
Town and Country bar, 77
trade, 40–42
Traditional Values Coalition, 137–138
Transgender Day of Remembrance, 159
transgender identity
   and AIDS crisis, 159, 166
   and construction of gender minority identities, 8
   and constructions of sexual and gender identities, 165
   and healthcare standards, 142–143, 144–145
   and historical examples of sexual and gender minorities, 6
   origins of trans movement, 111
   "transgender" term, 124, 158
   and transgression of gender norms, 34–35
   and transsexualism, 111, 124–125, 158
   and trans visibility, 95–96
Transsexual Phenomenon, The (Benjamin), 111
Transvestia, 95–96, 111
transvestism and transvestites, 95–96, 111, 117–118, 120–121, 126–127, 165
Trash and Filth Writings law, 24–25
Treaty of Dancing Rabbit Creek, 31–32
Trosse, Emma, 17
Trull, Teresa, 122–123
Trumbo, Dalton, 84
Turkey, 21
Turner, Frederick Jackson, 35
Tuskegee Airmen, 74–75
Twelve-Thirty Club, 60–61, 65–66, 77
21st Amendment, 58, 66–67
Twilight Men (Tellier), 52–53

Ubangi Club, 60
Ulrichs, Karl Heinrich, 11–14, 17, 37–38, 40–41, 43, 89–90
unemployment, 57, 66
Union Army, 33

Union for Lesbians and Gay Men, 135
United Church of Christ, 125
United Kingdom, 24–25
United Nations, 106–107
United Service Organizations, 76
Unity Fellowship Church, 153
University of Bern, 17–18
University of California, Berkeley, 115
University of Michigan, 139–140
University of Zürich, 17–18
"Unnameable Objects, Unspeakable Crimes" (Baldwin), 3
Uranism, 12–13, 18–19
urbanization, 25, 45, 54–55
Urnings, 12–14, 40–41, 43
US Army, 72–73, 74–76
US Congress
   and AIDS crisis, 147–148, 151, 154, 157–158
   and anti-abortion activism, 130–131
   and Carter presidency, 131
   and civil rights activism, 100–101
   isolationist sentiment, 69
   and Lavender Scare, 86
   and political response to Great Depression, 58
   and Red Scare, 84–85
   and Second World War, 70–71
US Constitution, 41–42, 45–46, 114–115, 130–131
US Department of State, 84–85, 106–107
US Food and Drug Administration (FDA), 150–151
US House of Representatives, 84, 99–100, 130–131, 151, 157–158
US Navy, 72–73, 76
US Postal Service, 34, 86, 92–93
US Supreme Court, 92–93, 99, 104, 114–115, 130–131, 155

Vaid, Urvashi, 156–158
Vanguard (youth organization), 104–105
variety shows, 76. *See also* drag
Velasquez, Loreta, 33
Veteran's Administration, 73–75
Veterans Benevolent Association, 89
Vice Versa, 79, 87
Vida/SIDA, 153
Vietnam, 102, 111–112, 114, 130
Village Voice, 108, 140
violence against gender and sexual minorities, 155
Virtual Equality (Vaid), 158

INDEX   207

Voeller, Bruce, 133–134
voting rights, 33–34, 41–42, 45–46, 54–55, 101, 163–164
Voting Rights Act of 1965, 101

Waldoff, Claire, 22, 28–29
Wallace, George, 113
Waller, Fats, 48–49
Warner, Jack, 84
"War on the Sex Criminal," 64
wartime mobilization, 33, 45–46, 54–55
Washington, DC
    and counterculture of the 1960s, 113
    and homophile activism, 165
    and Lavender Scare, 87
    and lesbian feminist groups, 122
    and Mattachine Society, 90–91
    and National March on Washington for Lesbian and Gay Rights, 143, 151–152
    and nondiscrimination ordinances, 132
    and police raids, 72–73
    and support networks for sexual and gender minorities, 104–106
    and wartime environment for sexual and gender minorities, 78, 164
Washington, Denzel, 154–155
Washington Post, 114
Watergate scandal, 114
Watts riots, 101
Weather Underground, 113
Weimar Republic, 21–26
Weiss, Ted, 143
Weldy, Ann (Ann Bannon), 88–89
Well of Loneliness, The (Hall), 14, 52–53
Wells Fargo, 33–34
Wenn die beste Freundin mit der besten Freundin, 22
West Germany, 29, 166–167
West Hollywood, California, 61–63, 66–67, 157–158
What Has Man Made of Woman, Child, and Himself (Elberskirchen), 17–18
"When Will the Ignorance End?" (Lorde), 141
White, Dan, 134, 136–137
White, Ryan, 154
white flight, 129–130
Whitehall Induction Center, 106–107

White House protests, 106–107
White Night Riot, 137
white supremacy, 96
Whitman, Walt, 36–38, 40, 43, 89–90
Whittaker, Bailey, 91–92
Wicker, Randy, 106–107
Wilchins, Riki, 159
Wilde, Oscar, 37–38
Williams, Cris, 122–123
Williams, Hosea, 101
Will Rogers State Beach, 79–80
winkte, 31
witch hunts, 73–74, 87, 164
Wittman, Carl, 123
Wojnarowicz, David, 154–155
Wolf, Irma, 91–92
"Woman-Identified Woman, The" (Lavender Menace manifesto), 121
Woman's Place, A (bookstore), 132
Women Accepted for Volunteer Emergency Service (WAVES), 72
Women's Army Corps, 72
Women's Barracks (Torres), 88–89
women's bookstores, 122–123, 132
women's colleges, 40, 43, 163
Women's Educational Equity Act of 1974, 114–115
women's movement, 112, 114–115, 156–157
women's music movement, 122
women's suffrage, 54–55, 163–164
Womyn's Music Festival, 132
Woodstock music festival, 113
Woolworth's lunch counter sit-ins, 100
World Health Organization (WHO), 153–154
"World of Tomorrow, The" (New York World's Fair), 59
Wounded Knee, South Dakota, 115–116

"Young, Gifted, and Black" (Simone), 110
Young Lords, 113
Youth Liberation Press, 139–140

"zaps," 120
Zeitschrift für Sexualwissenschaft, 15
Zola, Emile, 14–15
zoning discrimination, 129
Zoot Suit Riots, 74–75
Zuni people, 31